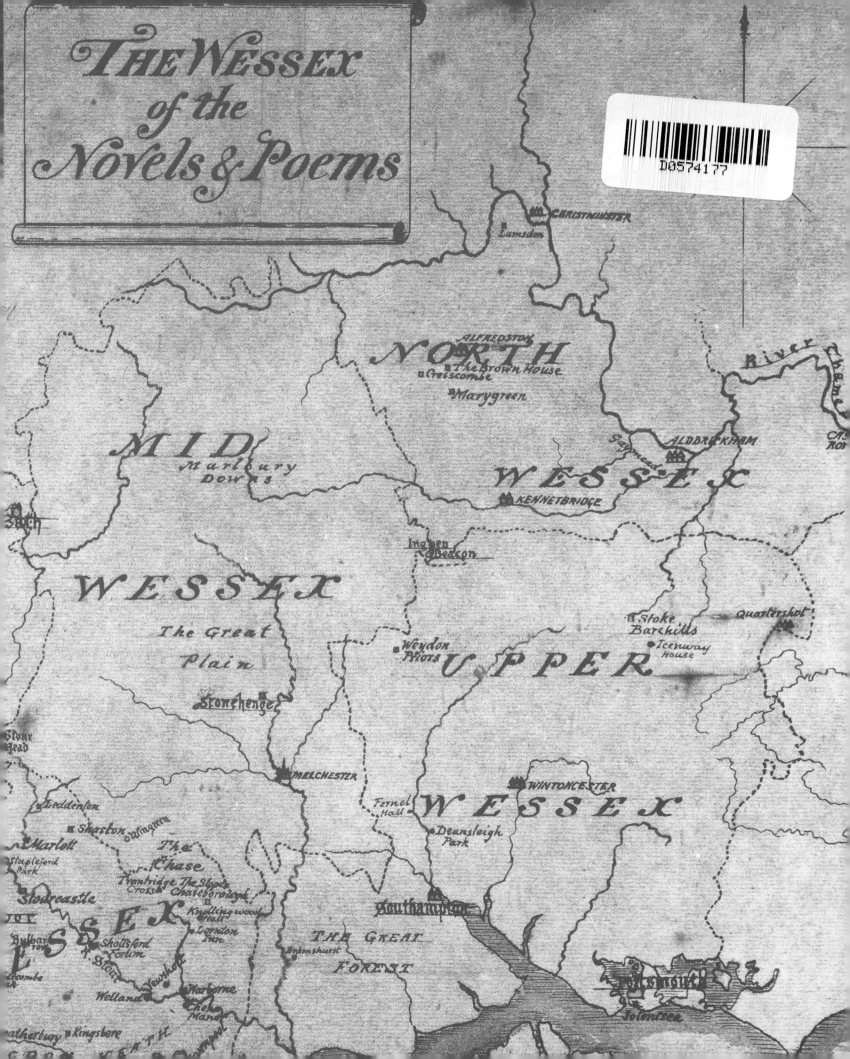

THE WESSEX of the Novels & Poems

NORTH
WESSEX

ALFREDSTON
The Brown House
Cresscombe
Marygreen

Seymead
ALDBRICKHAM

KENNETBRIDGE

Ingben
Beacon

MID
Marlbury
Downs

WESSEX
The Great
Plain

Stonehenge

Stoke
Barehills
Quartershot

Weydon
Priors

UPPER

Icenway
House

MELCHESTER

WINTONCESTER

Fernel
Hall

WESSEX

Deansleigh
Park

Bath

Stour
Head

Leddenton

Shaston
Oldsin-

The
Chase

Marlott
Stapleford
Park

Stourcastle

Trantridge
Cross

The Slopes
Chaseborough

Knollingwood
Hall
London
Inn

THE GREAT
FOREST

Bramshurst

Southampton

Portsmouth

Bulbar
row
Shottsford
Forum

combe

Newport

Welland

Kingsbere
Casterbridge

Marnhull

Chene
Manor

Solentsea

Lumsdon
CHRISTMINSTER

River Thames

CAS-
RO-

Thomas Hardy's World

THIS IS A CARLTON BOOK

Text © Molly Lefebure 1996
Design © Carlton Books Limited
20 St Anne's Court
Wardour Street
London
W1V 3AW

This edition published by Carlton Books Limited 1997

A CIP catalogue for this book is available from the British Library

ISBN 1 85868 245 2

Project Editor Sarah Larter
Project Art Direction Zoë Maggs
Picture Research Emily Hedges
Designer Rosamund Saunders
Production Sarah Schuman

Printed in Spain

Thomas Hardy's World

THE LIFE, TIMES AND WORKS OF
THE GREAT NOVELIST AND POET

Molly Lefebure

CARLTON

Contents

Introduction

1840 WAS AN AUSPICIOUS year for several reasons: the young Queen Victoria married her first cousin, Albert of Saxe-Coburg-Gotha; Rowland Hill introduced the Penny Post; Nelson's column was erected in Trafalgar Square; the can-can was first danced in Paris; the first photograph of the moon was taken in New York and Thomas Hardy was born in a remote cottage in the heart of a rural countryside that in due course he would immortalize as Wessex.

Hardy's life span (1840–1928) covered an era of enormous vitality in English literature, especially in the domain of the novel; an era extending from the Brontë sisters to the publication of D.H. Lawrence's *Lady Chatterley's Lover* in the year of Hardy's death. Hardy had not yet joined the infant class in his village school when William Makepeace Thackeray's immortal masterpiece, *Vanity Fair*, was being gobbled up by his readers in monthly instalments (1847–8) and Charles Dickens was settling into the full gallop of his dazzling career.

Thereafter came landmarks such as Elizabeth Gaskell's *North and South* (1855), Anthony Trollope's *Barchester Towers* (1857), Wilkie Collins's *Woman in White* (1860), George Eliot's *Middlemarch* (1871–2), and so to plunge into that glittering galaxy of Robert Louis Stevenson, George Gissing, Rudyard Kipling, JM Barrie, Joseph Conrad, Oscar Wilde, HG Wells; Henry James, Arnold Bennett, George Meredith, Somerset Maugham; EM Forster, Virginia Woolf, James Joyce – the list is endless.

Among these looms Hardy like a lonesome peak; not necessarily greater than any of these, but unique in his vision and his condemnatory rejection of modern civilization; in his pessimism – almost incomprehensible to his contemporary readership of mid-Victorians, cocooned as they were in smug and prosperous imperialism; furthermore a pessimism embedded in fatalism, entirely contrary to the British character. Hardy's choice of setting for his novels, a timeless framework of hills and moors, was not the cosy countryside of quiet lanes and friendly pubs but windswept empty heaths dominated by prehistoric barrows from which came muttering voices commanding the lighting of mystic fires, the playing out of ritualistic conflicts, which in turn were forever being interrupted, crossed, by accidents ruthlessly diverting the directives of the ghostly Neolithic chorus – accidents truly prompted by the pointing finger of an eternally subversive Fate, presiding over the Universe. No hope of escape. Certainly no hope of finding happiness founded on a nineteenth-century faith in the progress of critical reason; let alone a simple belief in the ultimate triumph of benevolence. Hardy's writing was haunted by the vision of a pitiless necessity.

Why was he, and how has he remained, so popular? One reason is his marvellous gift for narrative and his unerring instinct for a dramatic situation. The other reason is humankind's eternal need for catharsis, purgation; the release of pent-up subterranean emotion by drama; a need as essential to us as it was to the ancient Greeks who first identified it. Hardy presented his dramas in the form of novels, but these novels were, and are, as potent as Aristophanes. In modern times we put Hardy's novels on screen, witness the popularity of screen versions of *Far From the Madding Crowd*, *The Mayor of Casterbridge*, *Tess of the D'Urbervilles* and *Jude the Obscure*, and feel the truth of them perhaps more keenly than ever before.

Thomas Hardy's Life

1839

Thomas Hardy, builder and mason of Higher Bockhampton, Dorset, marries Jemima Hand, cook, at Melbury Osmund on December 22.

1840

Thomas Hardy, their eldest child, is born at Higher Bockhampton, June 2.

1848

He first attends village school. Later in the year Thomas pays his first visit to London, with his mother. A cholera outbreak in Dorset prompts his mother to keep him at home for rest of the year.

1849

Attends the British and Foreign School in Dorchester (formerly the Royal Lancasterian Society school).

1853–1856

Transfers to Isaac Last's independent "commercial academy". Begins learning Latin, French and German. Makes great strides.

1856

Leaves school, midsummer. Articled for three years to John Hicks, a Dorchester architect, to receive instruction in "architectural drawing and surveying." Hicks was primarily an ecclesiastical architect, a specialist in the rebuilding and restoring of Gothic churches, and this became Hardy's speciality. Continues classical studies with Horace Moule, eight years Hardy's senior and fourth son of the Reverend Henry Moule, vicar of Fordington St George.

1862

Leaves Dorchester for London, to work as assistant architect in the office of Arthur Blomfield.

1867

Poor health prompts Hardy to return to Higher Bockhampton and rejoin Hicks's office at Dorchester. Writes his first novel, *The Poor Man and the Lady* (unpublished). At about this time Hardy falls in love with his cousin Tryphena Sparks.

1868–69

The Poor Man and the Lady accepted by publishers Chapman and Hall, but their reader George Meredith advises Hardy not to publish. Following the sudden death of Hicks, Hardy goes to work for a Weymouth architect, G. R. Crickmay. Begins writing *Desperate Remedies*.

1870

Crickmay sends Hardy to St Juliot, Cornwall to make plans for the restoration of the church. Here Hardy meets Emma Lavinia Gifford, the rector's sister-in-law. Shortly afterward they become betrothed.

1871–74

Publishes *Desperate Remedies* 1871; *Under the Greenwood Tree*, 1872; *A Pair of Blue Eyes*, 1873; *Far From the Madding Crowd*, 1874. The latter is a tremendous success and allows Hardy to give up architecture in 1882. Finally Marries Emma Gifford on September 17, 1874.

1874–80

The Hardys spend two years "gypsying"; then in 1876 settle in Sturminster Newton. Hardy publishes *The Hand of Ethelberta*. 1876 sees publication of *The Return of the Native*. They remove back to London, living in Upper Tooting. *The Trumpet Major* published 1880. Hardy falls seriously ill and is bedridden for six months.

1881–85

A Laodicean published. The Hardys move to Wimbourne Minster, near Dorchester. Decision taken to build a house near Dorchester. *Two on a Tower* published 1882. 1883 move to Dorchester to supervise building the house, Max Gate. The Hardys move into Max Gate 1885.

1886–90

The Mayor of Casterbridge published 1886; *The Woodlanders*, 1887; short stories, *Wessex Tales*, 1888. In spring of 1887 the Hardys tour Italy.

1891

A Group of Noble Dames and *Tess of the d'Urbervilles* are published. The latter receives a hostile reception.

1892

Hardy's father dies.

1894

Life's Little Ironies published.

1896

Jude the Obscure published. The novel is received with such a storm of abuse that Hardy resolves to write no more novels.

1897

The Well-Beloved, is published having been written ten years earlier.

1898–1902

Hardy publishes his first collection of poetry, *Wessex Poems*, 1898. In 1902 *Poems of the Past and Present* appear. Begins work on *The Dynasts*.

1904

Hardy's mother dies.

1906–9

Two further parts of *The Dynasts* published in 1906 and 1908 respectively. *Poems, Time's Laughing Stocks*, published 1909.

1910

Awarded Order of Merit.

1912

Emma Hardy dies.

1914

Hardy marries Florence Emily Dugdale, previously his secretary.

1914–22

Outbreak of Great War. Publishes *Satires of Circumstance*, a collection of poems. Further collections, *Moments of Vision*, 1917, and *Late Lyrics and Earlier*, 1922.

1923–25

1923, verse play, *The Famous Tragedy of the Queen of Cornwall*. The final collection of poems to appear in his lifetime, *Human Shows*, is published in 1925. During these final years works on his autobiography, *The Early Life of Thomas Hardy*, burns old notebooks and private papers.

1928

Death of Thomas Hardy, January 11. Ashes placed in Poets' Corner, Westminster Abbey; his heart buried in the grave of his first wife, Emma, at Stinsford, next to the graves of his parents. Posthumous publication of collection of poems, *Winter Words*. Publication of his biograraphy *The Early Life of Thomas Hardy*, under the guise of having been written by Florence Hardy.

1 WHO WAS Thomas Hardy?

HARDY, LIKE ALL NOVELISTS, lived simultaneously in two worlds; one which most people supposed to be the real world, the other a world invented by him and inhabited by characters of his own creation. Between the shafts of limelight that streamed upon him with the advent of each new book he went to ground in his study and stayed hidden, writing poetry, working on his next novel; dedicating himself, he said, to "the exploration of reality."

He had received a remarkably good education for one of his relatively humble background, becoming a far from unsuccessful architect specializing in restoring country churches. Much of his success as a novelist stemmed from his ability to construct a narrative; from his architect's sense of equilibrium, of poise and counterpoise; his early days of training in the stonemason's yard, which he was fond of describing as "a centre of effort as worthy as that dignified by the name of scholarly study within the noblest of colleges." Similarly, he wrote about natural scenery and country life in a manner wholly direct that owed nothing to literature. His upbringing as a cottage child in a remote rural area had been the perfect grounding for the future novelist and poet who immortalized the region, "half dream, half reality" that was his "Wessex".

But none of this really answers the question, "Who was Thomas Hardy?" nor does it explain by what alchemy did he, fundamentally steeped in solitude and rusticity, come by the powers which made him one of the most famous and remarkable novelists of the age? Alone, in his rather spartan, unpretentious study, he conjured up the characters of Eustacia, Sue, Jude, Tess; landscapes of heath and forest, headland and cove, villages and towns and making it all more real for his readers than any place that they themselves lived in and the characters he was writing about more vivid and controversial than anybody actual who lived just round the corner.

Of course there were plenty who were ready to sneer; "Sex and Wessex" became a popular jibe with which to encapsulate Hardy. As is often the case, his own family, with heavy shakes of the head, insisted that he was not what the world thought him to be, or even what he claimed himself to be. For instance, when it came to women – he maintained that his novels revealed an extraordinarily accurate knowledge of women but his first wife, Emma, who shared close on forty years of increasingly fraught marriage with him, said of him that, "He understands only the women he invents – the others not at all." And indeed on his own admission Hardy didn't like what Emma called "real women." "Real woman is abhorrent to man?" he queried in a notebook. "Hence the failure of matrimony."

As a young man he was both hopelessly attracted and confused by the opposite sex. The Hardy family remembered him as being "outrageously flirtatious"; on more than one occasion courting a girl to the point of engagement, even buying a ring, but never giving it to her because at the last moment he developed cold feet, dropped her, and swerved to become engaged to someone else, the ring once more ending up in his own pocket. Not surprisingly the young Hardy gained a reputation as a "jilter". The family accounted for this behaviour by alleging that he was impotent. If true this could also explain his failure to give Emma the children she longed for. But this is a little too facile. And Hardy himself, indulging in sprightly reminiscence in his final years, insisted that he had remained capable of sexual intercourse until he was eighty-four. Nevertheless there is no firm evidence that he ever begat any children.

But what kind of information is this for people who wish to know what sort of man he *really* was? He was, and remained, what he chose to be for the outside world, an enigma. To quote his poem, "Not Known", in his final collection of poetry, *Winter Words*, which was published posthumously,

> *They know a phasm they name as me,*
> *In whom I should not find*
> *A single self-held quality*
> *Of body or mind.*

x

Roots

HARDY'S PARENTS JEMIMA AND THOMAS HARDY SENIOR. WED IN 1839; THESE PHOTOGRAPHS SHOW THEM FORTY YEARS LATER, STILL HAPPILY MARRIED.

THOMAS HARDY WAS born at Upper Bockhampton, Dorset, on the second day of June, 1840, less than five and a half months after his parents, Thomas Hardy, master-mason, and Jemima Hands, a cook, had been pronounced man and wife by the vicar of Melbury Osmond, also in Dorset.

Thomas Hardy Junior, when an acclaimed literary figure, liked to trace his ancestry back to the ancient le Hardy family of Jersey; linking his "branch", the Hardys of Owermoigne, Bockhampton, with these distinguished, albeit hazy, forerunners in the Channel Isles. However it had to be admitted that the name Hardy was a common one in Dorset and the novelist sensibly confined himself, in public, to remarking that he had firm knowledge that at least four generations of his direct paternal ancestors had all been master-masons. Hardy himself in a sense followed in this family tradition by training and practising as an architect before taking up full-time professional writing and as an author maintained a sound tradesman-like attitude to his work, relishing being considered "a good hand at a serial", just as he had formerly been proud of his reputation as a good hand at restoring and designing churches and rectory houses.

The Maternal Line

Hardy's maternal grandmother's family, the Swetmans of Melbury Osmond, had been, claimed Hardy, yeoman-farmers for countless generations before being "ruined" in 1685 for the part they had played in the Monmouth rebellion; losing their land and prosperity as retribution for this seditious conduct. Hardy's grandmother, born Elizabeth Swetman, came on her mother's side from another ancient Dorset line, of the name of Childs. The Childses of Thomas Hardy's day were engaged in the professions of medicine and publishing.

Whether or not Hardy had the blood of a medieval Clement le Hardy in his veins, together with that of sturdy English yeomanry reduced by supporting the losing side in an uprising, the fact that he believed in these Romantic antecedents was very important to his self-esteem.

Of different importance would be the more certain history of Elizabeth "Betty" Swetman who, against parental wish and heavily pregnant, married George Hand, a hired shepherd given to drink and violent behaviour. Betty's father had severed all connection with his daughter, cutting her off with the proverbial shilling. Eighteen years later George Hand died, leaving his widow penniless and with a large brood of young children to care for. She was obliged to "go on the parish" – seek Poor Relief – a great cause for shame in those days. Her sons took after their father in their drinking habits and were of little help or comfort to their mother.

Her daughter Jemima – Hardy's mother – was obliged to go into service while still little more than a child; she was found a place in the household of the Reverend Charles Redlynch Fox-Strangways, uncle of Lord Ilchester, the leading local landowner. Jemima became an outstandingly good cook, transferring in due course into another Strangways household, that of the Reverend Edward Murray, vicar of Stinsford and Lord Ilchester's brother in law. Murray was a staunch supporter of the Stinsford parish choir, in which a Thomas Hardy – destined to be the novelist's grandfather – played a significant role as bass-viol, flanked by the fiddles of his two sons, James and Thomas Junior.

Jemima and Thomas

The musicians often went to Stinsford House, abode of the vicar and his family, for rehearsals and it did not take long for the young cook Jemima and Thomas Hardy Junior to become acquainted, to a background music of cracked fiddles and antique flutes. Here is some, at least, of the material used for *Under the Greenwood Tree*. However, that novel, bowing to the ruling of Mrs Grundy, who controlled middle-class reading in Hardy's day, did not run true to the actual course of events; unlike the chaste courtship of Hardy's fictional lovers, young Dick Dewy and Fancy Drew, Jemima and her fiddle-flourishing swain, following the countryside tradition of their era made no attempt to wed until Jemima's pregnancy, with Thomas the novelist, forced matrimony upon them in 1840.

They made their home in the thatched cottage at Higher Bockhampton, which John Hardy (1755–1821) had built in 1800 for his eldest son Thomas Hardy and his bride, Mary Head of Fawley, Berkshire. This cottage, standing alone in woodland on the edge of a broad region of open heath, the Egdon Heath of Hardy's fictitious Wessex, was indeed a dwelling under the greenwood tree. The vista spread before the last Thomas Hardy, bosky woodland giving way to wide heathy horizons, was that of a rural countryside now utterly lost to us, but for him the living reality of his childhood and boyhood; a priceless inheritance from which he drew the fabric of his novels, the inspiration of so many of his poems. The thought of the le Hardys of Jersey may have soothed his always prickly pride, but shepherds and village fiddlers, hard rural circumstance and rustic tragedy would be the bloodstream of his genius.

HARDY'S BIRTHPLACE IN WINTER: "I ONLY NEED THE HOMELIEST OF HEARTSTRINGS."

THE Oral Tradition

HARDY'S MOTHER JEMIMA was undoubtedly the overriding influence in his life. Retaining a clear mind and powerful personality, she lived to be ninety, thereby not leaving her eldest and favourite child motherless until he himself was sixty-four. On his deathbed in 1928, he having survived

MARVELLOUS TALES AT GRANDMOTHER'S KNEE.

her by twenty-four years, he asked for a rasher of bacon to be grilled for him at the open fire in his bedroom as Jemima had cooked bacon in the old days in the cottage at Bockhampton: the old home from which she had refused to move in spite of Hardy's offers to buy her a more convenient modern residence. The smell of bacon cooking on the archetypal hearth; the sound of it sizzling in the pan; ancestral scents, sounds and memories shared by a succession of generations, the pattern of whose simple rustic lives had barely changed for centuries on end. Hardy wished his life to end as it had begun, eighty-eight years before, on a note of overwhelmingly powerful association.

Hardy has been described by one of his biographers Michael Millgate, as a "child of the oral tradition and perhaps, in England, that tradition's last and greatest product." He lived to be almost ninety himself; a span of years which witnessed the introduction into daily use of gas, electricity, modern plumbing, the automobile, the airplane, the telephone, and radio. 1928, the year in which Hardy died, saw the discovery of penicillin, while the BBC made its first successful experiments with televised pictures.

Yet he grew up in a world of horse-drawn traffic; he could remember mail-coaches clattering into Dorchester. People in their everyday lives, without giving it a second thought, walked what we today would call immense distances. The popular press had not yet arrived; and the telegram had only just made its first appearance. The darkness of night was illuminated by wax candles and oil-lamps in better class habitations; the poor still relied upon rush dips – rushes dipped in tallow – or home made candles, which dripped, guttered and at last bowed their heads before expiring.

The Twilight Hours

For this reason daylight was of the utmost importance and working folk rose at the crack of dawn to get through the day's labour. Similarly in the interest of economy, candles were not called into use too promptly in the evenings; there was a period, as dusk fell, of "enjoying the twilight" as straining the eyes and groping about for toasting-forks and tea-kettles was pleasantly called.

Old folk and small children were left to sit by firelight for hours on end; hence all the marvellous tales told to little people at grandmother's knee. While in the adult world, at the end of the day when candles guttered out

HARDY, IN THE POEM "ONE WE KNEW", TELLS HOW HE AND HIS SISTER MARY, TWELVE MONTHS HIS JUNIOR, USED TO SIT AT THEIR MATERNAL GRANDMOTHER'S KNEE, SHE LIVING WITH THEM AS ONE OF THE HOUSEHOLD, BY THE FIRESIDE:

*She told how they used to form for the country dances —
"The Triumph," "The New-rigged Ship" —
To the light of the guttering wax in the panelled manses,
And in cots to the blink of a dip ...*

*She showed us the spot where the maypole was yearly planted,
And where the bandsmen stood
While breeched and kerchiefed partners whirled, and panted
To choose one another for good ...*

*She told us of the far-back day when they learnt astound
Of the death of the King of France;
Of the Terror; and then of Bonaparte's unbounded
Ambition and arrogance.*

*Of how his threats woke warlike preparations
Along the southern strand,
And how each night brought tremors and trepidations
Lest morning should see him land.*

*She said she often heard the gibbet creaking
As it swayed in the lightning flash,
Had caught from the neighbouring town a small child's shrieking
At the cart under the lash ...*

*With cap-framed face and long gaze into the embers —
We seated around her knees —
She would dwell on such dead themes, not as one who remembers,
But rather as one who sees ...*

altogether and the fire burned low and people huddled close round the hearth to catch the last warmth, the hour arrived for telling tales and anecdotes: reminiscences of this and that; ghost stories, sagas of stealth and murder, to send everyone off to bed in a fine state of the shudders.

Twilight was the hour when romantic maidens daringly experimented with bibles and keys to find out whom they should marry: as did Bathsheba Everdene in *Far From The Madding Crowd*. It was also the hour when the desperate stole out of the house to elope, as did Avice Caro in *The Well-Beloved*.

Events both trivially domestic and earth-shaking alike were handed down from one generation to the next and thereby preserved for posterity with greater certainty, though doubtless less exactitude, than can ever be guaranteed for the photocopied texts, tape recordings and floppy disks of our era. Things written or otherwise technically preserved are always open to destruction by flood or fire, high-explosion or mice, whereas the handed-down spoken word must survive as long as humanity itself survives and people trouble to talk to one another.

And it is this which gives Thomas Hardy's novels their extraordinary quality of bone-marrow authenticity; their instinctive profundity, their tear-promoting poignancy and laughter-provoking humour. They are drawn from the oral tradition; from what Hardy himself called "the real", yet with aeons of human imagination and fantasy spread, like magic, over them. Herein lies the secret of their power.

Childhood

H ARDY'S FATHER, handsome, charming, easy going, though successful enough in the local building trade was a happy idler by inclination, given to roaming the countryside with his telescope, or music making with his fiddle, rather than furthering the worldly prospects of his family. The Bockhampton cottage of young Thomas Hardy's day never knew the pinch of want and it was a socially lively place despite its isolated situation, but it was a homestead very much dominated by what were then known as the

"womenfolk". Jemima Hardy knew that it was she, not her husband, who was head of the family and had to hold that family together in the face of what early experience had taught her was a hard world.

In Jemima Hardy fatalism mingled with an iron determination to see her children advance materially to a point where they need never fear the destitution which she had known in her early life. As a fatalist she believed in a mysterious "Something" planted in the path of mankind; that unbending image described in *Jude The Obscure*; "Something external to us which says, 'You shan't!'" In the face of this daemonic obstruction forever attempting to thrust humble souls back into the darkness from which they struggled to escape Jemima Hardy made a brave stand, gathering her flock around her, urging each and every one to stick together to the last, to live and fight as a clan. Remembering how family division and poverty all too

THE KITCHEN LIVING-ROOM IN HARDY'S COTTAGE; MUCH SPRUCED UP SINCE HIS DAY.

often resulted from ill-judged marriages she counselled her own children never to marry but to live together in pairs; Thomas with his sister Mary, and the two much younger children, Henry and Katherine, to do the same.

Mary Hardy

Mary was Thomas's sole regular child companion until he went to school at the age of eight. The two retained a warmly affectionate relationship throughout their lives, Mary died in 1915 at the age of seventy four, but they never domiciled together after they grew up – neither did Henry and Kate. Recessive and introspective, as was Hardy himself, Mary shared his love of the arts and of solitude. Understanding him perfectly she received all his confidences which he hesitated to make to others. She became a schoolteacher, remaining single all her life. After her death Thomas wrote two deeply poignant poems in her memory, "Logs on the Hearth" and "The Sun's Last Look on the Country Girl". His keenest memories of her were indeed associated with the Bockhampton hearth where he and Mary had sat at Granny Hardy's knee – their name for her – and had listened to her wonderful tales.

Shepherds and songs

Their other grandmother, "Granny from Melbury" as the children called her, the former Betty Swetman, born in 1778, died before Hardy was seven; nonetheless he retained a vivid memory of her and of the old songs she had sung, including "Shepherds, I have lost my love", a lament well suited for one whose personal history had been so tragically involved with a shepherd. It is not easy to unravel the workings of a poet-novelist's imagination, but clearly "Granny from Melbury" made a profound impression upon Hardy; his remarkable knowledge and understanding of sheep and shepherding, revealed in *Far From the Madding Crowd*, obviously owed their inspiration to his almost spellbound obsession with the tale of this paternal grandmother and her runaway marriage with the hired shepherd who with his drinking and violence ruined her life and the lives of her children, including the early years of the novelist's own mother. It is significant that in *Far From the Madding Crowd*, Hardy portrays his shepherd hero, Gabriel Oak, not as a drinking and violent man but, in reverse, a most humane and caring one; though in some respects firmly primitive and earthy, telling the time from the stars during his long night vigils among his sheep and measuring the progress of the year not from any printed calendar but the seasonal activities and near prehistoric festivals embedded in the endless round of his ageless shepherd's calling.

From his father Hardy learned all about the Stinsford parish choir, prototype for the Mellstock choir which figured so often in Hardy's writing. While Jemima early encouraged her little son to read, we are told that he was able to do so by the time he was three, Thomas Hardy Senior saw to it that the child showed equal precocity with the fiddle, which he was learning to play when he was four. He was still a schoolboy when he first accompanied his father to play at local fairs and dances and made quite a name for himself in the way he belied his frail appearance by the tireless enthusiasm with which he performed. Jemima herself sang a wide repertoire of old songs for the entertainment of her children; she was also an inspired gossip and one hears her voice and those of her friends and neighbours in those marvellous passages of rustic dialogue with which Hardy spiced his pages.

Hardy in retrospect would describe his childhood as having been solitary and rather uneventful; withdrawn and sickly he had been a spectator rather than a notably active participant. But his health improved steadily as he went along, and one suspects that he confined himself largely to

the role of spectator because he knew that watching and listening were more important for him than taking part.

Though he did not commence his official education at the village school until 1848 Hardy had by then, in fact, completed the better part of his essential learning. The great novels came not from the renowned man of letters, Thomas Hardy, Order of Merit, but from a small boy tucked in the corner of a fire-glowing inglenook, all eyes and ears, absorbing all he saw and heard, storing it away in readiness for the time when, not so very many years later, he should start penning his chronicles of Wessex: a place, as he put it, "half dream, half reality."

LAMBING TIME;
MIDNIGHT, MIDWINTER.
A TIMELESS SCENE.

THE
Seamy Side

THE WHITE SLAVES OF ENGLAND.

CHILD LABOUR IN A DERBYSHIRE COTTON-MILL, C.1840. ILLUSTRATION FROM FRANCES TROLLOPE'S "LIFE AND ADVENTURES OF MICHAEL ARMSTRONG THE FACTORY BOY".

THE RICK-BURNER'S HOME: LEACH CARTOON FROM "PUNCH" 1844; ONE OF A SERIES DEPICTING AGRICULTURAL DISTRESS.

RITING, IN 1912, a new preface for *Under the Greenwood Tree*, which had first appeared in 1872, Hardy remarked, "In rereading the narrative after a long interval there occurs the inevitable reflection that the realities out of which it was spun were material for another kind of study … than is found in the chapters here penned so lightly, even so farcically and flippantly at times. But circumstances would have rendered any aim at a deeper, more essential, more transcendent handling unadvisable at the date of writing." What he really meant was that, in 1872, there had still been too many people alive in the neighbourhood of Bockhampton, his Mellstock in the novel, for him to feel uninhibited in writing about the place warts and all, as he had truly known it.

Hardy, as a child, was well aware of the seamy side of rural life, as all children raised in such communities are bound to be, even if sheltered by the less abrasive circumstances of their own homes from experiencing the raw things at first hand.

Wretched Loves

Country life, even today, in some of its aspects is all but incomprehensible to the urban dweller and Dorset, even as late as Hardy's era, was to urban eyes a wild place: backward and undeveloped. The poverty and wretched living conditions of the Dorset agricultural labourer that

had prompted the march of the Tolpuddle Martyrs in 1834 still lingered in that part of the country, where, comparatively speaking, the Industrial Revolution had as yet made little impact and had brought few advantages to the local population which was still largely restricted to agriculture for wage earning opportunities – and agricultural wages remained very low. Hardy would never forget having heard talk as a child of a shepherd boy who had died of want and who, when he was opened up by the doctors, was found to have only raw turnip in his stomach. Not for nothing was the period known as the Hungry Forties.

THE HOME OF THE RICK-BURNER.

The picturesque villages and cottages that Hardy described so deliciously in his novels were, as he knew from having lived among them, riddled with filth and disease. As Ruskin wrote in *Modern Painters*, ruminating upon a morning spent sauntering and sketching in the picturesque streets of the French town of Amiens, the melancholy mien of the boatmen on the river winding through the town, a perfect subject for the artist, and the gloomy faces of the women who sat spinning at cottage doors, made him wonder "how many suffering persons must pay for my picturesque subject and happy walk." How many suffering persons paid for Hardy's early Wessex novels? Perhaps this was too simple a way to ask the question, but certainly, apart from the starving shepherd-boy, Hardy could recall all too well the rural poverty he saw around him in childhood; would remember the children who, unlike himself, could not attend regularly at the village school because they had to labour, to the best of their ability, to add to their family's miserable income; their hours spent in backbreaking gleaning, gathering and scraping for harvest leftovers with which to augment the subsistence-level fare on which they struggled to survive; their fetching and carrying; scaring rooks; drawing water from the well; endless drudgery.

Poverty bred alcoholism and alcoholism violence, as in the case of his own drunken shepherd grandfather. Wife beating was the pattern of daily life in many families; some of them being sunk in poverty. Sexual brutality and sexual licence were equally accepted as an inevitable part of domestic life. Hardy observed it all: "Visible to me … the wrinkles, creases, & cracks of life as then lived."

Village dances and junketings led to drunken brawls and not infrequently serious fights. Superstition was rife. Suspicion and distrust of one's neighbours lingered from darker feudal times. People who fell behind in the daily struggle for survival were pauperized; or, in the case of women, driven on to the streets as the only alternative to starvation. Minor transgressors found themselves in the stocks on the village green. Worse felonies resulted in flogging, transportation, and, as the ultimate, hanging on the gallows to the grisly entertainment of a vast crowd of people – Hardy himself witnessed two public executions.

A Romantic Vision

We should be wary of romantically supposing that the rural labouring population as a whole was worse off after the industrial revolution than before it, or that rustic life was automatically happier and less harsh than working class life in cities and industrial regions. Expanded industry brought more jobs, better wages and resultantly a higher standard of living. Rusticity automatically limited opportunities for improved circumstances: forward-looking country youths and maidens all over Britain drifted away to the industrial regions; though the enormous popularity of Hardy's novels in their rural settings revealed the incurable nostalgia for the countryside that was nursed by these immigrants to cities and coalfields, foundries and

dockyards. Remembering the honeysuckle draping the old cottage porch and the moss on the roof of the tumbledown privy it was easy to forget what a muddy, mucky, miserable, comfortless lot the jolly ploughman's had really been.

> *Under the greenwood tree*
> *Who will not lie with me*
> *And strike a merry note …*

Hardy, writing *Under the Greenwood Tree*, struck a determinedly merry note and his entranced readers accepted it as a true portrayal of rural life. Hardy's childhood and village schooldays had taught him better than that, but he was sensible enough to keep it to himself at the outset of his literary career. Later he would be condemned as "pessimistic". He argued that his experience of existence prompted him to believe that a pessimistic view was not necessarily erroneous. To recognize the seamy, as well as the merry side was to provide a "fairly comprehensive" picture of the whole.

AS THE STOOK'D CORN IS CARTED AWAY TO THE RICK YARD, THE LOCAL POOR GLEAN WHAT IS LEFT OF THE HARVEST.

THE SEAMY SIDE

Education

STABLISHED CHURCH and nonconformist chapel struggled energetically in young Hardy's day for the spiritual guidance of the people; church being regarded as a less stringent discipline than chapel, as Jan Coggan, master sheep-shearer, expounded to his drinking crony Mark Clark in *Far From the Madding Crowd*; "A man can belong to the Church and bide in his cheerful old inn, and never trouble or worry his mind about doctrines at all. But to be a meetinger, you must go to chapel in all winds and weathers, and make yourself as frantic as a skit".

The close of the eighteenth century had seen recognition of the need for a national system of day schools, but the revival of religious nonconformity as part of the impulse of radical thinking and industrial revolution resulted in controversy between nonconformist support, led by a young Quaker schoolmaster, Joseph Lancaster, for undenominational religious teaching, which later formed the basis of the 1870 Education Act, and the Anglican demand, led by Andrew Bell, for schools under the control of the parochial clergy. In 1808 the Royal Lancasterian Society was formed (later the British and Foreign School Society) in order to carry on the work of Lancaster, while in 1809 the National Society for promoting the education of the poor in the principles of the Established Church of England and Wales was founded, Bell becoming its superintendent. Both the British Schools and the National Schools used the monitorial plan of tuition by senior pupils themselves; later developed into the pupil-teacher system for

so long the basic method in the English elementary system. It was a practical solution to the universal shortage of trained teachers. The National and the British and Foreign schools jogged along in a state of uneasy mutual co-existence until the 1870 Act brought about compromise.

Thomas Goes to School

It was into the classroom of Bockhampton National, that is to say, Church of England School, newly opened in the village, that Thomas was shyly led in 1848: "Pink, tiny, crisp-curled", as he would describe himself years later in the poem, "He Revisits his First School." Two years later he was removed to the British and Foreign Society School in Dorchester; not because his mother, guardian of his progress, particularly favoured nonconformism but because of the high reputation of Isaac Last, the schoolmaster there.

But education, as already remarked, does not consist solely of schooling and before he transferred to Dorchester young Thomas had his first introduction to the major miracle of the age, the railway, and also had his first glimpse of London. George Stephenson's steam locomotive which, in the 1820s, had been introduced to haul the coal which formed the basis of Britain's industrial wealth, had further developed as a method of passenger conveyance. In 1843 there had been some 2000 miles of railway in Great Britain; by 1848 there were 5000. The railway reached Dorchester in 1847 and in 1849 Jemima Hardy took Thomas down to London by train to visit an aunt in Hatfield; an adventure which he never forgot.

When they returned to Bockhampton in the New Year of 1850 a cholera epidemic was raging and Thomas was kept at home out of the way of contagion. When he

CITY SLUMS LIKE THIS NOTORIOUS "ROOKERY" BEHIND LONDON'S OXFORD STREET WERE BREEDING GROUNDS FOR DISEASE.

A COURT FOR KING CHOLERA.

CHAPTER ONE

resumed school it was in Dorchester, where he flourished both physically and as a scholar. To and fro he walked, between Bockhampton and Dorchester, six miles in all, daily, rain or shine; considered no walking distance whatever in those days, and greatly beneficial to his health.

An Apprenticeship

In 1853 Isaac Last branched out independently, opening a "commercial academy" for older and more advanced pupils and to this Hardy went at his mother's instigation. Here he studied technical as well as scientific and classical subjects, including Latin. His love of church ritual and music had given him a deep desire to be ordained, but gradually he was forced to face the hard truth that he was not a sufficiently proficient classicist to be placed at university. So in 1856 he was articled for three years to John Hicks, a Dorchester architect, to receive instruction in "architectural drawing and surveying"; his mother once more being behind what she saw as a step towards his social and economic advancement. Hardy acquiesced in her choice of career for him, though never wholly ceasing to regret his lack of a university degree.

Hicks, a clergyman's son, specialized in the rebuilding and restoring of Gothic churches: the Gothic, together with all other manifestations of the medieval, being the rage with Victorian Romantics. Typically, the great breakthrough in modern building of the era was not Gothic but Joseph Paxton's Crystal Palace; a building of vast dimensions covering four times the area of St Peter's, Rome, and built of plate glass, iron, timber, and prefabricated elements produced in various factories across the country. Built to house the Great Exhibition in London's Hyde Park it was completed within a mere six months and was rightly greeted as "A revolution in architecture from which a new style will date." It far outdistanced the technical horizons of its time and its style was limited chiefly to the construction of market halls and major railway stations during the Victorian age. Nobody visualized the new Houses of Parliament or the Law Courts as crystal

palaces; these remained firmly rooted in the Gothic tradition, partly because that was the favoured architectural idiom of the day and also because it was argued that England's civil liberties rested on the achievements of the Middle Ages and therefore it was right to build these shrines of British Freedom in medieval Gothic, or at least Victorian medieval Gothic.

Hardy, as pupil of Hicks, naturally specialized in restoring and rebuilding Gothic churches in the footsteps of his master, revelling in every aspect of Gothic revival. He might have written about himself then as later he was to write of Jude, "He did not see that medievalism was as dead as a fern leaf in a lump of coal; that other developments were shaping the world around him, in which Gothic architecture and its associations had no place." When, in 1862, having again taken a train to London he was offered a job by the distinguished ecclesiastical architect Arthur Blomfield, who was in need of "a young Gothic draughtsman who could restore and design churches and rectory-houses", Hardy leapt with joy at the opportunity.

DAME-SCHOOL IN A COTTAGE KITCHEN; OFTEN THE ONLY EDUCATION THAT EARLY NINETEENTH CENTURY CHILDREN RECEIVED.

EDUCATION

Hardy THE Architect

H ARDY SPENT the next five years in London working with Blomfield. He quickly settled into London life, lodging with another of Blomfield's young assistants and tasting the joys of opera and theatre going. Hardy got on well with Blomfield, a sporty genial man in his early thirties; they shared a love of music as well as enthusiasm for ecclesias-

tical architecture and, perhaps even more importantly, the same sense of humour. Hardy, a gifted draughtsman, worked diligently at his drawing board; he joined the Architectural Association and before long had won an RIBA Silver Medal. It was a heady time in which to plunge into the world of London architects and architecture. The profession was still split by the running battle between Neo-Classicism and Gothic Revival, while the Pre-Raphaelite rebellion against "false and modern systems of thought and practice in art" added to the controversy.

Victorian England, immersed as it was in an advanced state of industrialization with all its squalid consequences, longed for the return of romanticism yet at the same time for stability. In the aftermath of the Napoleonic Wars and the depression of the Hungry Forties, the Victorian Romantics turned their backs on Neo-Classicism, or the Greek Revival, which had been the inspiration of Napoleon's "Empire" style and English "Regency", and so was associated with a war-devastated Europe and the emergence, in England's hitherto "green and pleasant land", of a spreading blot of "dark satanic mills". Resultantly, medieval Gothic appealed to a generation despairing of the power of revived Athenian Reason to reform the world. Away with the "Age of Reason"; welcome instead "The Age of Faith".

The High Victorian Dream

In 1836 the architect A.C. Pugin published *Contrasts: a Parallel Between the Architecture of the 15th and 19th Centuries*; a key document in the history of Gothic Revival, being not only a diatribe against Neo-Classicism but against the full ethos of bourgeois Liberalism. But not all Romantics were Tory. Romantic Socialists covered a wide spectrum; the feudal socialism of Thomas Carlyle, calling for the application of medieval virtues to cure the vices of modern society; John Ruskin, convinced of the moral superiority of the Middle Ages over a nineteenth century which, in its slavish pursuit of wealth, had "lost its soul"; William Morris, who believed that art had become insincere through the influence of Raphael's acclaimed "Grand Manner" of painting and that therefore it behoved artists to return to the medieval "Age of Faith". Accordingly Morris, with a group of friends, pre-eminently Edward Burne-Jones and Dante Gabriel Rossetti, formed the Pre-Raphaelite Brotherhood to lead a "crusade and holy warfare against the present age."

Poetry and music participated too in what has been called the High Victorian Dream; the impassioned plea was for commercialism to be replaced by a spirit of chivalry. Wagner's *Ring* was a battle cry against the evils of industrialism, his music, declared Burne-Jones, was the very embodiment of "the Dream". While Tennyson, in his *Idylls of the King*, escaped into the dreamland of Arthurian Wessex.

The star of the High Victorian Dream was William Burges; art-architect of unique genius, the culmination of whose career came with the restoration and rebuilding of Cardiff Castle and the recreation of the nearby Castell Coch, originally built in the thirteenth century by Gilbert the Red, Earl of Gloucester. With these two castles Burges revealed the full fantasy of Romantic Gothic imagination in architectural terms.

Probably the greatest triumph of Victorian "medievalism" was the rediscovery of medieval "pot metal" stained glass; carried out in the Whitefriars Studios, acquired by Powell of Bristol in 1834, where stained glass had been made for three centuries. It was the resuscitation of the "pot metal" process that made possible the deep hued glory of Powell's windows. Another distinguished glass making firm, Heaton, Butler and Bayne, was housed in a Gothic factory designed by Blomfield: Hardy was friends with Clement Heaton, a chemist instrumental in perfecting glass staining for these new "medieval" marvels; "A succession of images drawn from every point of the

human horizon conveyed with an ardour that ultimately exhausts the force of the emotions and lends them an indefinable anguish; a vast tapestry wrought by an imagination enthralled by the phantasmagoria of the ages." Such was the art of Victorian "medieval" stained glass and such was the art, though expressed in a very different genre, of Hardy's Wessex chronicles when he came to write them.

Thomas Hardy's arrival in London coincided with the International Exhibition of 1862 at South Kensington, where he spent much of his spare time. One of the novel features of this exhibition was the breaking down of artistic subdivisions, as urged by Burges who saw architecture as "the Great Art", necessitating that the architect should master the principles of all arts if he were to produce a perfect building. After viewing the 1862 exhibition Burges exulted, "Junior architects are following the example of the great men of the Middle Ages, and are gradually becoming artists as well as architects."

It is clear that Hardy took the precepts of Burges much to heart. He began studying the history of art and painting from the Renaissance onward, tried his hand at drawing from life, kept a busy sketchbook – street scenes, skyscapes, people, together with written observations. He embarked upon a course of serious reading. He had been writing poetry since his Dorchester days but now began working at his poems, redrafting, experimenting with styles, metres, words, phrases. He was not abandoning architecture for literature, but shaping himself in the Renaissance mould, mastering the principles of other arts. Had not Michelangelo been a poet?

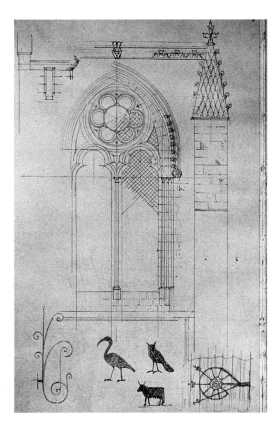

DETAILS FROM HARDY'S ARCHITECTURAL NOTEBOOK, (1862–72).

THE Poor Man AND THE Lady

BLOMFIELD, though a thoroughly respected and commercially successful Gothic Revivalist, belonged to the sober feet-on-the-ground league, far removed from the sphere of idiosyncratic genius inhabited by Burges. Blomfield had no multi-millionaire clients demanding a Castell Coch and would have poured cold water on such far-fetched schemes had they been put to him. Hardy, amusedly envisaging such an improbable situation, wrote an ironic, wickedly funny poem on the subject, part of which follows. Entitled "Heiress and Architect", Hardy dedicated it to Blomfield – whose robust sense of humour responded with snorts of glee,

NEW ST PANCRAS CHURCH; BRITAIN'S FIRST GREEK REVIVAL CHURCH, BUILT 1819–22.

…"A little chamber, then, with swan and dove
Ranged thickly, and engrailed with rare device
Of reds and purples, for a Paradise
Wherein my Love may greet me, I my Love,
When he shall know thereof?"

"This, too, is ill,"
He answered still,
The man who swayed her like a shade.
"An hour will come when sight of such sweet nook
Would bring a bitterness too sharp to brook,
When brighter eyes have won away his look,
For you will fade."

Then said she faintly, "O, contrive some way —
Some narrow winding turret, quite mine own,
To reach a loft where I may grieve alone
It is a slight thing; hence do not, I pray,
This last dear fancy slay"

"Such winding ways
Fit not your days,"
Said he, the man of measuring eye;
"I must even fashion as the rule declares,
To wit: Give space (since life ends unawares)
To hale a coffined corpse adown the stairs,
For you will die."

Hardy had been composing poetry since Dorchester, but now it became his habit to mark every step of his life's journey, every nuance of his thinking and feeling with a poem. This seemed to be as instinctive to him almost as breathing. Moreover, the first fumblings surmounted, it was marvellous poetry. Frequently, one suspects, it outdistanced in intensity the incident, or reaction, which inspired it. A rather dreary affair with a pious and bookish young woman, a lady's maid, Eliza Bright Nicholls, whose employer was daughter-in-law of the Archdeacon of Surrey, wound a depressing course towards an engagement. Her love for Hardy seems to have been soulfully clinging and clammy and he only escaped from it by adopting the desperate expedient of switching to an infatuation for her younger and prettier sister, which meant a broken heart for Eliza, shrugs and pouts from the sister, and, from Hardy, a deeply moving sequence of lyrics, "She to Him", which he wryly admitted, much later, were Eliza's letters to him transcribed into verse-form, "as having in them that living fire which no lubrication can reach."

Illness and Eroding Faith

These London years saw the gradual erosion of Hardy's religious faith, increasing perplexity as to whether he should abandon architecture for a risky venture into writing, and, in 1867, a deterioration in his health. Autumn 1866 saw him paying frequent visits to St Pancras cemetery to prevent irregularities during the removal of graves in the path of a new railway line: "Horrible Desecration of the Dead at St Pancras!" was typical of the outcry whipped up by the newspapers. It was one of those ghoulish episodes best treated as a joke by those involved; in later years Blomfield would greet his former assistant, by now a famous novelist, with a merry, "D'you remember how we found that man with two heads at St Pancras?" Whether or not St Pancras cemetery had anything to do with the vague, debilitating illness to which Hardy now succumbed is impossible to say; in greater likelihood it was nervous exhaustion, the result of jilting two sisters simultaneously, rather than the exhumation of a man with two heads. Whatever the cause, it was decided that Hardy should go home to Dorset to recuperate. Blomfield kept his job open for him, but instead Hardy resumed working for Hicks in Dorchester and after Hicks's sudden death, for G.R. Crickmay who took over the business.

By now Hardy had started work on a novel, *The Poor Man and the Lady*, "A Story with No Plot: Containing some original verses." Most of the verses had been written by Hardy while in London; they were linked by an episodic narrative concerning a radical young architect of peasant background, Will Strong, and his love for the squire's daughter. In the face of her father's opposition they marry secretly, whereupon she abruptly dies for no apparent reason other than meeting the demands of a plotless plot, which had earlier necessitated temporary blindness for the architect. Hardy sent the novel to Macmillan, who refused it but encouraged Hardy to persevere with writing as he showed promise of "power and purpose". *The Poor Man and the Lady* followed the course so often set by first novels: after having made the unsuccessful rounds of several publishing houses it was plundered by its author for subsequent books: in this instance for the Christmas scenes in the tranter's house in *Under the Greenwood Tree*.

TRYPHENA SPARKS,
WITH WHOM
HARDY FLIRTED.

Tryphena and Cassie

During this period Hardy conducted a flirtation with his cousin, Tryphena Sparks: rumours that they had an affair, that she bore him a child but that they could not wed because in reality they were uncle and niece, though appealing to sensation seekers fail to bear up under scrutiny. Hardy swiftly followed this flirtation with Tryphena by another, this time with a local servant, Cassie Pole; for her Hardy was said to have bought the engagement ring that he gave to Emma Gifford, by whom he was enchanted in an Arthurian setting fully worthy of any Castell Coch.

Emma AND Lyonesse

EMMA LAVINIA
GIFFORD, AS SHE
WAS WHEN HARDY
MET HER.

ARDY WAS still an architect, when he met his first wife, Emma Lavinia Gifford, in 1870 in the Cornish setting of St Juliot (pronounced Juliet), a hamlet neighboured by the smugglers' harbour of Boscastle, and Tintagel of Arthurian legend – nothing could have been more romantic. Cornwall in those days knew no tourists – wild, remote, a foreign country almost, its people still smuggling and wrecking whenever the opportunity presented itself, the outside world might have been a million miles away. Here Emma Lavinia, twenty-nine years of age but passing herself off as twenty-four, lived with her sister Helen, second wife of the Reverend Cadell Holder, rector of St Juliot. Hardy arrived there in early March, to "take a plan and particulars" of the hamlet's dilapidated, centuries-old church as a preliminary step to its restoration.

Emma Lavinia was as picturesque a figure as her name and location demanded. Blue-eyed, rosy-cheeked, graceful and slender, she wore her cornripe hair in a dramatic profusion of loose-flowing ringlets, with more ringlets arranged on the crown of her head and a rich fringe of curls framing a face not so much pretty as appealing; childlike, yet provocative; dreamy; a spontaneous warm-hearted friendliness about to break into a smile irradiating what might otherwise have seemed rather plain features. Not surprisingly Hardy thought her "very attractive". To add to her romantic appeal she was a dashing horse-woman. All this proved irresistible to the poet in Hardy and in no time at all he was in love with her.

I found her out there
On a slope few see,
That falls westwardly
To the salt-edged air,
Where the ocean breaks
On the purple strand,
And the hurricane shakes
The solid land.

Emma, for her part, was less carried away by Hardy's physical attractions – which admittedly were not great. But at twenty-nine and buried in such a remote spot she was privately anxious about finding a husband and quickly decided that she did not like handsome men; clever, well read ones were more to her taste. Monday, March 7 was the date on which they first met – and to this date after Emma's death forty-two years later the calendar on his desk was always set. It was March 11 when the two first kissed and voiced their love. Hardy was obliged to return to Dorset, but returned to St Juliot in August for a further three weeks of magical courtship.

Nonetheless four years elapsed before they could marry. Emma's father disapproved of the match, believing Hardy to be socially inferior to the middle-class Giffords, and to worsen matters his financial prospects were wretched: in 1872 gamely backed by Emma, Hardy had given up his promising career as an architect for a dubious career as a novelist. During this waiting period he and Emma kept their ardour alive with an exchange of love letters that Hardy, in old age, would recall as having been comparable to the love letters of Robert and Elizabeth Browning; the truth of this claim we shall never know for Emma, in the later unhappy years of their marriage, burned them.

The Emma Poems

Of all the poetry Hardy wrote in his writing career, none was more beautiful, moving or strange than the so-called "Emma Poems". Written for her during her life time and, more importantly, after her death the poems are in a vein that makes it almost impossible for the reader to be sure whether they are written for a real woman or a dream woman; a woman living, or a woman lost and gone, a memory, or a ghost.

The "Emma Poems" are haunting and haunted in the truest sense, expressing a great ache of loss, yet at the same time a sense of intense happiness discovered and known: poems unlike any others in the English language.

A DREAM OR NO

Why go to Saint-Juliot? What's Juliot to me?
Some strange necromancy
But charmed me to fancy
That much of my life claims the spot as its key.

Yes, I have had dreams of that place in the West,
And a maiden abiding
Thereat as in hiding;
Fair-eyed and white-shouldered, broad-browed and brown-tressed.

And of how, coastward bound on a night long ago,
There lonely I found her,
The sea-birds around her,
And other than nigh things uncaring to know.

So sweet her life there (in my thoughts it has seemed)
That quickly she drew me
To take her unto me,
And lodge her long years with me. Such have I dreamed.

But nought of that maid from Saint-Juliot I see;
Can she ever have been here,
And shed her life's sheen here,
The woman I thought a long housemate with me?

Does there even a place like Saint-Juliot exist?
Or a Vallency Valley
With stream and leafed ally,
Or Beeny, or Bos with its flounce flinging mist?

TINTAGEL:
"...THOSE HAUNTED HEIGHTS
THE ATLANTIC SMITES
AND THE BLIND GALES SWEEP."

CHAPTER TWO

2 Hardy Country

SOME WRITERS, especially poets, belong so intensely to their own native place that they are literally welded into it; unable to live or work satisfyingly when exiled from it. They live their homeland, rather than merely live in it. William and Dorothy Wordsworth lived the Lakes; Charles Lamb and Charles Dickens lived London; Sir Walter Scott lived Scotland; Emily Brontë lived the bleak Yorkshire heights and dales. Hardy lived Wessex; defined by him as "a province bounded on the north by the Thames, on the south by the English Channel, on the east by a line running from Hayling Island to Windsor Forest, and on the west by the Cornish coast." The name, Wessex, he took from the ancient heptarchy; the seven kingdoms of Angles and Saxons in Britain. This, as poet and novelist, was his kingdom, and such was the fame it acquired through him that already in his lifetime and ever since this corner of England, his Wessex, has been known as "Hardy Country": the heart of this realm being, of course, Hardy's native Dorset.

Hardy clove to Wessex not only because it was in his blood but also because he, as a powerful creative writer, felt the urgent need of the dramatic unities that he had so come to respect in his reading of the Greek tragic dramatists: dramas that, to quote his famous preface to the 1912 edition of his Wessex novels, "Evolve their action on a circumscribed scene." True, he continued, it may be argued that such tightly knit narratives "cannot be so inclusive in their exhibition of human nature as novels wherein the scenes cover large extents of country … even wander over the four quarters of the globe." But this, argued Hardy, was "untrue in respect of the elementary passions." Furthermore he considered that "Our magnificent heritage from the Greeks in dramatic literature found sufficient room for a large proportion of its action in an extent of their country not much larger than the half-dozen countries here

reunited under the old name of Wessex [and] anyhow, there was quite enough human nature in Wessex for one man's literary purpose."

But though choosing to confine himself in a circumscribed topographical space, Hardy was not thereby confined in any circumscribed space of time. It has been said of Hardy that he was one of those rare beings who can live two lives in time and many more in imagination.

The Wessex in which he set the action of his tales was essentially that of his own early childhood and his immediate forebears: a Wessex still remote and deeply rural, its inhabitants as yet barely touched by either industrial or agrarian revolution; a Wessex that was fast disappearing, much of which indeed had vanished for ever even as he began writing his first Wessex novels in his spartan little bedroom under the heavy thatched eaves of the Bockhampton cottage.

But the disappearance of the place about which he wrote meant nothing to Hardy; he lived it so intensely that for him it could not be lost – it would be real and present for him for ever. Sleepy villages and little towns respectively drowsing and bustling as they had drowsed and bustled for long centuries past; the pattering and plodding of footsteps; the clopping of horses' hooves and the rumbling of cart wheels; the flux of seasons, bringing with them their own particular rites and labours; the ploughing, lambing, harvesting; the feasts and festivals: an ever-changing calendar forever rooted in an eternal order of things. Rooted, too, in archetypal myths and superstitions reaching far far back in time; yet strangely accessible to Hardy who, in his genius, found the Wessex of the profound past, with its henge-sites and earthworks, its burial-mounds and long-barrows, its giants and horses carved white as ivory in the chalk of timeless hillsides, as real and immediate to him as the Victorian trappings of Dorchester Town Hall.

Hardy's Wessex

 ESSEX, declared Hardy, his Wessex, was meant to be any and every place; a region apparently local yet really universal. Yet this said, "At the dates represented in the various narrations things were like that in Wessex: the inhabitants lived in certain ways, engaged in certain occupations, kept alive certain customs", just as they were shown doing in the novels. It was a vanishing Wessex, perhaps an already lost Wessex, but nonetheless what his readers found in his pages was a fairly true record of that vanished life. "The description of these backgrounds has been done from the real." Hardy's tone was emphatic as he made this point.

Even if the backgrounds were "done from the real" there was no denying that the country of Wessex that Hardy was inviting his readers to enter with him was, as he constantly sighed, "half dream"; illusive, yet illusion with something real as its basis. The map that he drew of Wessex, for his readers, when he was engaged in writing *The Mayor of Casterbridge* was in part, no doubt, prompted by a shrewd professional realization that the time was ripe for the full exploitation of the regional setting of his novels and poems; the Wessex novels should be boldly named as such, he instructed his publisher: "I find that the name Wessex, which I was the first to use in fiction, is getting to be taken up everywhere: & it would be a pity for us to lose the right to it for want of asserting it." A map of his fictional region, firmly entitled "The Wessex of the Novels and Poems", greatly furthered a sense of reality, even though it was accompanied by the warning, "It is to be understood that this is an imaginative Wessex only, & that the places described under the names here given are

not portraits of any real places, but visionary places which may approximate to the real places more or less."

Two groups of names were used: some actual; some fictitious, or so ancient as to be unfamiliar. Among the real names appeared the Vale of Blackmoor or Blakemore, Hambledon Hill, Bulbarrow, Nettlecombe Tout, Dogbury Hill, High-Stoy, Bubb-Down Hill, The Devil's Kitchen,

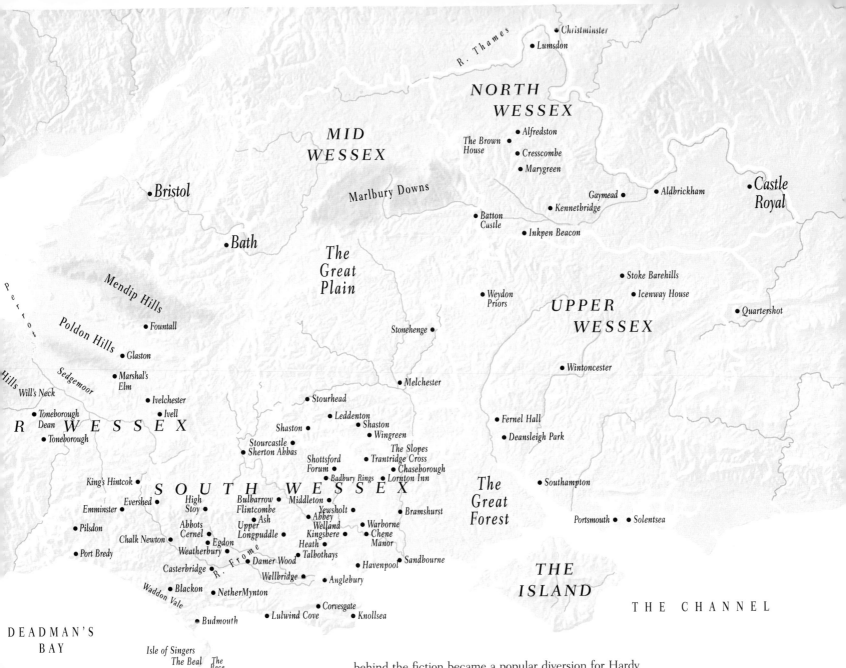

NORTH WESSEX

MID WESSEX

•Christminster
•Lumsden

R. Thames

The Brown House
•Alfredston
•Cresscombe
•Marygreen

•Bristol

Marlbury Downs

Gaymead• •Aldbrickham

•Castle Royal

•Kennetbridge

•Batton Castle

•Bath

•Inkpen Beacon

The Great Plain

•Stoke Barehills

•Weydon Priors

UPPER WESSEX

•Icenway House

•Quartershot

Mendip Hills

Perrot

Poldon Hills

•Fountall

•Stonehenge

•Wintoncester

•Glaston

Sedgemoor

•Marshal's Elm

•Melchester

•Fernel Hall

Hills Will's Neck

•Ivelchester

•Toneborough Dean

•Ivell

WESSEX

•Stourhead

•Deansleigh Park

•Toneborough

•Leddenton

Shaston•

•Shaston

•Wingreen

•Stourcastle

The Slopes

The Great Forest

•Sherton Abbas

Shottsford Forum•

•Trantridge Cross

•Chaseborough

•Badbury Rings •Lornton Inn

•King's Hintock

SOUTH WESSEX

•Southampton

Evershed•

High Stoy

Bulbarrow•

Flintcombe•

•Middleton

Yewsholt•

•Bramshurst

•Emminster

•Ash

Abbey•

•Warborne

•Portsmouth •Solentsea

•Pilsdon

Abbots Cernel

Upper Longpuddle

Welland•

Kingsbere•

•Chene Manor

Chalk Newton•

•Egdon

Heath•

•Weatherbury

R. Frome

•Talbothays

•Sandbourne

•Port Bredy

•Damer Wood

•Havenpool

Casterbridge•

Wellbridge•

•Anglebury

THE ISLAND

Waddon Vale

•Blackon

•NetherMynton

•Corvesgate

THE CHANNEL

•Budmouth

•Lulwind Cove

•Knollsea

DEADMAN'S BAY

Isle of Singers
The Beal The Race

Cross-in-Hand, Long-Ash Lane, Giant's Hill, Crimmercrock Lane, and Stonehenge: all obviously too good, as names in themselves, to be sacrificed to illusion. The rivers Froom, or Frome, and Stour, were retained together with large towns and other points helping to mark the outline of Wessex; these included Bath, Plymouth, The Start, Portland Bill, Southampton. Fictitious naming saw Dorchester become "Casterbridge", Salisbury Plain simply "The Great Plain", Shaftesbury changed to "Shaston", Sturminster Newton to "Stourcastle", Taunton to "Toneborough", Bournemouth to "Sandbourne", Winchester to "Wintoncester", Oxford to "Christminster", and so on. Of course keen readers were always writing to say that they clearly recognized the originals; spotting reality

behind the fiction became a popular diversion for Hardy fans, gratifying to the author if only because it boosted sales. "I do not contradict these keen hunters for the real; I am satisfied with their statements as at least an indication of their interest in the scenes."

More difficult to make convincing was the inclusion of the essentially Celtic Cornwall in the Anglo-Saxon Wessex. Hardy needed Cornwall for romantic and Arthurian reasons; on his map he showed with complete conviction a main section extending from Barnstaple to a line reaching between Portsmouth and just beyond Oxford and broke this up into Lower Wessex, Outer Wessex, Mid Wessex, North Wessex, Upper Wessex and South Wessex; Cornwall, which he named as "Lyonesse (or Off Wessex)", he placed in a smaller scale inset.

Prehistoric Wessex

N HARDY'S CHILDHOOD large tracts of heathland, lonely and uncultivated, still survived in Dorset: his own birthplace at Higher Bockhampton stood upon the edge of one such empty quarter; "Egdon Heath" it became, when the time arrived for him to create his Wessex. "A face upon which time makes but little impression," was how he introduced this "vast tract of unenclosed wild" at the start of *The Return of the Native*; the novel he centred around that Wessex of prehistory, which for him was so essentially part of the present. The story opens one November twilight and in a passage of ominous foreboding brings the Heath gradually to life, to brood over the reader like some fearsome jurassic monster, until a final heart-stopping image sets the full narrative in motion:

> *At this transitional point of its nightly roll into darkness the great and particular glory of the Egdon waste began, and nobody could be said to understand the heath who had not been there at such a time ... The place became full of a watchful intentness ... When other things sank brooding to sleep the heath appeared slowly to awake and listen. Every night its Titanic form seemed to await something; but it had waited thus, unmoved, during so many centuries, through the crises of so many things, that it could only be imagined to await one last crisis – the final overthrow.*

Hardy set his readers down in the heart of the heath: a scene of "hillocks, pits, ridges, acclivities, one behind the other", culminating in a great long-barrow, silhouetted against the still light sky. "It formed the pole and axis of this heathery world." Slowly, a figure rises from the giant mound: a woman. As if alarmed by something she glides out of view. "With her dropping out of sight a newcomer,

bearing a burden, protruded into the sky ... ascended the tumulus, and deposited the burden on the top. A second followed, then a third, a fourth, a fifth, and ultimately the whole barrow was peopled with burdened figures." The reader's blood runs cold. Here is prehistory "for real", as Hardy would say.

The Origin of Species

It was fifty years since Darwin's *The Origin of Species* had exploded like a fireball upon a shattered society; the search for "the missing link" was a quest of burning interest. The discovery, in 1907, of a massive lower jaw in a gravel pit at Mauer, in Germany, prompted H.G. Wells into "tormenting" speculation about the "Thing, shambling through the bleak wilderness, clambering to avoid the sabre-toothed tiger, watching the woolly rhinoceros in the woods." Could Man, stated by the Bible to have been created in the image of God, really be descended from this shambling Thing? Scientific-minded Wells was inclined to give the Thing the benefit of the doubt. More tormented doubts were prompted in 1908, by the excavation of a whole male Neanderthal fossil skeleton in France. To prevent it falling into the hands of the Darwinian-aligned École d'Anthropologie, which argued that Neanderthals, brutish things that they were, should be included in human ancestry, it was hurried away, upon the advice of the famous clerical palaeologist, the Abbé Breuil, to the Museum of Natural History in Paris, which in due course pronounced that it was anatomically impossible that *Homo sapiens* could have Neanderthal origins. Meanwhile, in 1912, a new "ancestor" had been unearthed in a gravel pit at Piltdown, Sussex: the skull, believed to be 50,000 years old, of a much brainier, lighter-built, fleet-footed counter-

part of the Thing from Mauer. For the next fifty years Neanderthal man was expelled from our ancestral tree. Eventually, in 1953, Piltdown Man was exposed as a forgery: the stained and filed-down jaw of a young orang-utan with a mediaeval cranium.

Now, archaeology has resources at its disposal unknown to Hardy's era. Carbon dating detected a Piltdown fraud and, applied to analyses of sediments, muds and oozes retrieved from lake beds and ocean floors, has brought an understanding of survival patterns of pre-historic man. Finds in Africa provide evidence of earliest homonids dating to about four million years ago. Pioneers from Africa arrived in Europe at least 730,000 years ago: European Neanderthal man is now believed to have derived directly from these pioneering Archaic *Homo sapiens* of the Middle Pleistocene – called "archaic" to differentiate them from later European man, *Homo sapiens sapiens* and the African earliest finds of *Homo erectus*. One fossilized specimen of Archaic *Homo sapiens* has been found in the Thames Valley, on the fringe of Hardy's Wessex.

Gradually the Neanderthals were absorbed by the moderns – a process of natural interrelation rather than mass genocide or direct conflict between the two populations; scenarios dear to writers of popular prehistory. This is far removed from Hardy's later Neolithic and Bronze-Age Wessex with its agrarian settlements, their surviving plough marks dating to at least 3500 BC, and its pottery, known as Groove Ware, associated with henge monuments such as Avebury, Darrington Walls and Stonehenge, which still retained symbolic power for the later Bell-Beaker people,(2560–1300 BC); named after the bell-shaped beakers placed in burial mounds.

Bell-Beaker culture took over in Wessex after a long struggle with the old order of things represented by the henge monuments: early Bell-Beaker burials were well distanced from these ceremonial sites as if indicating that these belonged to an inimical civilization. Later Bell-Beaker burials returned to the henge sites and involved an elaboration of Stonehenge, *c.*2000 BC, as a stone circle instead of the earth and timber monument it had been. Similar changes took place at Avebury, and West Kennet. Hardy spoke wistfully of the possibility that somewhere in the tract of Egdon Health might lie the territory of "that traditiony King of Wessex Lear." But when he came to people the great mound, which he, in his Wessex, called Rainbarrow, those he portrayed rising up from it were not kingly élitists arrayed with gold and amber jewellry and high-ly-crafted bronze daggers, as the Bell-Beaker people had become, but Neanderthal Things carrying bundles of furze to make bonfires celebrating an ancient witch-cult festival.

Superstition

"THE UNFATHOMABLE EXPERIENCE that humanity has symbolically expressed for millennia through myths, fables, rituals and ecstasies, remains one of the hidden centres of our culture, of the way we exist in this world," says Carlo Ginzburg in *Ecstasies: Deciphering the Witches Sabbath* (1990). Of this no writer

has been more aware than Hardy. So innately did he take this unfathomable experience for granted that he considered it natural to use material based on witchcraft and associated superstitions for his Wessex novels.

People said smugly, "Nobody believes in these things any more"; Hardy knew that these things were, in fact, still very much alive in his native homeland and would remain

alive: in 1913 Florence Dugdale, the future second Mrs Thomas Hardy, wrote to a friend of "The extraordinary case of witchcraft which has occurred at High Bockhampton in the next cottage to Mr Hardy's birthplace. Everyone in the village believes firmly in witchcraft."

The Little People

A particularly strong belief in witches and fairies persisted in Dorset. Perhaps not surprisingly the barrows were believed to be inhabited by Little People. We find one John Walsh of Netherberry, Dorset, arraigned for witchcraft in 1566, testifying that "when so disposed, he speaketh with them [fairies] upon hyls, where as there is great heapes of earth, as namely in Dorsetshire." Hardy's knowledge of witchcraft cults and archaic rites would have been remarkable in anybody other than he. For instance, one thinks of his extraordinarily vivid description of the pagan – probably fertility rite dance – introduced by him at the start of *The Return of the Native* when the turf cutters leap and bound among the dying embers of their fire on the long-barrow summit, an "outstep, ill-accounted place" and of the spellcasting of Susan Nunsuch, the wife of the son of a witch, when she works on a "ghastly invention of superstition, calculated to bring powerlessness, atrophy, and annihilation on any human being against whom it was directed ... A practice well known on Egdon at that date, and" adds Hardy darkly, "one that is not quite extinct at the present day." This in 1878. He describes this ghastly practice in detail, step by step.

Much superstition was attached to farm implements. If a man cut himself with a bill-hook or a scythe he took care to clean the blade carefully and to keep it bright and well oiled to prevent his injury from festering. If his horse ran a nail into its foot, or he ran one into his own, the important thing was to remove the nail-clean and grease or oil it and put it away carefully, to prevent the foot from festering, and while putting it away to repeat the name of the Father, of the Son, and of the Holy Ghost. But if you cut yourself with a knife then that knife had to be stuck in damp ground; your cut healed as the knife rusted.

A protection against magic was the wearing of a small red cloth bag next to the skin; the bag to contain some blessed salt and herbs and a bent steel nail – the nail acting as a sort of magic lightning conductor. Steel nails were considered particularly efficacious; doubtless because nails possessed a connotation with the nails used in Christ's crucifixion, just as the linen strips used for wrapping round injurious blades possessed a link with the linen of the Holy Shroud. The steel furthermore represented the witch's force while the bending symbolized the deflection of evil which it was hoped the force would be subjected to. Similarly to ward off evil spells cast against your house you hammered charmed steel nails into the wall. Within this context there lingered a strong belief that it "helped" a sickly tree to hammer a nail into it. Such superstitions were legion – and of course not only confined to Wessex. As a prevailing protection against witches you always planted a rowan tree near your front door and if things got seriously bad you buried a charmed toad in front of the house, or the stable if the mischief were being aimed at your horses, or the cowshed if a witch had made your cows run dry.

Hardy Witches

There were magic words known only to witches and used only for certain purposes, the most important being to raise the Devil. There were secret rites for rain-making, and fertility. Most of this lore was handed down orally; the more secret being closely guarded knowledge of certain families. One wonders if the Hardy clan of High Bockhampton may not have been one of these: the favoured family name of eldest sons, Thomas, is in itself

not without significance, being recorded as traditionally associated with members of witches' covens. Was Emma Hardy, with her unexpected but undoubted gift for inspired random perception, being wholly wild when she accused Hardy's sister Mary of being "a witch-like creature", adding, "I can imagine you and your mother and sister on your native heath raising a storm on Walpurgis night." Doubtless one of Emma's moments of dementia, but for all that a little chilling as a letter from one sister-in-law to another!

Books of magic, spells, love charms, recipes and fortune telling were handed down from one generation to the next in certain households: the possession of such a book was usually kept a secret for if ownership of it became known it marked the possessor as the Devil's own. Indeed, in a predominantly illiterate and deeply superstitious rural community the mere possession of any book roused

suspicion. Literacy, in mediaeval times and later, was commonly associated with wizardry. Owners of books of magic even frightened themselves – we should remember that Tess Durbyfield's family owned such a book, which was never kept in the house overnight but was always concealed in the thatch of the outhouse, lest the Devil came to claim it. The owner of such a book considered it so dangerous to handle that a hoop of iron was advisedly worn on the head while consulting the contents – though we do not find the Durbyfields going that far.

So distant in time is all of this to us and so contemptuous are we now of superstition that we dismiss the significance of these matters for Hardy, even if he no longer believed in any of it; which we must assume, because he wrote freely about it. Born when he was, in a profoundly rural and remote location in what was notoriously a bewitched corner of the country, it would have been truly amazing if he had not grown up steeped in superstition and ancient lore which, inevitably, surfaces repeatedly in his novels, even if we do not always recognize it.

CARTOON "WITCHES IN THE HAYLOFT" BY THOMAS ROWLANDSON (1756–1827).

Agriculture

ODAY WE READ HARDY'S WESSEX novels because we love their rural background, which is now so totally lost to us. The timelessness of his works enchants us; especially because we know what Hardy did not know, that this countryside would not last. Nostalgia is an essential ingredient of the success of the Wessex novels. The cults, rituals and superstitions recorded in them might be described as the instinctive sub-text of an agricultural tradition traceable in a line back to Neolithic times. Hardy encapsulated the seemingly eternal endurance of his rural England:

AGRICULTURAL
LABOURER SHARPENING
HIS SCYTHE.

Only a man harrowing clods
In a slow silent walk
With an old horse that stumbles and nods
Half asleep as they stalk.
Only thin smoke without flame
From the heaps of couch grass;
Yet this will go onward the same
Though Dynasties pass.

It was not to be so. With the outbreak of the Great War in 1914 not just Hardy's countryside but Hardy's world shattered. It was not so much a case of the lights of Europe going out one by one as the twentieth century clanging down like a guillotine blade, severing the past from the future, destroying all sense of the measured progression of things. In 1914 Thomas Hardy was seventy four. Nothing had much changed for man or beast on the agricultural scene since the Black Death (*c.*1348–49) which, though a distant date for most, was a date of significance to Hardy. A steady increase of population prior to that calamity had

resulted in a land-hungry thirteenth-century that had given the landowners the whip hand over the peasantry. The system of cultivation in early mediaeval times was by strip-holding, which combined individual labour and public control; it gave each a fair share in the better and worse land; it bound folk together in a community and gave even the humblest a voice in shaping the agricultural policy of the village. In short the peasant cultivators, in relation to one another, formed a self-governing democracy; but in relation to the lord of the manor they were serfs, "bound to the soil" by feudal law, which demanded service from all able-bodied individuals.

The Black Death carried off over a third of the population, creating a labour shortage that gave the peasantry bargaining power over the lord of the manor. He could no longer rely on the compulsory labour of serfs to cultivate the manorial lands; the peasants now demanded cash for their services. By saving, the peasant was then able to purchase his freedom. Because the price of labour was now so high, many landlords let their land out on lease to what was now a new social and economic factor – a middle-class formed of substantial yeoman farmers. The serf was becoming extinct: transforming himself into a yeoman tenant farmer or sinking into the status of landless hired labourer, however a class of yeoman freeholders *owning* their land did not emerge until several centuries later. Agriculturalists were now divided into two classes; employers and employed. This fourteenth-century divide still split rural England in Hardy's day. Writing in 1927 he recollected that "down to

NASTASSIA KINSKI AS
TESS AND PETER FIRTH
AS ANGEL CLARE IN THE
MILKING SCENE FROM
THE ROMAN POLANSKI
FILM "TESS".

the middle of the last century, country villagers were divided into two distinct castes, one being the artisans, traders, "liviers" (owners of freeholds) and the manor-house upper servants; the other "work-folk" i.e. "farm labourers." Hardy noted that these castes rarely intermarried, or socialized.

This explains why Hardy resented being referred to as a "peasant"; placing firm emphasis on his middle classness. This was not snobbishness, as many of his modern critics infer, but because he was essentially part of an historically established social fabric, which remained unshaken. To his honour he never accepted a knighthood, often as one was offered to him; but nor would he tolerate being referred to as a peasant. Here lies the key to his fondness for telling the world that his Swetman ancestors had been yeomen for generations, farming land that passed to the Earls of Ilchester. Their land had been Swetman owned, rasped Hardy, "when the Ilchesters were at plow." As for his Hardy ancestors, they "from time immemorial" had been master-masons; not "journey-men" but self-employed and independent.

Emma Hardy, née Gifford, daughter of a lawyer, prided herself upon a professional middle-class background. She was the niece of Dr Edwin Gifford, Canon of Windsor and later Archdeacon of London. On the strength of this she saw herself as belonging to the "aristocracy of the Church of England" and with scorn referred to her husband's kin as "peasants". But as Hardy saw it, his father's position as a master-mason, an employer, and lifelong tenant of a cottage with one-and-three-quarter acres of land, placed his family firmly in the established middle-class.

The agricultural landscape of Hardy's day matched these feudal sentiments. Teams of oxen, such as the Romans had used, drew ploughs of mediaeval design. Harrows, in appearance dating to the Iron Age, rattled over the ground. Teams of mowers, moving in long rhythmic lines, scythed the hay; harvesting was done with reap-hook and crook stick as in Biblical scenes. Corn was still flayed on threshing floors: a steampowered threshing machine was introduced in the 1880s but was regarded with ingrained rural suspicion. Old ways were best.

Village Life

A BUSY BLACKSMITH

FITTING A SHOE

ON A HORSE

WHILE ANOTHER

CUSTOMER WAITS.

HARDY COUNTRY

S HARDY HIMSELF made clear, the village was an essential part of the agricultural landscape and what went on in the village was part of the ages-old diurnal round that had dictated the habits of men and women among their flocks and herds and crops since earliest times. Village life depended on the hour of the day, in other words, what the sun was doing, and what the sun was doing depended on the season. Life for agricultural man was seasonal, as it was for the rest of nature: in the village in winter folk rose in the dark and retired in the dark; in the summer they rose with the sun and went to bed at nightfall, the long summer days stretching on for ever. The villages themselves seemed, to paraphrase Wordsworth's description of Westmorland, to be "the production of nature"; to have risen out of their native soil. Village and landscape reposed together in a timeless symbiosis.

The closeness of rural man to nature, even today, is all but incomprehensible to urban dwellers. In Hardy's era living off the land was, for the rustic, a truly earthy existence. Most villagers had a garden plot in which they kept a beehive or two, grew flowers and vegetables, and maintained a few fowls. And then there was the pig; quite one of the family until the time came to turn him into bacon, ham, sausages, chitterlings, pig's fry, brawn, trotters; not to mention the succulent white meat eaten roasted fresh after the kill, or pickled for keeping. Hardy described this ritual in vivid, almost too vivid, detail in *Jude the Obscure*. He knew it all first-hand: we find his father writing to the youngest daughter, Katherine, absent

from home at college, "We are going to kill the pig round about next Thursday", adding that the girl would therefore be home in time to make black-pudding the following Monday "and just in time for the White Meat."

How cosy they look in retrospect, those little communities of thatched cottages, often occupying sites where men had clustered their habitations since the Middle Ages at least! However, we should remind ourselves that in the mid-1800s, the life expectancy of a rural manual labourer was 38 – but in London's Whitechapel, however, it was just 29. Infectious diseases and epidemics were rife in the 1800s and 1900s as the population explosion resulted in overcrowded, insanitary living conditions. Even in cities homes had no running water or decent sanitation, and humble cottages, however picturesque, were often death traps. Smallpox and tuberculosis were particularly feared, although the first was to some degree brought under control by vaccination; introduced in 1796 by Edward Jenner. This said, Jenner had no clear idea as to what he was really doing, as bacteria had not yet been discovered, infectious diseases were not understood. For that reason tuberculosis as a disease was known long before its cause was identified, or its contagious nature recognized. Cottages were a particularly encouraging environment for the tubercle bacillus, coughed into the air of the small, smoky and dusty rooms; perfect places to promote infection. Village life was squalid, hazardous and scourged with pulmonary tuberculosis, the dreaded "consumption", which carried off entire families to early graves. The disease was far from being confined to one class, it was too highly contagious for that, but the poor, by the very nature of their cramped and unhygenic living conditions, were especially afflicted.

The Brighter Side

To look at the brighter side, the village would doubtless be blessed with a general store selling a wondrous variety of goods ranging loaf-sugar to hair-pins and mouse-traps. Butchers, bakers and grocers in larger villages or the small towns served their more rural customers by dispatching vans, really small travelling shops, to outlying districts.

A wide range of services were offered by itinerant tradesmen who travelled the countryside in vagrant fashion; knife-grinders, basket-makers, brush and broom men, pedlars, men who rushed and caned chairs, others who sold herbal remedies and almanacks – there was no end to them. The era, unlike ours, was not one of death-dated articles, to be thrown away when worn out. Life was frugal; nothing was allowed to wear out until the bitter end; there was not an article of use that was not patched, welded, stitched, sewn, rivetted or in some way or other repaired, often to be handed down from one generation to the next. The cobbler and the blacksmith, the tinker and the tailor were essential members of a community, showing skill and ingenuity in breathing new life into the outworn. Then there were men selling rabbit and mole skins; and clarified adder's fat for sprains and rheumatism. Nothing was wasted. Somewhere in the offing there was always a bone-setter, a midwife, and one of those faceless females who, for a penny or two, was prepared to do anything from child-minding to laying out the dead.

The big house, the church, the tavern and the school; were the four main points of the village compass. The pump was the chief focal point, from whence radiated the gossip that bound the place together in a web of information – or misinformation. Gossip was a village's life blood, as Hardy knew when he portrayed villagers and village life.

Country Towns

THE VILLAGE WAS part and parcel of the landscape, a feature of it rather than an intrusion. The country towns *complemented* the rural life around, rather than appearing as urban opposites. At all events, this was the point made by Hardy in his description of the Dorchester of his youth, disguised as "Casterbridge", in his novel about the mayor of that ancient county town. Butterflies, Hardy assures us, still flew down the main street on fine summer days.

When we look at old photographs of these country towns, with their thoroughfares so wonderfully uncongested, not a mechanized vehicle in sight, but only the occasional horse-drawn vehicle – dray or waggon, gig or dog-cart, chaise or break – we sigh for their civilized tranquillity, their freedom from stress and pollution. They look so deliciously quiet, those country towns, so clean and secure and orderly. A bit sleepy perhaps? Well, that might make a pleasant change!

DORCHESTER HIGH STREET. HARDY IMMORTALIZED DORCHESTER AS CASTERBRIDGE.

The Merchants of a Country Town

There are plenty of shops, but all giving on to nice uncrowded pavements, and you can cross the road wherever you wish without cars parked in your way all along the kerbside, and once you are in the roadway there is absolutely no danger of being knocked down by an oncoming vehicle. The shop-keepers are all neatly arrayed in spruce white aprons, apart from the butchers who wear striped blue and white ones. The shops include a corn chandler's which may also sell dry goods in general, including candles, and, tucked well away from the open

premises, paraffin. If not, then the hardware shop will stock these things, together with paraffin lamps, their glass funnels and shades which are so easily broken, and wicks: all so important in households without either gaslight or electricity. There will be a combined wholesale and family grocer; a butcher's shop with livestock depot and abattoir attached – though out of sight and hearing; a wet fish-shop, if the sea is not too far distant; a chemist and apothecary's, with enormous ornamental glass flagons filled with red, blue, violet and green fluid which the naive suppose to be actual physick – as medicine was then always called, placed in the window. There will be a draper's and haberdasher's; a bakery complete with bakehouse on the premises; maybe a toy shop; and in every likelihood, tucked away somewhere, an old woman will sell homemade toffee and humbugs – and maybe even lace – in a tiny shop set up in her own front parlour. The town will boast a cobbler and bootmaker; a farrier; a joiner and undertaker; a sweep; a saddler and harness maker; a coal-yard; a saw-mill; perhaps a tannery. There may also be a brewery. Certainly there will be a goodly choice of inns, taverns, and humble pot-houses. There will a post-office, a fire-station and a police-station with lock-up. If you are in a county town there will not only be a Town Hall but also a court-house and the county gaol.

There will be a doctor or two; a firm of solicitors; a vet. There will of course be a church, possibly one of historic fame and beauty; there will be two or three non-conformist chapels. There will be schools; a drill hall; an auction mart; a work-house. There will be a private circulating library and, in later Victorian times, a public library. If a small town there may be a cottage hospital while a county town will almost certainly have an infirmary. Somewhere or other, probably behind the graveyard, there will be a mortuary. There will be various clubs and societies and much public spirit.

In looking back on those distant days before mechanism and freneticism took over we should be on our guard against becoming too eloquent about the absence of noise and pollution. A street on busy market days, or when the Assize courts were sitting, full of horse-drawn traffic with its clipping, clopping, jingling, jangling, the shouts of drivers and the rumbling and scraping of wheels was in reality far from quiet. And above all, what we do forget, was the prodigious quantity of horse dung forever being deposited in the streets; the smell; the flies in summer; the horrible liquefied ooze and mud that resulted whenever it rained. Highly necessary crossing-sweepers were found at every street corner and any other popular crossing spot.

Crossing Sweepers

Crossing-sweepers were more often than not self-employed, though some were engaged by banks, larger shops and other prosperous businesses on behalf of their customers – and partly in self-interest to prevent mud from forever being brought into their premises. The sweepers drew their ranks mainly from members of the servant and stable-hand class who had met with accident, illness or in any other unforeseen way had fallen on hard times. There were also child crossing-sweepers of either sex; usually orphans or former workhouse inmates. All that was needed to set up business as a crossing-sweeper was a broom; and a crossing to sweep. Brooms cost tuppence ha'penny each and didn't last more than a week in really wet weather. It wasn't, one sweeper informed a questioner, an "easy situation to work into as most of the good crossings was bespoke" and once you had made a successful bid you stuck to that crossing, in some cases for years on end. It was all a matter of luck and keeping a sharp eye for a crossing to fall vacant. If you did the job well you would most likely receive protection from the police, or the Town Hall, it being in the interest of the municipality to have clean streets. And, as aforesaid, banks

and business premises would employ sweepers. As it was a wet weather occupation sweepers found other jobs on fine days; running errands, collecting parcels, posting letters; or helping out in genteel households cleaning knives, boots, windows.

The earnings, or takings, on a crossing varied. In a largish town you were lucky to earn ten or twelve shillings a week; eighteen pence a day was considered an average "decent taking." The usual gratuity was a ha'penny. Male passers-by were more generous than females. Crossing-sweepers were considered "deserving poor", and honest. As one astringent observer ruminated, "Nearly all of them have had their minds so subdued by affliction, that they have been tamed so as to be incapable of mischief."

A KIND LADY LEADS A POOR OLD MAN ACROSS A BUSY CITY STREET AND GIVES A CROSSING SWEEPER A PENNY. UNCONSCIOUS SOCIAL COMMENT HERE!

Fairs AND Markets

THERE WERE CERTAIN DAYS of the year when the country towns became amazingly overcrowded and noisy; these were the market and fair days.

Markets were of various kinds, their frequency depending on their nature. Many towns then had, as they still do today, weekly markets in the traditional market square; not infrequently a widened place where the high street passed through the town centre. At this weekly market all kinds of farm and regional produce was sold; butter, cheese, cream, eggs, fruit, honey, poultry plucked and trussed ready for cooking; bacon, hams and sausages; pies and pasties; brawns and black-puddings; bunches of flowers; vegetables; knitted socks and stockings; pots and pans.

Itinerant folk were present selling goods, or offering services, of every kind and description. The weekly market, as it remains today, was a good general shopping venue. Also it enabled neighbours who didn't see each other that often to meet old friends and enjoy a good gossip.

Unlike today's weekly shopping markets there would also be a decent amount of dealing in grain going on at the same time. Hardy has left us a wonderful account of such a market, "lively as an ant-hill", with farmers trading with one another among the stalls of fruit and vegetables:

The farmers as a rule preferred the open carrefour for their transactions, despite its inconvenient jostlings and the danger from crossing vehicles, to the gloomy sheltered market-room provided for them. Here they surged on this one day of the week, forming a little world of leggings, switches, and sample-bags; men of extensive stomachs, sloping like mountain sides ... who in conversing varied their attitudes much, lowering themselves by spreading their knees, and thrusting their hands into the pockets of remote inner jackets. Their faces radiated tropical warmth; for though when at home their countenances varied with the seasons, their market-faces all the year round were glowing little fires. Some [were careless in their dress], appearing in suits which were historical records of their wearer's deeds, sun-scorchings, and daily struggles for many years past. Yet many carried ruffled cheque-books in their pockets which regulated at the bank hard by a balance of never less than four figures.

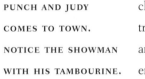

Plus ça change. Readers who frequent our more remote country markets will recognize much of this, even today.

Markets were not so large, or so specific in the commodity dealt in, as the fairs. Horse fairs, sheep fairs, agricultural shows; each had, and still has, where such fairs continue to exist, its own particular sounds, its own smells, and attracts its own type of attendance. A country town at fair time would be a seething mass of people and animals, and a constant uproar of sound. We are told that on the occasion of Marlborough's great annual sheep fair, at which there were often as many as twenty thousand sheep, it was impossible to sleep at night because of the noise they made. Agricultural shows were much as they are now, though smaller and not calculated to attract crowds of holiday makers from outside. There would be a prize ring for stock; with cattle and draught horses being led round for appraisal by the judges; and sheep and pigs being judged in pens; and probably another ring for the showing of sheepdogs, hounds and terriers. There would be side-shows; a fortune-teller's tent; and a flower-show and another of home produce – vegetables, honey, bread, jam, pickles, cakes and baking. There might be a Punch and Judy show, and swing-boats. There would be wrestling bouts; and running and jumping contests; a greasy pole up which hopeful youths sweated and slid to win the flower and-ribbon bedecked gammon of bacon perched on top of it; sack races; three-legged races. And of course there would be a beer tent.

Hiring Fairs

The two most important dates in the year for the agricultural population were the hiring fairs, held at Candlemas (February 2) and Martinmas (November 11). All those wishing for employment attended these fairs: again we do not have a better description of one that than given by Hardy in *Far From the Madding Crowd*, when Gabriel Oak the shepherd goes to the Candlemas hiring fair at Casterbridge: "Carters and waggoners were distinguished by having a piece of whip-cord twisted round their hats; thatchers wore a fragment of woven straw; shepherds held their sheep-crooks in their hands; and thus the situation required was known to hirers at a glance."

Quarter Days

The quarter days were still based on the ancient, presolstitial division of the year: Candlemas; Rood Day (Whitsun) on May 15; Lammas (August 1) and Martinmas – these quarter days have survived in Scotland. Frazer, in his famous work *The Golden Bough*, suggests that these festivals were connected with the breeding seasons of flocks and herds and date to neolithic times. The later, solstitial divisions of the year, which in course of time had Christian festivals laid over them, were: the shortest day, *c.*December 22, the feast of St Thomas; the great festival and quarter day, Yule, December 25, said by some experts to be the mid-winter red meat, or slaughter, season – the arrival of Christianity saw Yule renamed Christmas. The vernal equinox of *c.*March 20 became the Christian festival of Lady Day, March 25; Midsummer saw the great pagan feast of Beltane, on the longest day (*c.*June 21) with its fires of magical power. This became official Midsummer Day, June 24, the feast of St John the Baptist and the fires known as St John's Fire. Finally came the autumn equinox, *c.*September 13; which became the Christian festival of Michaelmas, September 29. The country fairs were originally set for saints' and feast days, which in turn concealed the old pagan feasts and festivals. Thus, beneath the bustling, jostling high days and holidays, fair days and show days of the present, there flowed always an undercurrent of the inescapable past.

CATTLE ARRIVING FOR MARKET. THE PEDESTRIANS HAVE TAKEN REFUGE IN THE MARKET HOUSE UNTIL THE PHOTOGRAPHER HAS GOT HIS PICTURE AND BUSINESS CAN BE RESUMED.

Maypoles
 AND Mummers

VER THE QUARTER OF A CENTURY during which Hardy's Wessex novels were appearing (1872–1896) interest in subjects such as folklore and mythology progressed from a popular fondness for quaint old customs and legends into an awakening serious interest in these studies and the realization of their importance within the context of the origins of ceremonial ritual and religious observance. One of the chief reasons for this was the immense furore aroused by the publication, in 1890, of a two volume work, *The Golden Bough: a Study in Magic and Religion* by James Frazer (1854–1941), classical scholar and professor of anthropology at Liverpool University. So great was the impact of *The Golden Bough* that it was expanded into a twelve volume treatise, published between 1907–15, and later, at popular demand, appeared as an abridged single volume in 1922; though not surprisingly a pretty hefty single volume. Hardy, in 1891, began an intent perusal of the first edition and immediately noticed the correspondence of Dorset folklore and the customs and beliefs discussed by Frazer. Others noticed this too and it was largely because of this that the Wessex novels gained a serious importance that might otherwise have eluded them had their interest been confined to readers of popular fiction.

The First of May

CHIMNEY Sweeps' Day, Blackbird is gay,
Here he is singing, you see, in the "May."
He has feathers as black as a chimney sweep's coat,
So on Chimney Sweeps' Day he must pipe a glad note.

JACK IN THE GREEN

Jack-in-the-Green from door to door
Capers along with his followers four,
As May Day mummers are seldom seen,
Let us all give a copper to Jack-In-the-Green.

18

"POPULAR FONDNESS FOR QUAINT OLD CUSTOMS": KATE GREENAWAY-STYLE TREATMENT OF JACK I' THE GREEN.

By the mid nineteenth-century the rustic rituals and revels so vividly described by Hardy belonged, to all intents and purposes, to the past, or, if still kept up through force of superstitious habit, were performed by persons who had wholly forgotten the origin of these ceremonies and celebrations and their true intention. Having started as solemn rites, upon the observance of which the welfare and even the life of the community depended, they had degenerated into light hearted pageants, mummeries and diversions. The little children dancing prettily round a maypole, or embarrassed adolescents dressing up as mummers, hadn't the first notion of what they were really involved with, enthusiastically as they might throw themselves into it all. The enthusiasm was in itself an indication of how artificial the thing had become. For as Hardy remarked of the mummers in *The Return of the Native*,

A traditional pastime is to be distinguished from a mere revival in no more striking feature than this, that while in the revival all is excitement and fervour, the survival is carried on with a stolidity and absence of stir which sets one wondering why a thing that is done so perfunctorily should be kept up at all … This manner of performance is the true ring by which a fossilized survival may be known from a spurious reproduction.

The May Day Festival

The maypole around which innocent children prance while their parents look on with indulgent smiles is the central feature of the May Day festival which was anciently the biggest fertility rite of the year. The maypole was more than mere phallic symbol, being simultaneously a tree spirit itself and the abode of a tree spirit. Tree spirits gave rain and sunshine, thereby causing crops to grow, flocks and herds to multiply and women to be blessed with offspring. A Tudor historian recorded how, on May Eve (April 30) all the countryfolk were "gadding out overnight enjoying pleasant pastimes" (resulting in at least a third of the young maidens finding themselves pregnant); everyone brought back with them branches of greenery with which to deck their homesteads. Above all they brought back to their village the maypole; reverently decked with flowers and bound round with coloured ribbons from top to bottom and drawn by twenty to thirty yoke of oxen, their horns tipped with nosegays. In Tudor times a fresh tree was fetched in, green and sappy, every year, to be set up on the village green, but later the maypole became, as a stark undressed object, a permanent fixture; being redecked each year for the May Day holiday merry-making. Things were no longer quite the same.

So much for the tree spirit as a presence in the tree; the original primitive concept. This developed into a tree spirit which detached itself from the tree to be represented in human form; an anthropomorphic variation on the original theme which became popular with the peasantry across the face of Europe, resulting in mummers, or play actors, performing dramas, pantomimes almost, based on the myths relating to these spirits in human form. Characters usually included a May Queen, or a Little May Rose, and always a youth bedecked in green leaves, called Father May, or, in England, Jack-in-the-Green; a chimney-sweeper traditionally encased in a pyramidal wickerwork frame (shades of the Druids!) covered with holly and ivy and surmounted by a crown of flowers and ribbons. Thus arrayed he danced at the head of a proces-

sion of chimney sweeps, or at least youths with blackened faces impersonating sweeps. In truth they represented Satan the Prince of Hell, who anciently superintended May Day revels. The procession usually included a white

MAY-DAY FESTIVAL   EASTINGTON. 1909.

clad, flower bedecked Queen of the May; sometimes a lord and lady or bridegroom and bride, sometimes the whole lot, depending on the mood of the village. Sometimes there was a clown with a white beard and wearing his clothes inside out. But these embellishments belonged to later times when things were slipping: the true traditional May Day mummers' cavalcade demanded Jack-in-the-Green, perhaps or perhaps not a queen; certainly a Moorish king with a sooty face and a crown on his head; a Dr Iron-Beard, a corporal, and an executioner; all bedecked with ribbons. The drama entailed a confrontation between the king and Dr Iron-Beard, the arrest of the king by the corporal, and the decapitation of the prisoner by the executioner. Which, Frazer tells us, represented the archaic ritual of ceremoniously putting the man-god, the King of the Wood, to death as the only means of preserving him from the inevitable decay of age: killed so that the divine spirit, incarnate in him, might be transferred in all its integrity to his successor.

VILLAGE MAY DAY
CELBRATIONS C.1880:
CHILDREN DANCE
AROUND THE MAYPOLE.

3 Apprenticed to the Pen

HARDY'S FIRST CONSCIOUS STEP in apprenticing himself to literature was to embark on a concentrated study of poetry – most importantly Shakespeare, Spenser and Wordsworth; with particular attention to Wordsworth's 1805 preface to *Lyrical Ballads* and *The Excursion*, 1814, a nine-book marathon of profound influence upon the earlier Victorian era. Among poets of his own generation Hardy responded with particular enthusiasm to Swinburne. He was rigorous in schooling himself in the discipline of poetry, which he rightly saw as a process akin to the training of a mason, allowing no wayward self-indulgence when it came to the crunch: a poem, like a built edifice, must either stand, or fall. Hardy also knew that reading is, for a writer, both essential nourishment and on-going confirmation. So he read. And continued to read for the rest of his life.

He early realized that he was a poet. There came, too, the realization that a man cannot support himself by poetry alone. So he turned to the novel. Following disappointment with his first attempt, *The Poor Man and the Lady*, he started on his second, *Desperate Remedies*, most of which he wrote while still working for Crickmay. *Desperate Remedies*, an intricately plotted "sensation novel" modelled on Wilkie Collins's famous tale in that genre, *The Woman in White*, (1860), was rejected by Macmillan as "far too sensational", "disgusting" and "extravagant." Hardy then offered it to William Tinsley, who offered to publish it if the author would guarantee £75. This Hardy agreed to and the novel was published anonymously in March 1871 in three volumes. Its interest for modern critics lies in the remarkable lesbian scene between Miss Addclyffe and her maid, Cytherea, which, in its stark candour combined with subtlety of writing, bears comparison with Colette: a remarkable achievement for the young Hardy. Despite this episode, which was passed over, *The Athenaeum* and the *Morning Post* gave *Desperate Measures* favourable reviews, seeing the anonymous author as "powerful and promising". *The Spectator*, on the other hand, hammered it, albeit concluding with a crumb of backhanded comfort for the author: "If we step in silence over the corrupt body of the tale … we hope to spur him to better things."

Hardy's first reaction was to "wish himself dead" in the face of such harsh words, but he quickly pulled himself together and like a real pro-in the-making resumed work on a novel which he had started before *Desperate Remedies* and which he felt would in no way be found sensational or disgusting: *Under the Greenwood Tree*, a pastoral study. Again he offered it to Tinsley, who in turn made an offer of £30 for the copyright which Hardy, to his later great regret, accepted. He was still green in his attitude to publishing and publishers.

The two-volume first edition was published in early June 1872 to an enthusiastic reception by reviewers. Tinsley wrote asking for a serial to begin the September number of *Tinsley's Magazine* and Hardy, tempted by the offer of £200 that Tinsley made as payment for the serial, began writing *A Pair of Blue Eyes*. However he had been studying the copyright law and now he did not dispose of the copyright but only of the right to serialization and the three volume first edition. The blue eyes which had inspired the theme of the novel belonged, of course, to Emma Gifford, with whom Hardy was now once more in Cornwall. During this visit Hardy was offered a further engagement by T. Roger Smith, a distinguished London architect, with whom Hardy had worked briefly just before Easter of that year. With Emma loyally supporting the momentous decision, Hardy declined Smith's offer and instead cast his bread upon the waters literature. This faith in the power of his pen was not misplaced; in December he received a request for a serial from Leslie Stephen, the editor of the prestigious *Cornhill Magazine*. The result would be *Far From The Madding Crowd*.

Monthly Magazines

TESS AND ALEC AS PORTRAYED FOR "THE GRAPHIC" SERIALIZATION 1891.

HE POPULAR monthly magazines of the nineteenth and first half of the twentieth century (World War Two virtually brought about their demise, though some struggled on into the 1960s) were an important source of income for authors, particularly novelists and short story writers. To be financially rewarding, nov-

els needed to be sold initially for serialization in one of the monthly magazines, George Eliot's *Romola* had been serialized in the *Cornhill Magazine* for a sum little short of £1,500; a huge fee in her day. The routine for successful novelists was to have their work first serialized, then put on the market in three volume form at 31 shillings and 6 pence. A further source of income awaited those books which then went on the lists of the popular lending libraries.

The monthly magazines, by and large, were intended for family reading, which of necessity placed a fair degree of restraint upon what might, or might not, be included in their fiction. Hardy was not the only author who learned to bow to the censorship imposed by domestic audiences, fond of gathering round while papa read aloud in the evening. The dodge was, on publication in book form, to reinsert the offensive passages back into the texts; at least within the bounds of reasonable discretion. This was the line that Hardy took.

The popular magazines might be seen as the down-market offspring of the early nineteenth-century critical journals, of which the first, the *Edinburgh Review* (1802–1929), famous for its attacks on Wordsworth and his fellow Lake Poets, was established by Sydney Smith, Henry Brougham and Francis Jeffrey and issued in the buff and blue colours of the Whig party which it supported. Its contributors included William Hazlitt, Thomas Carlyle and Macaulay. Its rival, the Tory *Quarterly Review*, was launched in 1809 by John Murray at the urging of Sir Walter Scott. Last of this brilliant trio of nineteenth-century critical periodicals was *Blackwood's Edinburgh Magazine*, notable for its association with Thomas De Quincey: nonetheless his famous *Confessions of an English Opium Eater* first came out in the pages of Blackwood's rival, *The London Magazine*, in 1821. Rivalry was the spice of life for periodicals from the word go.

The great forerunner in the field of popular magazines was *The Gentleman's Magazine* (1731–1907), designed for diversion as much as information and containing a medley of essays, news stories, murder trials, poems and reviews: "A happy mixture of indolence and study," Hazlitt called it. It still makes marvellously entertaining reading. Its outstanding rival was *The Monthly Magazine and British Register*, (1796–1843), which numbered amongst its earlier contributors names like William Godwin and William Wordsworth, as well as the celebrated *Ellenore*, William Taylor's translation of Bürger's ballad *Lenore*, in which a soldier returns from the dead to carry off his living bride on horseback, and Scott's first ballads, *The Chase* and *William and Helen*. Samuel Taylor Coleridge was also a contributor, and his *Rime of the Ancient Marinere*, as the poem was called in its earliest version, was originally intended for the *Monthly*, before finding its way into *Lyrical Ballads*.

1822 saw the appearance of the *Mirror*, an innovatory twopenny illustrated magazine, which enjoyed a lifespan of twenty-seven years. In 1832 came the famous *Chambers's Journal*, long conducted by the Chamberses, father and son. Knight's *Penny Magazine* (1832–1846) and the *Saturday Magazine*, (1832–1844), issued by the Society for the Promotion of Christian Knowledge, together with Chambers found their way into innumerable households hitherto unused to regular reading.

Fraser's Magazine, (1830–1882), was famous for publishing some of the best of Thomas Carlyle and much early Thackeray. Charles Dickens had his own periodical, *Household Words*, (1850–59), which serialized Mrs Henry Wood's first wildly successful weepies. *All the Year Round*, (1859–95) was an even more successful follow-up period-

LESLIE STEPHEN WITH HIS DAUGHTER, VIRGINIA WOOLF.

ical launched by Dickens. *Temple Bar*, edited by G.A. Sala, ran from 1860–1906 and enjoyed immense popularity.

The era of the profusely illustrated magazines was now at hand. The *English Illustrated Magazine* (1883–1913) is generally thought of as the parent of illustrated monthlies: the famous *Illustrated London News*, launched in 1842, was the pioneer of illustrated weeklies in which illustrations took pride of place over the letterpress. The *Strand Magazine* (1891–1950), immortalized as the publication in which Sherlock Holmes made his bow, was seen as dangerously extravagant in furnishing no fewer than a hundred and ten illustrations in a single number. The gamble paid off.

The *Cornhill* (1860–1839) was first edited by Thackeray, then by GH Lewes, partner of George Eliot; by Hardy's day the editor was Leslie Stephen, father of Virginia Woolf. The *Cornhill* had published not only Thackeray himself, but George Eliot, Trollope, Reade, Collins, and Mrs Gaskell, among notable authors. Its circulation was some fifty thousand, with a readership far exceeding that. To be asked to write a serial for the *Cornhill* meant that Thomas Hardy had arrived.

Under THE Greenwood Tree

HE ENTHUSIASTIC RECEPTION given to *Under the Greenwood Tree*, the first of Hardy's Wessex chronicles, paved the way for the breathtaking success of *Far From the Madding Crowd*. Even though *Under the Greenwood Tree* was never serialized it became a favourite from the start. Its plot was too insubstantial for serial treatment; indeed this novel might have been written as a pastoral narrative poem, rather than in prose form. Both in language and content it reveals Wordsworth's influence upon Hardy: *Under the Greenwood Tree* skims the borderline of *Lyrical Ballads* – Wordsworth's famous poems of rural life dealing with everyday situations and written in language as close as possible to that spoken by

ordinary people, as he put it in his Preface to the poems: that Preface which had made such a strong impression upon Hardy when he had read it during his Blomfield days.

Hardy's aim was that *Under the Greenwood Tree* should conform to Wordsworth's intentions for *Lyrical Ballads*; this he made clear on the title-page of the novel:

UNDER THE GREENWOOD TREE,
or THE MELLSTOCK QUIRE
A Rural Painting of the Dutch School

By "a rural painting of the Dutch school" Hardy meant that his readers would find in this novel writing of a vigour and precision analogous to good genre painting; in this case of the Dutch and Flemish schools of the seventeenth century. This he brilliantly achieved, vignette after vignette, to be fixed upon the memory; such as this scene on a country road: a farmer and two passengers, one his wife, travelling in a spring-cart: "The farmer's wife sat flattened between the two men, who bulged out over each end of the seat to give her room till they almost sat upon their respective wheels." Presently "the wheels … jogged into a depression running across the road, giving the cart a twist, whereupon all three nodded to the left, and on coming out of it all three nodded to the right, and went on jerking their backs in and out as usual." Or take this description of Fancy Day's step-mother's indignant response to discovering that the best tablecloth hadn't been used when Fancy brought Dick Dewy home for the first time. The rest of them were already eating their dinner without Mrs Day; described by her husband Geoffrey as belonging "to that class of womankind that become second wives: a rum class rather." Shortly afterward:

THE REAL THING.
"MELLSTOCK PARISH QUIRE": SKETCH FROM HARDY'S NOTEBOOK.

The second Mrs Day appeared, looking fixedly at the table as she advanced upon it … She showed herself to possess an ordinary woman's face, iron-grey hair, hardly any hips, and a great deal of cleanliness in a broad white apron-string as it appeared upon the waist of her dark stuff dress. "'People will run away with a story now, I suppose,' she began saying, "that Jane Day's tablecloths are as poor and ragged as any union beggar's!' Dick now perceived that the tablecloth was a little worse for wear, and reflected that 'people' in step-mother language probably meant himself. Mrs Day vanished, to return "with an armful of new damask-linen table-cloths folded square and hard as boards by long compression. These she flounced down into a chair; then took one, shook it out from its folds, and spread it on the table by instalments, transferring the plates and dishes one by one from the old to the new cloth.

That this scene is drawn from life the reader never doubts for an instant. Take, lastly, this famous paragraph with which the novel opens: "To dwellers in a wood almost every species of tree has its voice as well as its feature. At the passing of the breeze the fir-trees sob and moan no less distinctly than they rock; the holly whistles as it battles with itself; the ash hisses amid its quiverings: the beech rustles while its flat boughs rise and fall." Hardy, from the first passage of his first Wessex novel stood revealed as unique. Here was an author with the countryside absorbed into his system, the very fabric of his existence; his rustic domestic interiors steeped in affectionate observation; his descriptions of landscape guided by a caring eye and heightened by an intimate ear.

Character and Environment

Under the Greenwood Tree was, as Hardy phrased it, a "Novel of Character and Environment". It told the tale of the Mellstock parish quire, or choir, and was intended, to quote Hardy writing in 1912, as "A fairly true picture, at first hand, of the personages, ways, and customs which were common in our villages fifty or sixty years ago." The

novel described how Mellstock quire, in common with all such antique rustic church quires, was at last displaced in favour of a solo organist, in this case Fancy Day, the pretty young schoolteacher. This story of the demise of the choir was amplified into a rustic courtship, touchingly ten-

der and amusingly naive, between Fancy and a village lad, Dick Dewy: a story with a true Hardy twist to it, inasmuch as while Dick is straightforward and sincere in all he says and does in his courtship of Fancy she, the archetypal Eve, dallies secretly with the vicar behind her suitor's back. Of all Hardy's novels, *Under the Greenwood Tree* remains the freshest, the happiest, and resultantly the one whose popularity is, generally speaking, the most lasting. Well-loved novels confer immortality upon their characters. The voice of young Dick Dewy still rings out into the starry night as he walks home to Mellstock, singing as he goes,

With the rose and the lily
And the daffodowndilly
The lads and the lasses a-sheep-shearing go.

"UNDER THE GREEN-
WOOD TREE": BRITAIN'S
SECOND "TALKIE",
1928, FEATURING
MARGUERITE ALLEN
AND JOHN BATTEN,
DIRECTED BY HARRY
LACHMAN. FANCY DAY
IS SERENADED BY THE
MELLSTOCK QUIRE.

UNDER THE GREENWOOD TREE

Far FROM THE Madding Crowd

THE 1967 FILM,
"FAR FROM THE
MADDING CROWD",
TERENCE STAMP AS
SERGEANT TROY
HYPNOTIZES BATHSHEBA
EVERDENE (JULIE
CHRISTIE) WITH
HIS FAMOUS
SWORD-EXERCISE.

*L*ESLIE STEPHEN WAS constantly pointing out to Hardy the importance of remembering that novels which "came out in numbers" – that was, in serialization – were essentially for family reading and the greatest care should be taken not to offend subscribers on sexual or religious grounds. "Remember the vicar's daughters'" was a famous editorial line. Stephen admitted that he was ashamed of his "excessive prudery" but added that it was forced upon him. Hardy, at that point in his career, was understandably ready to compromise. "Perhaps I may have higher aims one day, and be a great stickler for the proper balance of the completed work, but for the present I wish merely to be considered a good hand at a serial."

Sweet, Bright Bathsheba

In *Far From the Madding Crowd* Hardy invented the first of his famous heroines: in this instance Bathsheba Everdene; beautiful, enticing, "wilful and fascinating … the embodiment of all that was sweet and bright and hopeless," to quote Hardy himself. We cannot be sure whether he means "hopeless" in the sense of being a near nut-case, which Hardy perceived as natural in a female, or as a conquest. Probably he subconsciously meant both.

We should never ignore Emma Hardy's comment upon the man who, above all other Englishmen, was celebrated for his portrayals of "the sex", as he referred to women in the nauseating jargon of his day. Hardy was writing at a time when women's long struggle for emancipation was at last taking a truly positive stride forward, yet: "His opinions on the Woman Question are not in her favour", Emma disclosed to a friend. Why should they have been? Hardy was writing professional popular fic-

tion – with the vicar's daughters, as well as umpteen other genteel persons, forever huddled at the back of his mind. To sell, his fiction had to be exciting; yet never give offence. Excitement could be guaranteed by writing about women who, as the saying went, "sailed close to the wind", without actually capsizing. Hardy's supreme skill was the balancing act: how to nearly capsize but never quite. Sexually, he was the high-wire star of his era, so far as writing went at least. He carried explicit sex further than any contemporary English novelist had dared to take it; always making the point that the woman was not to blame.

Hardy sagely exploited the accepted sexual climate of his day: women were to be treated as objects, either to be ground underfoot, or placed, mute and motionless, on a

FROM THE SAME FILM:
BATHSHEBA AND
GABRIEL OAK
(ALAN BATES).

APPRENTICED TO THE PEN

PAGE 52

pedestal. They were not considered living realities in the sense that men were. Women were designed for one purpose only. The "strong-minded woman", a bugaboo with cropped hair, sturdy boots and skirts a little too clear of her ankles, her gaze fixed on the goal of university education for her sex, was a character Hardy steered clear of – such women were dreary material when compared with the wayward, untutored Bathshebas. Essentially Hardy's heroines were wild ponies, the so-called heathcroppers. "I've danced at your skittish heels, my beautiful Bathsheba, for many a long mile, and many a long day," says Gabriel Oak, taking her in his arms two pages before the end of the book. Caught at last! It must be confessed that it makes, even for the strong minded, rivetting reading.

Contradictory Woman

As *Far From the Madding Crowd* came out in numbers, it had to be constructed round cliff-hangers. These included Bathsheba's impulsive marriage to the dubious, dazzling womanizer, Sergeant Troy, who is murdered by a besotted rival for Bathsheba's hand, the forbidding Boldwood, who in turn receives a life-sentence and conveniently vanishes behind bars for ever, leaving the way open for Oak.

What a labyrinth of contradictions did Hardy love his women to be! "We now," says Hardy, as Bathsheba dithers from one out-of-character idiocy to the next and Oak crouches on tenterhooks in his sheepfold, "see the element of folly distinctly mingling with the many varying particulars which made up the character of Bathsheba … Though she had too much understanding to be entirely governed by her womanliness, Bathsheba, had too much womanliness to use her understanding to the best advantage." By womanliness Hardy meant, of course, what later cynics would call "the poor-little-me" syndrome.

Bathsheba had courage, both physical and social; she became a farmer in her own right. She had the good sense, in the end, to employ Oak as her bailiff, having tried her hand at it, and proved that she could do it, but deciding to let him carry on with the hard work, feeling

masterful, while she, the real boss, gave herself time to explore the many other possibilities in life. In short, both she and Oak believed, privately, that they had had the last laugh. Hardy, however, kept this strictly as a silent subtext. We should note that he thought their marriage, unlike most, would work.

Far From the Madding Crowd is an unforgettable book; written with formidable power, it made Hardy famous overnight. It contains one of the great passages in English pastoral literature: Gabriel Oak alone on Norcome Hill at night, tending his lambing ewes in their pens, lamp in his hand, stars wheeling the hours of vigil away overhead. Hardy may not have known as much as he supposed about women, but he did know about sheep and shepherding. Even Bathsheba improves with keeping, as the saying goes. There she sits in the first chapter, perched on a pile of furniture in a cart, smilingly surveying herself in a newly-purchased swing-mirror, while Oak surreptitiously surveys her from over a hedge. And then, to our pleasure, they sit together on the final page, newly wed but sensibly not bothering to go away on honeymoon but instead, after the ceremony, walking back to her house, which they will now be sharing. She puts on the kettle and is soon pouring him a cup of tea. Things are exactly as they should be.

AN ENDANGERED FLOCK "ON THE KENTISH CLIFFS": THOMAS SIDNEY (1803–1902).

A Quiet Nook

OMERSET MAUGHAM, ruminating upon Hardy, renamed Driffield, a pivotal figure in Maugham's satirical novel, *Cakes and Ale*, produced a *tour de force* of pen-portraiture. Maugham, in real life, had been scarcely acquainted with Hardy, yet with the uncanny insight of the novelist he "divined" him unerringly. "The face that you saw was a mask and the actions performed were without significance. I had an impression that the real man, to his death unknown and lonely, was a wraith that went a silent way unseen between the writer of his books and the man who led his life, and smiled with ironical detachment at the two puppets that the world took for Edward Driffield." We recall the lines of self-portraiture written by Hardy at the close of his life,

> *They know a phasm they name as me,*
> *In whom I should not find*
> *A single self-held quality*
> *Of body or mind.*

Maugham had put his finger on Hardy with exactitude, though, for reasons of discretion, he would of course insist that he had founded Driffield on an obscure writer.

Never a Sign...

At Sturminster Newton, that "quiet nook", Hardy still believed in the possibility of things being real and in himself as being real. The "two seasons" spent at Riverside Villa overlooking the Stour swept "like summertime wind on our ways", wrote Hardy, in his immensely moving poem, "A Two Years' Idyll". So confident were he and Emma of their continuing bliss that they saw it as no more than a preface to even greater happinesses, "lifefraught", soon to come. But these bright expectations were not realized. Maugham pin-pointed the loss of Driffield's first and only child as the calamity of his life. Rosie Driffield could bear no more children. Driffield, though devastated, used the death of his child as the shockingly chilling high point of one of his "shocking" novels.

Hardy and Emma longed for children and at the Sturminster period of their marriage must still have looked forward to parenthood as a very real possibility. But though their unmarried servant girl became pregnant and gave birth to an unwanted infant, "Never a sign of one is there for us," commented Hardy poignantly. Nor did one ever arrive. Theirs was a childless union; and both felt blighted by it. This, of course, makes nonsense of the theory that Hardy was impotent; clearly he was fully confident of fatherhood. Whether the failure to have a child lay with him, or with Emma, we do not know. No more did they. Hoping and hoping, they at length resigned themselves and lavished their frustrated parental love on cats.

Whenever a writer has anything on his mind, said Maugham, in explanation of Driffield's cold-blooded use of his child's death, he has only to put it down in black and white, using it as a theme of a story, to forget all about it. "He is the only free man." The childless Hardy may, or may not, have been ridding himself of a hidden anguish when he destroyed Jude's three beloved little children in one fell and awful swoop because they were "too menny". Was there here a prolonged smouldering resentment that some had too many, while he had none?

"RIVERSIDE", STURMIN-STER NEWTON WHERE THE HARDYS LIVED (1875–7) IN THE NEAR-ER OF THE TWO SEMI-DETACHED VILLAS.

To live in a world of fantasy, which is essentially what the novelist does, though he may excuse it as hypersensitive reality, is a form of neurosis, productive as it may be – protective it certainly is. Sturminster, idyllic as it was, saw Hardy's cruellest struggles with the stranglehold of professional writing. In his new novel, *The Return of the Native*, he aspired after "art". He would preserve that sacred thing, "the integrity of the writer". Nothing would prevent him from writing truly about his native Egdon Heath; the dark and extraordinary streams of ancient faith and superstition interwoven to produce waywardness, frustration, chaos and tragedy in human lives even to this day. He wrote; he dispatched what he had written to editor after editor. Nobody would touch it. What he had written was "dangerous" for a family magazine. Hardy was a professional; he relied upon his writing, so he rewrote *The Return of the Native*; routinely it went into serialization, then book form. He did not make as much money as he had hoped, and the reviews disappointed: "Too tragic"; "tried to be too clever"; failed to "amuse". This was what came of conforming to rules that themselves had no virtue. He might as well have stuck to his guns in the first place – but he hadn't. His books had to sell and he vowed that his next one should.

A Team of Two

At Sturminster Newton Hardy and Emma had worked as a team; which made her very happy, and her happiness kept him happy. He entrusted her with the job of writing-up his "literary notebook", or commonplace book; a collection of transcriptions and cuttings from current books and periodicals, to be used in *The Return of the Native*. Emma would continue to do this work for him for many years: she insisted, and there is no reason to disbelieve her, that they discussed together this material, which subsequently appeared as allusions in the novels; that she put forward ideas and suggestions for their use; that it was a reciprocative process which she, rightly, saw as "contributing to his novels." Any contribution to his work on her part Hardy subsequently angrily denied. As he saw it, Emma's

"*Far from the madding crowd*"

toil was insignificant ground work; there was a point beyond which she could not pass, and that was the point where it really all began – the point where Hardy took off. Until that moment he was fiddling around in his mind with notes, quotes, classical allusions, a jumble of half-formed aspirations and recollections: then, he was up, soaring, and not looking down again. Emma, earthbound, might wave to him like crazy, but he'd never notice. Still, they were happy. In their quiet nook, they shared at least some of his labour; he looked ahead to novels of integrity, ranking as literary art. And there would be children. Sons. Posterity.

It didn't happen that way. Hardy decided that to be a successful professional they must leave their nook and establish themselves in London. This they did forthwith, on March 22, 1878. Their new address was "The Larches", in Upper Tooting, not far from Wandsworth Common. Hardy hurled himself into London literary circles; Emma did her best to join in. But nothing was ever quite the same again. Hardy conformed to the rules; hit the big time; vanished into a wraith.

THE HARDYS' FONDNESS FOR BOATING ON THE RIVER STOUR MAY BE SEEN AS THE INSPIRATION FOR THIS DELIGHTFUL WIMSY.

The Return OF THE Native

EXPERTS TELL US THAT, after close examination of Hardy's early drafts of *The Return of the Native*, though these differed considerably from the final version, there was never any indication that the novel was intended to be linked to themes of "satanism"or that Eustacia, the heroine, was any more "satanic" in earlier versions than the later. The problem of not accepting *The Return of the Native* as a deeply superstitious work, based on ancient rituals and, not to put too fine a point on it, witchcraft, is that you are left asking, what is it about?

A young man, Clym Yeobright, born and bred on a wild and spooky Wessex heathland, Egdon Heath, returns from Paris where he has become a diamond merchant. But he is the thoughtful type and has become impregnated by the Utopian socialism of Proudhon, the *dernier cri* of intellectual Paris at that time (the 1840s). Clym is determined to bring enlightenment to the furze-cutters of Egdon. His mother, a worthy widow of great force of character, receives him dotingly. His cousin, Thomasin, meanwhile has been making a silly of herself with the local herbalist; Damon Wildeve, and has been jilted by him at the altar, thus damaging her reputation on Egdon. She has been befriended and brought home by Diggory Venn, a reddleman (Hardy takes it for granted that his readers will know what a reddleman is, and never elucidates beyond saying that he is red). Also on the heath lives a wayward, mysterious beauty of nineteen, Eustacia, who roams among the barrows, mostly in the dark, telescope in one hand and hour-glass in the other. She lives in a lonesome cottage with her grand-father, an old seafaring man. She is half Corfiote and has a local reputation as a witch. She loves the unscrupulous Wildeve. Clym meets Eustacia, described unequivocally by Hardy as Artemis, who under

her other name, Hecate, was queen of the witches. He could hardly have made things plainer. She enchants Clym and, desperate to escape Egdon Heath, agrees to wed him in the hope that he will take her to Paris. Damon, stung that Eustacia has abandoned him for Clym, decides to "wring her heart" and marries Thomasin. Clym and Eustacia take up residence in another lonely cabin on the heath. Here Clym all but blinds himself reading hours on end by candlelight, in pursuit of learning. Clym becomes gradually estranged from his mother on account of his marriage – something is very wrong. Old Mrs Yeobright summons her strength and goes to confront Eustacia, who puts Clym under such a powerful spell that he lies insensible when his mother calls, unable to respond to her appeal that they quarrel no more. Eustacia will not open the door; instead she glares at Mrs Yeobright through the window. Mrs Yeobright, unable to summon the strength to retaliate, dwindles, peaks and pines virtually on the very spot, is bitten by an adder, doubtless summoned by Eustacia, and expires. Meantime a primitive neighbour, Susan Nunsuch, who fears that Eustacia has bewitched her own child, is sticking pins in a wax effigy of Eustacia and melting it, while reciting the Lord's Prayer backward. She also sticks a long needle into Eustacia's arm during church to see if she bleeds, for a witch will only bleed in church. Eustacia bleeds. Eustacia, planning to run away with Damon, succumbs to the violent shakes and fearful depression: sure sign that the de-witching process is working on her .On a pitch black night, she flings herself in the river. Damon leaps in after her to save her. Clym follows. Damon and Eustacia drown. Clym survives and becomes an itinerant preacher. Thomasin marries Diggory Venn, who has given up his reddling and returned to prosperous dairy-farming, into which he was born.

Why did Hardy, a highly intelligent man and creative genius, write this farrago? Especially bearing in mind that he intended it as "writing of integrity" and organized it with infinite care so that it might truly say what he wanted to say. The second Mrs Hardy, in 1913, spoke of an "extraordinary case of witchcraft" which had recently occurred in the cottage next to Hardy's birthplace. "Everyone in the village believes firmly in witchcraft," she added. Hardy, even if he no longer believed in it himself, fully realized the part which such ingrained beliefs play in communities.

The timespan of the novel covers the ages old magic period of a year and a day: in this case from November 5 till November 6; the twelvemonth span of the prehistoric pastoral calender based on the breeding rhythm of flocks. The narrative opens with the bonfires of Hallowe'en, the 31st October – such pagan festivals matching the Old Style of reckoning, pre-dating the change in the calender in 1752, when by Act of Parliament dates were advanced by eleven days to bring us in line with the rest of Europe. Thus, the fires of November 5 with which the novel opens really belong to the original Hallowe'en, a fire festival marking the start of the prehistoric pastoral year, the time of the annual rut when ewes are put to the tup. Hallowe'en festivities extended over a period of several days, rising to the climax of the Hallow Even, the 31st, a night not only of bonfires, but fertility dances and rites. It is perfectly correct that Hardy's opening scenario should include the reddleman; an itinerant salesman of the ruddle or reddle, the blood-coloured pigment with which the rams were smeared on chest and underparts so that they stained the rumps of the ewes when they mounted them, thereby establishing which ewes had been tupped. This practise extended all over the Old World, from places as far apart as Cumbria and Turkey; and was said to symbolize the blood of ceremonial sheep sacrifice. A reddleman carried, therefore, both pagan pastoral and Biblical connotations as he travelled from farm to farm, selling his redding stuff, which in the old days was made from red earth or soil, mixed with oil. Later it could be bought as a ready preparation from chemists and reddlemen disappeared.

The bonfires were lit on the highest points of Egdon Heath; as the dying embers glowed the people formed pairs and danced the stamping, leaping fertility dance handed down the ages since heaven knows when; at sight and sound of which the aptly named Christian Cantle hugged himself in dread:"They ought not to do it … t'is tempting the Wicked One, 'tis."

Hardy intended that the reddleman should disappear as mysteriously as he came, but convention demanded a happy ending to a serial and so, to please his public, and ensure sales, Hardy married him to Thomasin. He made other alterations too, bowdlerizing and gentrifying the story. Today, when we take anthropology seriously, we should see this astonishing witchcraft epic in a different light from that in which Hardy's contemporaries viewed it. And we should understand why Diggory Venn, forced into conformity for the sake of magazine sales, utters his desperately cynical, "I am given up body and soul to the making of money."

THE Woman Question

T IS ALL TOO OFTEN EASILY assumed that until the Women's Suffrage movement got under way in the early twentieth-century all women had always been immured in a Victorian-style prison house existence. But this is far from true; the position of women in society has always fluctuated from era to era. When the English grammar schools came into being in Tudor times, many of them provided education for girls as well as boys. But it was more difficult, for domestic reasons, for girls to attend school as regularly over an extended course of time as their brothers and so, gradually, females became ousted from these schools, which resultantly came to be seen as institutions traditionally reserved for the education of boys; a belief which persisted down the centuries and hardened into an established masculine opposition to the education of females as a matter of principle.

The daughters of the working poor were never educated beyond dame school, if that. Their role in life was seen as domestic labour and this role was further exploited and brutalized by the industrial revolution. But there was always some kind of education for girls from the wealthier and more leisured homes. Over-all, the seventeenth and eighteenth centuries gradually saw an advance in the literacy and general education of females

and with the Enlightenment, soon known as the Age of Reason, redolent with the voice of Rousseau and finally crowned by the influences of the French Revolution, the liberation of women exploded briefly into virtually uninhibited activity. Advanced young women of the middle-classes were discussing Tom Paine's *Rights of Man* (1791) and Mary Wollstonecroft's response, A *Vindication of the Rights of Women*, which appeared in 1792. It would be wrong to suppose that Wollstonecroft's celebrated book was lobbed into a society wholly unprepared for serious consideration of women's rights. A middle-class feminine protest movement had been steadily building up throughout the era of the Enlightenment. By 1790, for instance, women were speaking on the platforms of the London debating societies on subjects relating to "The Woman Question".

Mary Wollstonecraft was a genuine product of her age inasmuch as she entertained the deepest regard for the doctrines and writings of Rousseau; but it was a regard tempered by one strong reservation; Rousseau, she emphatically stated, was essentially the enemy of women, maintaining as he did that woman's role intended by nature, was exclusively to please men, to be useful to them, to advise, console and in general render the lives of men easy and agreeable.

Rights of Women is not about "rights" in the combative sense in which we use that word today, but about the desirability of an equal participation by both sexes in a society oriented upon a two sex and not a single sex axis. It is not about sexual equality as we popularly construe that greatly abused idea; as Wollstonecraft correctly saw it, equality of women with men assumes an implicit superiority of the masculine standard; she was urging the equality of men and women *with each other* – she did not fall into the trap that women should merely be imitation men.

She was urging a view of women's rights within the moral and social concept of a regenerated, revolutionized society; where there would be equal participation by men and women in common rights and common duties. This would entail the world seeing women in a new light; the light of truth instead of prejudice. Said Mary, "I have thrown down my gauntlet, and deny the existence of sexual virtues … For men and women, truth, if I understand the meaning of that word, must be the same … Women, I allow, may have different duties to fulfil; but they are human duties, and the principles that should regulate the discharge of them, I sturdily maintain, must be the same."

To bring about this change, continued Mary, women must be educated: herein lay the answer to the condemnation, by men, that women were incapable of playing an equal role in society. "Contending for the rights of woman," declared Mary, "my main argument is built on this simple principle, that if she be not prepared to be the companion of man, rather than his plaything or mistress, then she will stop the progress of knowledge and virtue; for truth must be common to all." The battlecry for women became, "Wisdom is the principal thing: therefore get wisdom." Wollstonecraft's greatest contribution to the emancipation of her sex was the persistency with which she urged that women, as a first step toward achievement of the goal of equal rights and equal participation in a socially regenerated society, must first win the right to *the same levels* of education as those enjoyed by males. This, over the next century, remained the paramount goal for women; the vote was seen as a natural corollary. The 1790s was a decade in which female emancipation rode on a wave of advancement not to be experienced again until well into the twentieth century.

MARY WOLLSTONECRAFT AFTER HER MARRIAGE TO WILLIAM GODWIN, PREGNANT WITH HER SECOND DAUGHTER THE FUTURE MARY SHELLEY.

The arrival of the nineteenth century saw the liberation of women borne away on an ebb tide and lost to view, apart from a band of "blue stockings", as they were derisively called, who kept the flag flying. The 1840s saw signs of the tide once more turning as talk of higher education for women was revived. 1850 saw the breakthrough with the founding, by Frances Mary Buss, of the North London Collegiate, where girls would receive an education on the level of that available for their brothers. Emily Davies, future founder of Girton College, Cambridge, battled for university education for her sex. Elizabeth Garrett, in the face of refusal by the medical schools to take a female student, received private tuition and in spite of continuing opposition, qualified to practise medicine in 1865; while Eliza Lynn, first full-time female journalist in Fleet Street, spoke for the New Woman, as the pioneers of emancipation were now being called. It was by a strange twist of Fate that the New Woman, in the popular mind, came in due course to be associated with Hardy's Bathshebas and Eustacias; wild ponies needing to be brought to heel. Not what Miss Buss and her legions intended at all – and not quite how it worked out in the end.

THE British Museum

ONE GREAT ADVANTAGE for Hardy, back in London, was that he had access to the famous Reading Room at the British Museum. The novel on which he was now working, *The Trumpet-Major*, was set during the Napoleonic wars and during 1878–79, Hardy made several visits to the Reading Room, researching for this novel, accompanied by Emma, who continued to be his enthusiastic collaborator, painstakingly unearthing facts, reminiscences and descriptions and entering them in what became known as "The Trumpet-Major Notebook".

The Reading Room

The Reading Room was founded in 1753 as part of the British Museum; one of the flood of museums which resulted from the wealth created by the Industrial Revolution and the great private collections made by the leading names in industry; these were subsequently donated to learned Societies that in turn endowed the new municipal museums. The British Museum and Library emerged on the scene in 1753, following the bequest of Hans Sloane's library and museum to the nation. To his library was added the Cotton collection of 1700, and the royal library of George II. To house these treasures, now national possessions, Montagu House in Bloomsbury, was bought for £10,000, an enormous sum in those days. This once famous palace, of which the diarist John Evelyn wrote that there was "nothing more glorious in England", then stood on the outskirts of London with nothing but farms and fields stretching away to distant Hampstead Heath. The remoteness of Montagu House was held against it as the reason why it should not become the new British Museum, but the British Museum it

became. Having been a private house it could not be made suitable for use as a national institution without further outlay, which brought its total cost to the nation up to the then gigantic sum of £23,000. In January 1759 the splendidly refurbished edifice, was thrown open for public inspection. The library of this institution enjoyed the privilege that the Royal Library had acquired in the reign of Queen Anne, of being supplied with a copy of every publication entered at Stationers' Hall. The reading room, in a basement corner, with twenty chairs and one "proper wainscoat table covered with green bays" furnished "more than sufficient accommodation for all demands."

A second royal collection of books was presented to the nation by George IV. For this an extension, the King's Library, was built, but the library went on growing; in 1838 more rooms were added, including a new reading room for 170 readers. A year later it was planned to pull down the high wall around the Museum and to make radical changes to the front of the building. In October 1850 *The Times* announced that, "The British Museum is finished." Meanwhile the Reading Room was in increasing use and by 1852 the "new reading room" was being called "the Black Hole", so overcrowded had it become. Clearly, a new reading room had to be built. In May 1857 the new New Reading Room was opened for a week of public viewing – 162,489 people queued to see it. After which, with the exception of one day a week, it was closed against sightseers and strictly reserved for the use of 300 readers.

The Reading Room was a marvel. The great dome was only two feet less than the Roman Pantheon, and "exceeded that of St Peter's by one foot." By day the reading room was suffused by light from twenty immense windows. Then, as after dark on winter evenings, "arc lights shine in the dome, and shaded incandescent lamps light up every table and desk, with their fittings of adjustable book-rests, ink, pens, blotting-pads, paper-weights, and even pencleaners. At every reader's feet is the warmth of hot-water pipes."

Revolutionary Readers

The Reading Room became a godsend to the radical refugees who arrived in London following the abortive revolutions of the 1840s. Open long hours; with its endless supply of comforts, it was no wonder that every revolutionary writer of any account was installed there, scrawling acres of seditious literature: Karl Marx and Lenin were probably the most famous. There was scarcely a name in letters or politics who did not use the pens and ink and thank whoever it was that had thought of the hot-water pipes.

The Reading Room became the scene of several romances, as it was a splendid rendezvous for intellectuals involved in amorous intrigues. One of the most celebrated liaisons was that of Marx's youngest daughter, Eleanor, and Edward Aveling; Doctor of Science, Marxist, militant atheist; known for the sincerity of his socialist convictions, and equally as a seducer of women – Bernard Shaw said he reminded him of a lizard. Shaw, then young and a flaming Marxist, met Eleanor in the Reading Room, where she worked as a literary hack. Shaw fell in love with this striking and very clever girl, but before he could make headway with her she had been snatched up by Aveling; who, having deserted his wife, carried Eleanor off to live with him. Eleanor devoted herself to him and to socialist causes. When Aveling's wife died it was taken for granted that the Marx-Aveling union would be legalized; but Eleanor discovered that he had, with incredible speed, married somebody else. Eleanor committed suicide.

Meanwhile more and more books flooded into the library; more and more readers thronged to the well-appointed desks. By 1895, an article in *Strand Magazine* tells us, a daily average of 650 readers were applying for the 458 available seats; 1,402,815 books were read in one year alone, excluding thousands of reference works. And, "New forces must surely be reckoned with in the twentieth century." So it has proved. A new library has been built at an expense that makes the sums of the past seem trivial. But those who believe in ghosts have no doubt that the shade of Karl Marx turns up regularly at Great Russell Street as of old, to claim his customary desk with its customary blotter and to warm his poor refugee feet on the hot-water pipes.

ELEANOR MARX: "VERY STRIKING IN APPEARANCE AND VERY CLEVER," WROTE BERNARD SHAW.

THE READING ROOM: IN 1895 IT HAD A DAILY AVERAGE OF 650 READERS.

Literary Lions

THE SOCIETY OF AUTHORS was founded by Walter Besant in 1884, to protect authors' rights. Hardy was among those who joined, together with many other illustrious literary names. In 1909 he was asked to become President of the Society as succes-

"KING OF THE LIONS". THACKERAY IN 1867, PAINTED BY SAMUEL LAURENCE (1812–84).

sor to George Meredith. This appointment Hardy did his best to refuse, but the Society continued to press him for acceptance and to this pressure he finally succumbed. Forty years after he had apprenticed himself to the pen he had at last become king, as it were, of the literary lions.

Hardy's first glimpse of a true literary lion had been in 1868, when he had had the seventy-three year old Thomas Carlyle pointed out to him by the publisher, Frederick Chapman, in the publisher's shop. The young Hardy had felt greatly indignant on Carlyle's behalf that he had not been attended to by Chapman himself, but by one of the clerks. It was no way, Hardy felt, that Britain's greatest living author should be treated.

The following year, 1869, Hardy was still hoping that Chapman might buy *The Poor Man and the Lady*, the reason for the first visit to that publishing house. Chapman invited the aspiring author to call once again "to meet Mr Chapman & the gentleman who read your manuscript". This turned out to be George Meredith, a handsome bearded man wearing "a frock coat buttoned at the waist and loose above", Hardy was to recall. Meredith, his tone "trenchant, turning kind", advised Hardy either to make radical changes to the novel or abandon it entirely and attempt something else with a stronger plot. Accordingly Hardy wrote *Desperate Remedies*. He did not meet Meredith again until 1886, by which time Hardy was well established on the literary scene.

Meredith, Thackeray and Dickens

George Meredith (1828–1909), though now almost entirely forgotten, was one of the major literary lions in his day: a novelist more famous than Hardy himself. He had much about him that was reminiscent of Hardy; one of the early Meredith novels, *The Ordeal of Richard Feverel* (1859), has as themes the force of instinct, and the primitive wisdom embodied in the individual being. As with Hardy, fate, chance and circumstance were forces continually at work, but the real drama, for Meredith, was consciousness, finding expression in passions and wills. His literary career rather fell into two distinct halves, not without relationship to his personal life. His first marriage, following which he gave up the Bar for literature and journalism, was to the daughter of Thomas Love Peacock ; it was not a happy union and his novels during that period never truly scored a resounding success either. He and his wife separated in in 1858, she died four years later, and in 1866 Meredith married Marie Vulliamy. He was happy, and the fresh spate of novels which now flowed from his pen made him famous: *Beauchamp's Career*, (1876); *The Egoist*, (1877); *The Tragic Comedians*, (1880), and *Diana of the Crossways*, (1885); this last the most famous of all. A further group of novels were less successful. He also wrote poems, short stories, and critical essays; all of which were well received. He was strongly influenced by French manners, history and literature and was as highly appreciated in France as on his native side of the Channel. Hailed by his public and peers alike as a master, he was still publishing at the time of his death at the age of eighty-one; it has been said of him that he was at the zenith of his fame on the morrow of his death. His name has now sunk into near oblivion, though some still believe that the future will recognize him as one of the greatest writers of his time. It is interesting that his reputation has faded in the way it has, when that of Hardy has remained so strong. During the late Victorian period their names were constantly coupled in literary context, with Meredith's generally regarded as the greater of the two.

Thackeray (1811–1863), whose novels *Vanity Fair*, *Pendennis* and *The Newcomes* had placed him in the front rank of novelists of his era, was deceased by the time Hardy was attempting literature; he had to be content with meeting the great man's daughters, one of whom, Minna, was Leslie Stephen's first wife. She was a kindly hostess to the young Hardy on more than one occasion. Dickens was another heavily maned lion whom Hardy never met, apart from attending some of the celebrated readings, in London in 1863.

The Savile Club

Hardy first started to mingle with literary figures on something like equal terms in 1878; when his friend and publisher, Charles Kegan Paul, put him up for the Savile Club, at 107 Piccadilly; the leading literary club of the day. Here Hardy found himself meeting poets like Tennyson, the Poet Laureate; Robert Browning, and Matthew Arnold. He also met Edmund Gosse (1849–1928), famed critic, and author of that small but wonderful book *Father and Son*: Gosse would play a double-edged role in Hardy's life. Also at the Savile, Hardy met James Barrie (1860–1937), who would become one of his greatest friends, and Rudyard Kipling (1865–1936), whom Hardy always liked and admired, apart from his politics.

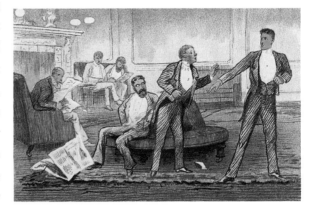

A LIVELY LITERARY CONVERSATION? C. 1884.

Women were not admitted as members of the Savile. This rule applied, of course, to George Eliot; ridiculous as that now seems. It has been said that Hardy, who found himself frequently compared with her, felt "too close to her for comfort", so it must have been a relief to him not to meet her there – the last straw came, for him, when she borrowed the name "Wessex" in *Daniel Deronda*. It was probably this "theft", that prompted Hardy's suggestion to his publisher that his books should be sold under the general title of "The Wessex Novels": "I was the first to use it ..."; adding crossly that it was now "being taken up everywhere." Finally, "It would be a pity for us to lose the right to it." Thus do literary lions, even the greatest of them, snarl among themselves.

Victoria

F ANYONE QUALIFIES to be called a Victorian then surely it must be Thomas Hardy. Fifty-nine years of his life were covered by her sixty-four year reign. The question is, what does "Victorian" really mean? It is impossible to attach a single descriptive label to such a long period of time. And equally impossible to suppose that Victoria herself didn't change, or that the meaning and function of the monarchy remained for ever the same.

The daughter of the Duke of Kent, fourth son of George III, Victoria began her reign in 1837 with firm liberal principles, a Whig ministry, and an intense dislike of Tories. Almost pure German by birth and German speaking when at home in Kensington Palace with her impoverished mother, Princess Mary Louise Victoria of Saxe-Coburg-Gotha, Victoria, whose father had died when she was an infant, was brought up frugally and simply. Consequently when she became queen she thought her new life thrilling; especially enjoying the glittering balls at which she danced tirelessly. It became clear that this mercurial little creature needed a husband and her cousin, Prince Albert of Saxe-Coburg-Gotha, was fetched to England. She fell ardently in love with him at first sight. Contrary to today's popular image of her, Victoria had a passionate nature and a personality verging on the salty; on naval occasions she was notable for downing her

tot of rum with a zest which greatly endeared her to the Fleet. According to the Duke of Wellington, Prince Albert was "extremely straight-laced and a great stickler for morality whereas she was rather the other way. He insisted on spotless character, the Queen not caring a straw about it." Under Albert's influence, she became an unimpeachable wife and bore nine children. The British public grumbled that the Royal pair's ever expanding family was costing the nation a fortune. All the same a large family and spotless domestic virtue, the so-called "Albertine moral code", became the established middle class pattern.

The Influence of Albert

At first Victoria was insistent that Albert should have no share in governing the country but gradually, at the urging of Lord Melbourne, her Prime Minister, she agreed that Albert must play a more responsible role. In course of time he became her private secretary, informally describing himself as her "Permanent Minister". Under his guidance the monarchy gradually changed; in place of a brittle prerogative, acquiring a carefully undefined but potent influence. Victoria had relatives and personal contacts throughout Europe and gradually across the world and Albert saw to it that she set up a species of private overseas intelligence service, while at home there was an unobtrusive but increasing participation in ministry making.

Against this political background there was also, under Albert's cultural influence, a lively encouragement of industry, the sciences and the arts; these three spheres being seen as altogether more homogeneous than is generally the case today. As early as 1851 Albert made himself largely responsible for the huge success of the Great Exhibition in Paxton's innovatory "Crystal Palace", 1862 saw Victoria opening the International Exhibition in South Kensington, predecessor to the Victoria and Albert Museum for art treasures. Paxton had been firmly dropped for Gothic Revival. Social conscience became increasingly aroused and there was a general thrust towards the improvement of the lot of ordinary people: the Factory Act defined legal working hours; municipal libraries were endowed and government grants made toward evening schools; Working Men's Associations were promoted; public health became a major issue. Albert was never able to make himself popular with the British but the dedication of himself and the queen to the interests of the people, albeit with Albert always steering Victoria toward conservatism, made the monarchy less unpopular than it hitherto had been.

Albert's death in 1861 left Victoria devastated. She suffered what modern medicine recognizes as a profound nervous breakdown. Her mourning was pathological. Ever after, until her own death, she slept with a photograph of him on his deathbed over her head; every night at Windsor his clothes were laid out and every morning fresh water was placed in his wash-stand basin. For years she secluded herself. As a result, the tide of republicanism ran high.

Behind the scenes she tried to carry on as Albert had trained her; and she gradually re-emerged – if restrainedly so. Her dislike of Gladstone and her sympathy with Disraeli moved her further toward conservatism as she was determined not to become what she believed Gladstone wished her to be, "The Sovereign of a Democratic Monarchy." Yet, inexorably the tide of time bore her toward this very thing.

Increasingly recognized as a woman of great ability whose long experience of affairs of state made her a valuable person to consult, she won mounting respect from her ministers. She displayed an uncanny understanding of her subjects; uncanny because, as it was remarked after her death, this understanding did not come from any close personal contact. But as the two jubilees of 1887 and 1897 revealed, the link between the queen and her people was unmistakably there. Though she appeared formidable and self-confident, privately she always felt the need of a supportive man in her life. Being at heart totally devoid of social snobbery or race or colour prejudice she found these male stalwarts in unexpected guises. Her favourite protector, after Albert's death, was his former Highland gillie, John Brown; the successor to Brown was her favourite Indian attendant, the self-styled *munshi*, a choice highly unpopular with her Court; and finally her personal physician, Sir James Reid, in whose respectfully professional arms she died in 1901 at Osborne. She was clad in white, and scattered with flowers as she lay in her coffin; she wished to go to Albert, as she had gone to him before – a bride.

VICTORIA OPENS THE GREAT EXHIBITION AT THE CRYSTAL PALACE, MAY 1 1851. OSLER'S FAMOUS CRYSTAL FOUNTAIN IS IN THE FOREGROUND. THE QUEEN STANDS WITH THE PRINCE CONSORT AND THEIR TWO ELDEST CHILDREN ON A CANOPIED DIAS.

Max Gate

**MAX GATE C.1900:
HARDY WITH HIS
BICYCLE, EMMA AND
HER NEPHEW, GORDON
GIFFORD, BY THE
ROLLER. BLOMFIELD
WHEN HE VISITED
APPROVED OF THE
DESIGN OF THE HOUSE.**

B Y EARLY 1880 the Hardys had realized that their decision to move to London had been a mistake. They were now contemplating buying a plot of ground just outside Dorchester, in the vicinity of the old tolbooth, Mack's Gate. Here it was proposed that Hardy's brother, Henry, should build them a house. This plan was delayed for several reasons, one of which was that Hardy fell seriously ill, in the autumn of that year, with a urinary infection. At home, in Tooting, Emma nursed him devotedly. He had a deadline to meet for his new novel, *A Laodician*, the serial rights of which he had sold to the *Atlantic Monthly*, a magazine that appeared in London as well as in America. Tom's innate professionalism meant that he would risk death rather than not meet the deadline – somehow, with Emma's dedicated assistance, it was met. Hardy, confined to bed and at times semi-delirious, dictated the story to Emma who scribbled away and nursed him simultaneously. He was in great pain and compelled to lie on an inclined plane with his head lower than his pelvis. This state of affairs lasted for six months; by which time a rough draft of the novel had been completed – "It was an awful job," he said. Slowly he recovered.

In April 1881 the Hardys left London for Dorset. For the next two years they lived in Wimbourne Minster, near Bournemouth. They threw themselves enthusiastically into local social activity, as they had while in Sturminster. *A Laodicean* – not one of Hardy's greatest successes – was followed by *Two on a Tower*; a deliberately slight and light-hearted novel, full of somewhat schoolboyish sexual innuendos; or so at least we would think them today. This, too, was serialized in the *Atlantic Monthly* and published in book form by Sampson, Low. After which the Hardys relaxed in Paris, where they rented a small apartment on the Left Bank. They then returned to England and moved to Dorchester to supervise the building of their house.

Return to Dorchester

Hardy was also planning his new "Wessex" novel, *The Mayor of Casterbridge* – Casterbridge being his "Wessex" name for Dorchester. For this purpose he began a systematic reading of the back-files of the *Dorset County Chronicle*. Among the notes which he made was an account of a wife-selling; to become the famous opening action of *The Mayor of Casterbridge*. The novel was written ("on and off", Hardy said) between 1884 and mid-April 1885. On 29 June 1885 the Hardys moved into the at last completed Max Gate – an obvious play on Mack's Gate. Max Gate was in an exposed position on open heath: Hardy planted Austrian pines designed, in due course, to screen the house from wind and the eyes of the curious. Close by, in full view of the windows, was a large Bronze Age burial mound, surmounted by a crest of trees. During the course of digging the foundations some skeletons were unearthed, said to be British-Romano; though possibly considerably earlier. In 1890, or thereabouts, a

MAX GATE TODAY,
A NATIONAL
TRUST PROPERTY.

so-called "Druid stone" was dug up in the garden of Max Gate, where it was duly erected as what today would be called "a feature". In 1987 excavation next door to Max Gate discovered half a Neolithic enclosure; the other half lying in Hardy's garden, surrounding the house. Of this enclosure, used for the disposal of the dead and dating from about 3000 BC., Hardy of course knew nothing. His cherished "Druid stone" must have been part of it. One begins to understand why the author of *The Return of the Native* felt so instinctively at home at Max Gate.

A Strange, Victorian Dwelling

The house was generally considered by visitors as strangely inappropriate for a poet's dwelling. They supposed that the man who wrote *Far From the Madding Crowd* would be living in something picturesque and thatched. But the house had been built for the Hardys by the family firm of Hardy and Son, and Hardy Senior and his sons had been born and reared in a late eighteenth-century cottage, "mud walls and thatched", small mullioned windows under heavy over-hanging eaves, infested with bats and mice, all water having to be fetched in from outside-well or pump, no sanitation except for an earth-closet in the garden: so that it was

natural that when they built Tom his new house it was up-to-date; uncompromising in its Victorian architecture; wholly a building of its time, the 1880s. It had a turret – later two turrets: but what is a Victorian house without a turret? It was well-built; a house for a family firm to be proud of. Hardy had designed the interior, and the windows, himself; with an eye upon letting in all the light possible – that thirty years later he was refusing to cut down the trees, by then blotting out the light, was another side of his complex character. Fashions go round in circles: today Max Gate would be thought very pleasant. It is true that there were no mod cons as we understand them, or indeed as the second Mrs Hardy understood them, when she became mistress of Max Gate in 1914; but that was because Hardy, by now set in his ways, never noticed, or cared, that Max Gate had become sadly out-of-date.

Understandably, in 1885 when it was raw, Max Gate must have looked a little incongruous in comparison to the surrounding heathland and wonderful vistas. May O'Rourke, Hardy's secretary, found it "the solidification in brick of Hardy's intermittent mood of helplessness at the Ugliness in life." But we may be quite certain that that was not how Hardy & Son of Bockhampton, Builders, saw it. Max House, for them, was their crowning achievement.

THE COMMEMORATIVE
SUN DIAL ON THE WALL
OF MAX GATE.

A VICTORIAN
Household

ALL HOT WATER FOR
WASHING HAD TO BE
FETCHED UPSTAIRS.

F WE WANT to understand something of the Victorian house, we could not do better than take a detailed look at Max Gate itself. The house was built upon a west-east axis, the living-room, or drawing-room — it was a combination of both — faced south, and had a window low enough so that those sitting inside might see out, the corresponding window of the dining-room was high, to prevent those outside from seeing in. Not altogether surprisingly there was something slightly ecclesiastical about the general appearance of the building; it might quite easily have been a country vicarage. There was a quite impressive front porch, with a garden and sundial facing it. A generous entrance hall led into a dining room on the left and the rather larger living-room on the right. At the rear was a good sized kitchen, and a scullery. The first floor consisted of two bedrooms, the front one being decidedly the bigger and better; the room above the living-room was Hardy's study; a large, pleasant room with a fine view. A fourth, much smaller room, could be used as bachelor spare bedroom, sewing-room, box room; in short, a general purpose place. There was also a distinctly up-to-date touch in the shape of a water-closet: these were not perfected until the 1870s, after which they were slowly introduced into middle-class homes. Bathrooms were as yet unknown; the plumbing could not have coped with them. The installation of a roof tank at Max Gate meant that there could be cold running water in the kitchen and a flushing w.c. on the first floor. In the 1880s this was all very advanced. However all hot water for washing had to be heated on the kitchen range and fetched upstairs in hot-water cans or, if larger quantities were required, metal buckets with flap-lids. Baths were taken in the form of hip-baths, placed in front of a coal-fire lit in the bedroom, with towels warming on a wooden clothes-horse ready to hand. There was also the invention known as the saucer-bath; a kind of large, shallow dish, rather resembling a bird-bath, in which the decent citizen, avid for cleanliness — or the wretched coerced child — huddled in extreme discomfort, flannel in one hand, soap in the other, attempting to wash whatever part of the anatomy might be reached without upsetting the perilous receptacle all over the floor. One had to be keen to be clean. It should be remembered that these horrid ablutions, inferior to anything the Romans knew, had a moral, as well as hygenic, purpose and were usually taken in cold water, upon jumping out of bed and shedding your nightshirt.

The Servants' Quarters

Above the study, bedrooms and box-room were the attics where the Max Gate servants slept; their numbers varied over the years between two and four, and of course there would have been others, such as chars, washer-women, handymen and the like, who were not resident. There was a gardener, and a gardener's boy; they too would have lived elsewhere. There was a carriagehouse and stabling for two horses; but the Hardys seem not to have kept a carriage but to have hired horses and vehicles when required.

Central heating of course was unheard of. Fires, with the exception of the kitchen-range, were open coal fires, for which coal had to be endlessly fetched, and ashes cleared and carried away; and every morning there was the ritual of cleaning and blackleading the grates. The house was supplied by its own well and pump; unlike so many houses, at Max Gate both well and pump were indoors, in the back premises. Water was pumped each morning into the tank in the roof; a wearisome labour. A

THE DRAWING ROOM
AT MAX GATE.

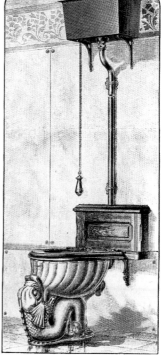

"ELEGANT AND

FUNCTIONAL":

A VICTORIAN

SELF-FLUSHING

WATER-CLOSET.

cess-pit in the grounds dealt with the problem of sewage. All lighting was by candles and oil-lamps. Servants in no way denoted social snobbery, or luxury; they were a necessity in a world entirely without domestic appliances. Even the humblest of homes usually employed at least one servant girl; often greatly to be pitied. The usual quota of resident servants in a household like that of Max Gate would be a cook, a parlour-maid, and two housemaids. At one time there was a boy employed as a "buttons", to announce visitors, but this extra effort at gracious living was a failure as the child was so taken up with staring at the guests that he mostly left them entirely unannounced!

There was a tradesmen's entrance at the back of the premises and inside the house were two separate staircases; one for use by the family – meaning in this case the Hardys – and the other for the domestics; for ever clambering up and down stairs with coal-scuttles or peat, much of which was dug in the region of Dorchester and therefore consumed in household grates, and cans of hot water and buckets of emptied slops. There was no end to the daily labour entailed in a Victorian household.

Coal was stored, for convenience of domestic handling, in a cellar inside the house; usually underneath the front steps, immediately next to which there would be a coal-shoot down which the delivery sacks were emptied directly into the cellar. Every effort was made to keep the nitty-gritty of domestic servicing out of view of the gentry: following the abolition of chimney sweep children these were no longer fetched into the house and put up the chimneys at crack of dawn before the family was up, but instead the flues were reached by the sweep himself using brushes inserted into little metal doors at intervals into an outside wall. On wash-days, in the Victorian era once weekly, clothes and bedding washing being such a palaver, the laundry was boiled in the copper, scrubbed, wrung out, mangled, starched, dried, ironed; it was like a military exercise.

Households tinkled with bells, summoning servants; each bell having a slightly different sound, in order to be recognizable. "There goes the missus, needing me the parlour!" "That's the master; I'll wager he's spilt the ink!" "Who's that on the front-door bell? I hope it's not that Mr Kipling turned up out of the blue!"

Gardens

F VICTORIAN HOUSES were innovatory with their running water, flushing lavatories and well-ventilated rooms, Victorian gardens were also a break with the past. The architect Reginald Blomfield, as it happened, the son of Hardy's old friend and employer Arthur Blomfield, with his book, *The Formal Garden in England* (1892) exercised a strong influence upon late Victorian thinking about gardens, which in turn has influenced much of our thinking about gardens today. Reginald Blomfield lamented the break with gardening tradition and the past which the early and mid-Victorians had brought about with such gusto. However, the gardens that Blomfield was lamenting were much earlier in date than those of Capability Brown or Repton. The gardens he mourned were those of the seventeenth-century; when, to quote him, "Garden design took its place in the great art of architecture", resulting in that well-ordered harmony that was characteristic of the house and garden in England down to the middle of the eighteenth-century." After which, in Blomfield's view, everything had gone wrong. By then, garden design had reached the fullest development of which it was capable; it then became stereotyped. Worse still, "It became familiar, though incomprehensible, to the man of letters and the amateur, who at once set to work to pull it to pieces." To copy Nature now became all the rage. William Kent, insisted Blomfield, was particularly to blame for this. Kent

(1684–1740) had been, as Blomfield freely admitted, an unusually gifted architect, but:

lent himself to the fancies of the fashionable. He endeavoured, to the best of his ability, to reproduce the landscapes of Claude and Poussin … In the words of Horace Walpole, 'The living landscape was chastened and polished' … The chastening of nature was rather severe … it consisted in wholesale destruction of trees, alteration of ground, building up of rocks and, for a crowning effort of genius, in planting dead trees 'to heighten the allusion to natural woods.'"

Kent might, snorted Blomfield, have nailed stuffed nightingales to the boughs while he was about it! Capability Brown's notion of landscape, continued the vitriolic Blomfield:

consisted of a park encircled by a belt of trees, a piece of ornamental water, and a clump … on these lines he proceeded to cut down avenues and embellish nature with the utmost aplomb. He … was succeeded by Humphrey Repton … who … irrevocably destroyed some of the finest gardens in England.

High Victorian Gardening

It might have then been thought that a halt would be called to this alleged vandalism; but no, Blomfield had worse to comment on. Joseph Paxton had appeared on the scene with his ingenious waterscapes, cyclopean aqueduct and giant conservatory, constructed for the

Duke of Devonshire at Chatsworth at the commencement of Victoria's reign. Paxton's inventive genius culminated, of course, in the Crystal Palace, foreshadowing an era when engineering devoid of any influence of stylistic architecture would wed with English romantic landscape to become an art that was plainly Victorian: except that Blomfield would not recognize it as art. "It shows a total insensibility to what has been done in the past … but what else are we to expect from a mind stored with the ideas of the Great Exhibition of 1851". He continues to describe the effects of High-Victorian gardening; known to us because the style survives in parks and public places.

Kiosques and cast-iron fountains … bandstands … urns … peppered all over with shrubs and statues and interminable paths leading nowhere. … If there were any truth in his cant about nature would the landscape gardener bed out asters and geraniums, would he make the lawn hideous with patches of brilliant red varied by streaks of purple blue, and add his finishing touch in the magenta of his choicest dahlia? … It is impossible to take his profession seriously when he flies in the face of nature..

The longed for change was at hand with the arrival on the scene of Edwin Lutyens (1869–1944). He turned to the past for ideas, becoming the leading architectural exponent of the William Morris-founded Arts and Crafts Movement, He put into practise Blomfield's maxim that the object of formal gardening was to bring the house and its surroundings into harmony, to make the house grow out of its surroundings. "The building cannot resemble anything in nature, … on the other hand you can lay out the grounds and so control and modify them as to bring nature into harmony with the house, if you cannot bring the house into harmony with nature." Through his feeling for period, his inventiveness, and technical mastery of natural materials Lutyens, it has been rightly said, delighted the senses without sentimentality. He recaptured essences from the past without resorting to pastiche; houses and gardens at one with another. Some of his buildings were

medieval in conception; others basically Tudor, with Italian overlay; here would be a wholly romantic castle, there a rill-garden drawn from the thirteenth-century. He was blessed by working in partnership with a gardener of genius: Gertrude Jekyll (1843–1932), a painter turned to fulfillment of her eye for form and colour by collaborating with Lutyens and developing her gift for relating plant to plant to achieve her effects. She wrote several influential books, probably the most important being *Colour Schemes for the Flower Garden* (1914). Her *tour de force* was a garden with a sequence of orange, grey, gold, blue and green sections. She wrote with charm and immense authority:

After the grey plants, the Gold garden looks extremely bright and sunny. A few minutes suffice to fill the eye with the yellow influence, and then we pass to the Blue garden, where there is another delightful shock of eye pleasure. The brilliancy and purity of colour are almost incredible. Surely no blue flowers were ever so blue before! … all the blue flowers used, with the exception of Eryngium and Clematis davidiana, are quite pure blues … There are no purple-blues, such as the bluest of the Campanulas and the perennial Lupins; they would not be admissable.

"BUILDING AND SURROUNDINGS IN PERFECT HARMONY". THE IDEAL OF LATE VICTORIAN GARDENERS.

GARDENS

Entertaining

ENTERTAINING IN HARDY'S WORLD was a formal matter, once one entered what was known as "polite society." In the old days, at Bockhampton, as we learn in *Under the Greenwood Tree*, when entertaining was done on any special occasion the fare was hearty; ham and fowls and pies and brawns, custards, puddings and tarts. There was dancing and plenty of home-brewed cider. There was, however, no great refinement about it. But in the circles in which Hardy would have found himself moving as he climbed the social ladder, in Sturminster Newton, for instance, or Dorchester, things would have been different.

People, *en famille*, ate plainly, and we are told that often they ate frugally, meaning that sometimes there wasn't quite enough. For this reason dropping in unexpectedly for a meal just wasn't done, you didn't know what you might find people were eating – or perhaps not eating at all. High-tea in many households was a rule rather than an exception; when alone together the Hardys often enjoyed high-tea and would occasionally invite friends to join them. Tea again, or cocoa, with cake or biscuits, would be served later, before going to bed. Dinner was rarely eaten in the evening in middle-class homes, unless it was for a rarely given dinner-party. Sometimes people would be invited round for cards and then a light supper would be offered. When there were young people in the house there would be musical evenings, and then you might

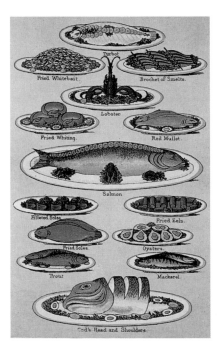

THE FISH COURSE: ILLUSTRATION FROM MRS BEETON.

expect coffee, and rissoles or veal-and-ham pie, followed by a fruit tart and custard, or bavaria cream or, in season, a gooseberry-fool or something similar.

Afternoon Tea

Afternoon tea, when done properly was anything but a simple meal. There had to be two kinds of bread-and-butter, white and brown, and usually fruit-loaf too; all cut thin as tea had to be dainty. Then there would be scones, served with butter and jam, and there might be muffins, or pikelets, or little Scotch pancakes; again all kept warm upon dishes with matching, or silver, lids. Then there also had to be sandwiches. Upon these Mrs Beeton is enlightening: to have sandwiches in perfection, she says "the bread should be not new, but not more than one day old. Cut very thin, and spread lightly with creamed butter", this being easier to spread. "Savoury anchovy, lobster, prawn, and shrimp butters may be usefully employed to give piquancy and variety to other substances; they are also used alone in preparation of rolled sandwiches, which consist of single slices of bread and butter spread with some prepared substance, and then lightly rolled." Sandwich fillings might be ham, egg-and-cress, cucumber, watercress, potted meat, potted shrimps, smoked salmon, pounded smoked goose, flaked and shredded smoked haddock, shredded lobster, crab – there was no end to it. There would be at least four kinds of cake; fruit, chocolate or coffee cake, Victoria sponge; Battenburg cake was popular, but had to be of highest quality, as had marble-cake. Then there would be a selection of fancy cakes; sponge fingers; shortbread; macaroons; madeleines; ginger snaps. And several kinds of tea on offer; Indian, China, of differing blends. Gentlemen were kept busy, handing round. Conversation, like the food, had to be light.

Luncheon parties were popular with ladies. They might start with oyster patties; quenelles in cream sauce; stuffed soft herring roes; poached fillets of sole served in various ways, with grapes, or crayfish tails and truffles, or simply with Mornay sauce, then perhaps there would be the highly popular *oeufs à la tripe* with chicken, or blanquette of veal, or pigeon pie; perhaps a timbale of chicken and veal. Then Bavarian creams with various kinds of fruit; mousses; compotes; meringues; frapfen; floating islands. What a delicious world we have forgotten: let us hope they were not also dining-out in the evening.

Dinner is Served

Dinner parties were vast undertakings for the hostess. First, *hors d'oeuvre*; cold trifles, says Mrs Beeton lightly, before going on to detail a formidable list. Then soup; first one clear, then one thick, each different in colour. Then fish, two sorts; the first large and boiled or poached, then smaller fish, fried or grilled. If cold salmon were served it was *after* the hot fish. Throughout dinner; there was no repeating of any ingredient, flavour, or colour. Then came *entrées*; with which the cook revealed their skill. Rissoles, croquettes, quenelles; then the more substantial fillets and cutlets. *Entrées* were the most important part of the repast; tasteful dishing and decoration were important; but over-ornamentation was in bad taste.

Then the *pièce de résistance*, a saddle of mutton or sirloin of beef, or venison, or poultry accompanied by plain vegetables. At a grand dinner there next came a roast of game; partridge, grouse, pheasant, whatever was in season. After which came *entremets*, properly three in num-

A MUSICAL EVENING.

ber; first various kinds of dressed vegetables such as asparagus with one sauce or the other; cauliflower *au gratin*; stuffed tomatoes; vegetable-marrow fritters. Then came savoury jellies and pastries; then salads, prawns, lobsters. Then the sweets: hot first, then cold: puddings; creams, jellies, babas, savarins. Large ice-cream puddings might be included in this course; smaller ices were preferably served with dessert. After the sweets came the savouries: to prepare the palate for the choice wines to follow. Strong, appetizing flavours were essential for savouries, of which a wide variety ensured that you didn't eat as a savoury an exact replica of what you had first enjoyed as *hors d'oeuvre*. Then cheese arrived; and after cheese, dessert – fresh, dried and crystallized fruits; bons-bons, *petits-fours*, fancy biscuits, and dessert ices.

Needless to say the ordinary middle-class hostess couldn't manage all this, but she did her best to keep up appearances. Alas, too often the man of the house let her down when the time came to carve the joint at table: a must, if he were to stand revealed as a real male. Mrs Beeton remorselessly devoted a whole section to the average gentleman's lack of skill while carving.

THE Mayor OF Casterbridge

PLAQUE ON THE "MAYOR OF CASTERBRIDGE'S HOUSE", HIGH STREET, DORCHESTER.

This house is reputed to have been lived in by the MAYOR of CASTERBRIDGE in THOMAS HARDY'S story of that name written in 1885

HAY TRUSSING: DETAIL FROM "THE HAY CART"; BY BLYANDT.

he Mayor of Casterbridge is increasingly seen as not only Hardy's finest novel, but as one of the outstanding achievements of English fiction. It is a profoundly tragic work, in a way that the more celebrated *Jude the Obscure* is not. Jude is doomed from the start, essentially a symbol, rather than a flesh-and-blood man. Hardy created Jude for a purpose. He did not so create Henchard, the Mayor of Casterbridge. Henchard was there, ready, awaiting Hardy. Michael Henchard comes intensely, grippingly alive from the moment we first see him, walking along a dusty highway in the company of a woman carrying a tiny girl. The man's:

measured, springless, walk was the walk of a skilled country man as distinct from the desultory shamble of the general labourer,
while in the turn and plant of each foot there was, further, a dogged and cynical indifference personal to himself, showing its presence even in the regularly interchanging fustian folds, now in the left leg, now in the right, as he paced along.

So he walks toward us; so in due course he will walk away. But we, having met him, will never be quite the same again. In *The Mayor of Casterbridge* we don't watch an author capturing reality; we experience human truth presented through the medium of art. As to whether we come to like Henchard or not that doesn't matter. What signifies is that he has come, and gone, leaving behind him some unforgettable force.

After establishing the characters, there follows the famous scene when they reach a fair, the man drinks too much rum and sells his wife for five guineas to a sailor. She and her child depart submissively with him; Henchard is left to sleep off his drink. Next day, overcome with disgust, Henchard swears an oath on the Bible that he will avoid all strong drink for the space of twenty-one years, a year for each year that he has so far lived. Then he kisses the Bible and sets off to search for his wife and child; presently coming to a sea-port he learns that they and the sailor have emigrated. Whereupon Henchard starts walking again and "reaches the town of Casterbridge, in a far distant part of Wessex." This introductory sequence is beautifully written, carrying total conviction. And so the novel continues, as it has begun: an exploration of "character as fate."

We next meet Henchard, eighteen years later, a successful grain merchant and Mayor of Casterbridge. Now Henchard's wife and daughter turn up at Casterbridge; Newson, the sailor, having been lost at sea. The woman has succumbed to a desire to find out what happened to the husband who had sold her to the sailor. Her daughter knows nothing of this past history and supposes herself to be the daughter of the sailor, whom she loved dearly. Simultaneously there also appears a charming and clever young Scot, Donald Farfrae. He meets Henchard by chance, reminds him in appearance of his dead brother, and with his knowledge of grain, business sense, and attractive personality so wins Henchard's interest and approval and becomes his partner. Thus, unforseen Henchard brings upon himself the chain of disasters which follow one after the other, struggle as he may.

Elizabeth-Jane

Henchard reconciles with his wife and meets Elizabeth-Jane, his daughter. She is the most convincing of all Hardy's heroines, since he gives her a reasoning mind and allows her to use it. She is also ambitious to learn and so teaches herself Latin and develops a scholarly bent. A former sweetheart of Henchard's, Lucetta Templeman, arrives in Casterbridge, intent on marrying him, while he is intent on avoiding her. The death of his wife leaves him free for Lucetta, but she marries Farfrae instead, despite the fact that he has been courting Elizabeth-Jane. Complicated as all this sounds, it happens quite convincingly. Henchard's business fails; Farfrae buys him out; Henchard scandalous past actions are revealed and he is displaced by Farfrae as mayor.

The supremely touching element in this narrative is the development of Henchard's fatherly love for Elizabeth-Jane. But even she cannot be his; Newson turns up; overjoyed to be reunited with Elizabeth-Jane who – of course – is his rightful daughter, the original Elizabeth-Jane having died shortly after having been sold. Henchard has now lost everything. To crown his defeat, the twenty-one years of his vowed abstinence from drink have now expired and he returns to the bottle. In a final blow to Henchard, Lucetta dies and her widower soon leads Elizabeth-Jane to the altar. The reader may find this difficult to recognize as the stuff of a great novel, but there is more to a book than its plot. *The Mayor of Casterbridge*, once taken up, cannot be put down.

Hardy doesn't make Henchard an attractive man; in most respects he comes across as the reverse; he is a forceful and, at his zenith, a powerful man, but one understands why when he topples nobody runs forward to catch him. Nobody but Elizabeth-Jane, that is. She sees he needs her love and support. But his weight is too great

for her. And though he needs love, he doesn't want pity. So solitary and penniless, he re-equips himself as a hay-trusser and walks away from Casterbridge, alone except for Elizabeth-Jane watching him. "She watched his form diminish across the moor, the yellow rush-basket at his back moving up and down with each tread, and the creases behind his knees coming and going till she could no longer see them." He dies not long after, broken hearted, in a dilapidated cottage attended by the crazy Abel Whittle who hands Elizabeth-Jane Henchard's will:

> . . . that I be not buried in consecrated ground.
> & that no sexton be asked to toll the bell.
> & that nobody is wished to see my dead body.
> & that no mourners walk behind me to my funeral.
> & that no flours [sic] be planted on my grave.
> & that no man remember me.
> To this I put my name. Michael Henchard.

Elizabeth-Jane respected these wishes: she knew "that the man who wrote them meant what he said. She knew the directions to be a piece of the same stuff that his whole life was made of, and hence were not to be tampered with."

ALAN BATES AS HENCHARD IN THE 1978 TELEVISION ADAPTATION OF THE NOVEL.

THE
Woodlanders

ARDY OFTEN REMARKED that he liked *The Woodlanders*, as a story, best of all his novels. For many of his readers, too, it was, and today remains, the favourite Wessex novel. The reception of *The Mayor of Casterbridge*, though polite, did little real justice to it, though Hardy was delighted by the praise which Robert Louis Stevenson lavished upon it in a personal letter. The problem for Hardy was what to write next? Clearly *The Mayor* had not satisfied an audience always hoping for another *Far From the Madding Crowd*. Hardy looked round for a plot likely to provide the desired peg; finally he decided that he could not better one he had

mulled over prior to *The Hand of Ethelberta*, suitably modified and transposed into a deeply rural corner of "Hardy's Wessex". There would, of course, be a "greek chorus" of comic rustics; his Bockhampton relatives and former neighbours, remorselessly exploited to amuse his readership of sophisticated urbanites – it is no small wonder that Hardy made himself not much liked back home in his native haunts! And then there would be, as intrinsic to the work, anthropological allusions and mysteries indigenous to the woodland setting that Hardy was now envisaging.

A Forest Tale

The Return of the Native had been set on Egdon Heath; *The Woodlanders*, as the title suggested, would be a forest tale. Hardy's devotion to trees was almost akin to a form of worship; they filled him with reverence and awe which Havelock Ellis, in an essay on Hardy's work, in 1883, traced to "lingering echoes of the old tree-worship." No wonder Hardy couldn't cut down trees! But despite this tree fixation or perhaps because of it, Hardy chose, as one of the leading characters in his new novel, a timber-merchant, George Melbury, and furthermore presented him in comic vein, though his trade kept him felling green and living trees to be sold as dead, dry, sapless timber. Melbury not only brought down trees in their prime; he would be instrumental in bringing down his daughter in all her vernal springtime and imprisoning her in a cruelly loveless marriage. Not so much the Man with the Scythe, as the Man with an Axe.

There are various ways of looking at *The Woodlanders* and one is to see it as Hardy's variation upon the Don Juan theme. Eldred Fitzpiers, a doctor of medicine and amateur transcendental metaphysician, reputed locally to be in league with the devil, as anyone with any pretensions to learning invariably was said to be in the rural England of those days, is the villain in this woodland piece. A born satyr, pathological in his addiction, he may also of course be seen as a Jack i' the Green, and therefore perfectly suited to Hardy's woodland setting and giving the novel a deeper layer of meaning than at first it appears to have.

The plot is claustrophobic, like the forest itself. Marty South, a village lass, loves Giles Winterborne, an apple and cider dealer, who loves Grace, daughter of George Melbury, timber-merchant. But Grace is attracted by Fitzpiers. Grace's father, a successful self-made man, is anxious to crown his advancement in the world by seeing his daughter cap his endeavours by achieving the social status of a lady. To this end he gives her an expensive education. She returns home from finishing school to discover that she has both intellectually and socially outdistanced poor Giles Winterborne, with whom she has shared an "understanding." In any case her ambitious father is set upon seeing her married to Fitzpiers.

She marries him, but is rapidly disillusioned. But there is no way in which she can be released from this disastrous marriage; the new divorce law, upon which she pins her hopes, does not cover her predicament. She flees from the appalling Fitzpiers and takes refuge in the cottage of the man whom she still truly loves: Giles Winterborne. Anxious not to compromise the good name of the woman whose love he reciprocates, he sleeps out of doors: which we, today, recognize as a completely daft thing to have done, for she has already compromised herself, in Victorian terms, by running to him, and since the cottage is buried in the depths of the forest, anyway, who is to notice the gallant gesture which Giles is making? Tongues will simply go on wagging. But sleep out he does and resultantly gives himself pneumonia and dies, despite all that Fitzpiers, summoned to him in a medical capacity by the distracted Grace, can do for him.

Felice Charmond, a local landowner and another of Fitzpiers' conquests, is shot by her former lover from South Carolina (to satisfy the vicar, if not his daughters).

Marty mourns Giles. Grace goes back to Fitzpiers – there is really no other course open to her as things are. In real life, of course, the climax of the story would be her discovery that she had caught syphilis from him; but that was the end for Ibsen to write, not Hardy, who was seeking realities of a more transcendental kind. He maintained, we should remember, that he had matured beyond what was popularly recognised as realism. "He only writes for Art, though ethics show up," Emma's dry comment, would be made a few years later: at present Hardy was still thinking it advantageous to trim his sails when discretion so demanded, though he in his heart knew where truth lay.

In spite of all the bowderization and trimming that his professional stance necessitated, *The Woodlanders* not only was an artistic success, but emerged as a gripping and intricate chronicle of a countryside community into which outsiders had introduced themselves, bringing with them sophisticated complications. People delighted in its poetic descriptions and the delicious – there is no other word for it – rustic sequences. You can smell the cider, taste the apples. And for those with an eye for it, there is a very nice strain of irony.

"APPLE PICKERS", BY THE IMPRESSIONIST CAMILLE PISSARRO.

THE WOODLANDERS

Hardy's Years of Fame

THE SUCCESS OF *The Woodlanders*, though not altogether approaching that of *Far From the Madding Crowd*, went a long way to restore Hardy's reputation as master of the rustic novel. Always fearful of reviews, instead of waiting to be put on the rack by "the crits" as they came out one by one, he and Emma left England immediately *The Woodlanders* was published and remained abroad for several weeks touring Italy. As it turned out, the reviews were good. Financially, too, Hardy had reason to be satisfied. He had signed an agreement to sell Tillotson & Sons' Newspaper Fiction Bureau the serial rights of his next novel for one thousand guineas; in today's money, well over £25,000.

It would be correct to say that Hardy, at least in his native country, was a well-known author rather than a famous one. In the United States he had a readership that though still restricted made up for lack of numbers by its enormous enthusiasm. In England both public and critics alike showed greater reserve. As early as 1875 Hardy had been the subject of a lengthy and appreciative essay by Léon Boucher in the *Revue des Deux Mondes*. The following year Kegan Paul attempted to do Hardy justice on the English side of the Channel with a piece on him, published anonymously, in the *Examiner*. At last, in 1879, the *New Quarterley* presented a full evaluation of Hardy's work; saying that in *Far From the Madding Crowd* he had introduced a "new sensation" into the art of the novel. With *The Woodlanders* Hardy succeeded in recapturing that sensation to the

satisfaction of his reading public. Nevertheless he had to write *Tess of the d'Urbervilles* to find himself really famous. After publication of this celebrated novel, in 1891, life for Hardy was never the same again. His name entered the public domain. To be sure, the media as we know it today was still in infancy, but nevertheless there were moments when Hardy felt hard-pressed with the attention he received and was known to sigh that he sometimes thought he might have been happier if he had remained a country architect.

Over the four years following the publication of *Tess*, a serialization titled *The Well-Beloved* and two collections of short stories, one of which was the provocative *A Group of Noble Dames*, kept Hardy's name in the public eye. In 1896 *Jude the Obscure* burst upon a stunned readership, with a rusticity no longer cheery with clowns and gentle with lambs, but brutally unvarnished; backcloth for the bleakest love-story in English fiction; three hauntingly ghastly corpses, and an aftermath of abnegation and despair. This extraordinary masterpiece crowned Hardy with some discerning acclaim and a public storm of indignant uproar at times approaching hysteria.

Jude was Hardy's last novel, apart from a much-revised *The Well-Beloved* published in book form. In 1898 he brought out *Wessex Poems*, and stood revealed as his intrinsic self, a poet. But the fame that had come to him as a novelist did not evaporate: the public continued to rave, or rant, over his books. In short the world went, and remained, Hardy mad.

Galleries

SIR FREDERICK
LEIGHTON, PRESIDENT
OF THE ROYAL
ACADEMY FROM 1878.

THE GALLERIES, MUSEUMS and collections made available to the public during the nineteenth century was one of the era's greatest achievements. Museums at first followed the pattern of the Ashmolean in Oxford and were general in their coverage of culture; but as the century advanced, more collections concentrated upon specific branches of science and the arts. Thanks to generous bequests, great private art collections became public galleries; such as the National Gallery (1824), the Tate Gallery (for British works of art, 1841), and the National Portrait Gallery (1857). The provinces followed; notable examples including Glasgow (1856), Edinburgh (1859), Birmingham (1867), Liverpool (1877), Manchester (1882) and Leeds (1888).

Hardy was a great gallery-goer from his first arrival in London. Being an exceptionally gifted draughtsman himself, Hardy's interest in drawings, paintings and engravings might be described as professional, as well as being illuminated by his poet's imagination. He and Emma, spending part of every year in London, visited all the major collections and exhibitions that the metropolis had to offer. Season after season we find them also looking at pictures on their frequent visits to Paris, and revelling in the works of art they saw during their travels in Italy.

The great revolutionary and innovatory period covering the last decades of the eighteenth century into the first decades of the twentieth witnessed experimentation and breakthrough in every conceivable direction, together with processes of integration between the sciences and the arts which subsequently have become largely lost to view. This spirit of integration sprang initially and chiefly from the two great transcendentalists, Goethe in Germany and Coleridge in England. Hardy was blessed, as an artist, in having been born into an age still under their influence, capable of grappling with ideas and idioms, visions and philosophies. It was his grasp of the concept of the oneness of all artistic endeavour that fetched him from his writing-desk into the museums and picture galleries. As with many great exponents of the creative arts, a moment arrived for Hardy when he found himself all but overwhelmed by problems of reality: "What is reality" asked Michelangelo; the same question, only put differently, that Tolstoy asked, "What is art?" How does the artist – poet, sculptor, painter, or novelist, through his visions, his symbols, his putting of words together, create a reality, a truth, as opposed to a deception; however beautiful, beguiling, entertaining, that deception may be? Hardy had been experimenting with this problem in *The Return of the Native* (truth as expressed through myth or ritual); he had thought it through in *The Mayor of Casterbridge* (fate arising from the hard realities of character); then, with *The Woodlanders*, he had found himself in sloughs of depression as he wrestled not only with the finding of reality behind the face of this new novel, but with the question that presented itself to him ever more forcibly with each fresh novel he undertook –"What was he *really doing*?"

Hardy described himself wryly as "resigned to novel-writing as a trade." He had to confess to himself that he went about the business mechanically. In due course he would present a copy of *The Woodlanders* to Sir Frederick Leighton, president of the Royal Academy. Why to Leighton? "My art," explained Hardy, "is to intensify the expression of things as is done by Crivelli, Bellini etc., so that the heart and inner meaning is made vividly visible."

The paintings he gazed at so intently in the many galleries he visited were of vital assistance to him in thinking about his art as a novelist, as apart from the mechanics of writing best-sellers, and even more so as a poet. In March 1885 he was musingly jotting in his notebook,

Novel writing as an art cannot go backward. Having reached the analytic stage it must transcend it by going still further in the same direction. Why not by rendering it as visible essences, spectres, etc., the abstract thoughts of the analytic school? … The human race is to be shown as one great network or tissue, which quivers in every part when one point is shaken, like a spider's web if touched … The Realities to be the true realities of life, hitherto called abstractions. The old / [sic] material realities to be placed behind the former, as shadowy accessories.

Among those painters whose work said most to him Turner was paramount; especially in his late watercolours, those that drew popular ridicule; visionary, abstract, more suggestion than reality, yet capturing suggestion in a way beyond the reach of any other painter. This Hardy almost rapturously perceived a reality. It was Ruskin who had first, in *Modern Painters*, pointed out that Turner was a realist, whose power rests on truth to nature. Turner's contemporary, Charles Kingsley, commented on the realistic naturalism of Turner, his "actual representation", even in his final work; so different from anything else seen that it passed the comprehension of most who saw it. It was felt that he had gone beyond reality. Turner recognized the need for a new realism that could describe phenomena of greater emotional power than any that had been painted in the past: a realism that would release the imagination to discover deeper insights. Hardy, like Turner, wanted "to see the the deeper reality underlying the scenic". "The simply natural," wrote Hardy, "is interesting no longer. The much decried, mad, late-Turner rendering is now necessary to create my interest. The exact truth as to material fact ceases to be of importance in art". After visiting a Turner exhibition at the Royal Academy in 1889 Hardy noted:

Turner's watercolours: each is a landscape plus a man's soul … What he paints chiefly is light modified by objects. He first recognizes the impossibility of really reproducing on canvas all that is in a landscape … Hence, one may say, Art is the secret of how to produce by a false thing the effect of a true.

"COAST NEAR FOLKESTONE", 1845, BY J.M.W. TURNER.

At the very time Hardy was jotting these notes, the French painter, Claude Monet, was struggling with his problems of reality on the other side of the Channel; painting his famous series of grainstacks, stack after stack, day after day, at all hours of the day, in all seasons, explaining that he was trying to make statements of *"ce que j'éprouve"*. In short, in this instance, to confront reality through the exploration of the dimensions of self, both conscious and unconscious, in conjunction with strenuous exploration of the haystacks: a mysterious process – but, said Monet, for him reality stemmed from "mystery and allusion." "To arrive at a higher level of awareness – that is the perfect use of mystery." Whether Hardy ever saw Monet's stacks is uncertain; mixing in the company of painters and poets on either side of the Channel he must have heard of them. Both he and Monet were striving, through different mediums, to achieve the same end. Certainly Monet knew of Hardy: he had his novels in his library at Giverny.

THE Theatre

ARDY WAS TWENTY-TWO and working for Blomfield when he began his first serious theatre-going. He became a fan of the veteran eminent Shakespearean actor-manager, Samuel Phelps who had made history when, in 1844, together with Mary Warner, he had taken over the management of Sadler's Wells in "the hope of eventually rendering it what a theatre ought to be – a place for justly representing the works of our great dramatic poets."

The breaking of the monopoly of the Patent Theatres, granted to Thomas Killigrew and Sir William Davenant by Charles II on his return from exile in 1660, made it possible for the Minor Theatres, as they were called, to present the plays of Shakespeare. The patent granted to Thomas Killlgrew had brought the Theatre Royal, Drury Lane, into being, while that granted to Davenant created the Duke's Theatre, forerunner of Covent Garden – originally straight theatre rather than opera house. In this way the famous rivalry of the two theatres was established.

SADLER'S WELLS IN ITS EARLY YEARS IN A THEN GREEN AND LEAFY ISLINGTON.

Their monopoly of the legitimate drama was not broken until 1843, when Phelps took advantage by making Sadler's Wells the home of purist productions of Shakespeare; eschewing the adaptations and "versions" of the Bard which had become habitual during the Restoration, with the authority of Dryden, and had continued with ever-growing insensitivity during the eighteenth century. Phelps reverted to the Shakespearean text itself. His transformation of the Wells into a home for legitimate drama had indeed been a bold one; for close on two hundred years the Wells had had a reputation of providing the lowest forms of dramatic entertainment and attracting the roughest audiences in London.

Phelps presented thirty-four of the plays while at the Wells; commencing with *Macbeth*. Mary Warner retired from the partnership in 1846; the Wells then was placed under the joint management of Phelps and Greenwood. Greenwood retired in 1860; Phelps terminated his management two years later. At the time of his retirement he had given between three and four thousand performances in all. His revival of *Anthony and Cleopatra* had been the first for over a century; his *Pericles* in 1854 had been the first since the Restoration.

But retirement from the Wells did not mean that he retired from the stage; for a further fifteen years he continued to magnetize audiences, appearing for various managements both in Shakespearean roles and highly successful adaptations of Scott's novels, these from the pen of Andrew Halliday. Hardy saw him play Falstaff, Othello, and Macbeth; as well as in *Cymbeline* and *King John*.

Hardy the Actor?

Did Phelps inspire Hardy with an ambition to tread the boards? Certainly we find him, in 1866, obtaining a "walk on" part for the evening (the equivalent of film-extras signing on for a day) at Covent Garden in Gilbert à Beckett's pantomime, *Ali-Baba and the Forty Thieves*. Not content with this, Hardy also contrived a "walk on" in the celebrated Oxford and Cambridge Boat Race scene in *Formosa*, at Drury Lane. He explained this as "getting stage experience" to prepare him for the writing of blank verse!

The Stars of the Day

Hardy's long lifespan covered a remarkable era in the English theatre. In 1865 the Bancroft management at the Prince of Wales put on *Society*; the first of the celebrated comedies of T.W. Robertson. Under the Bancroft *regime* a new school of realistic staging was launched in revolt against what has been called "the wild fustian" of the general drama of the period – Phelps honourably excluded. Unfortunately Robertson, the chief playwright in this experiment, lacked successors; the theatre of the early and mid-Victorian period clung nostalgically to fustian, abhorring anything resembling real life. Resultantly the theatre became divorced from the mainstream of national culture.

The Bancrofts gave up their management of the Prince of Wales in 1880. Their company had included, at various times, famous names such as Ellen and Marion Terry, Forbes-Robertson, Madge Robertson and her husband W.H. Kendal, Arthur Cecil and John Clayton. The Bancrofts moved to the Haymarket. One of their achievements was to reintroduce the theatre to the prosperous middle class as a respectable place of entertainment; their other great achievement was the reorganization of the theatre in the provinces by sending out touring companies. By the close of the nineteenth century all the leading London actors and famous foreign *artistes* like Sarah Bernhardt habitually took themselves and their companies on tour. The centralization of theatrical activity in London was healthily diminished.

Because of the absence of good playwrights during the mid-Victorian period there was a compensatory explosion of great acting. Until the renaissance of English drama in the late 1880s, when Oscar Wilde, Henry Arthur Jones and A.W. Pinero burst into view, with Bernard Shaw following on their heels, the English theatre was predominantly an actors' theatre, with Henry Irving and Ellen Terry as the sovereign partnership, in reign at the Lyceum (1878–99). The leading theatre critic of the day, before he took to writing plays instead, was George Bernard Shaw. He professed to have no time for Shakespeare and urged

actor-managers, above all, Irving, to put on Ibsen in preference to the immortal Bard. Ibsen was then unknown to the English theatre: why did Irving persist, reiterated Shaw, in playing outworn parts like Shylock and Hamlet when, instead, he might be the first man on the English stage to peel Peer Gynt's famous onion? At length, in 1889, Ibsen's *The Doll's House* was performed in London. Audiences gasped and shuddered as Nora slammed the notorious front door in her husband's face. As Shaw had predicted, the English stage was never the same again. The New Woman had arrived, along with the New Drama.

"THE DIVINE SARAH!": BERNHARDT IN A TYPICALLY SEDUCTIVE POSE.

THE THEATRE

Music

CARICATURE OF THE
YOUNG HENRY WOOD,
RAISING HIS BATON AT
A PROM.

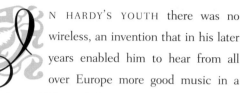

I N HARDY'S YOUTH there was no wireless, an invention that in his later years enabled him to hear from all over Europe more good music in a week than he could formerly have heard in two years. Nor was there any gramophone, or phonograph as the invention was first called when Edison patented it in 1877. It was not until 1894 that a horizontal disc, rather than a cylinder, could be used as a record. And even that was far from meaning that everyone had a gramophone; if you wanted music you either had to make it yourself, or find other people able to do it for you. For Hardy, thanks to his family's involvement in the village quire, his continuing devotion to the violin, and Emma's fondness for playing the piano, there was always music available, first-hand, in his household. There is a reality in playing an instrument, or being in the same room where an instrument is being played that is lacking when the sound is recorded. The recorded music may be infinitely better than any first-hand performance, but the first-hand has the virtue of immediacy. Hardy grew up with the immediacy of music as part of his life.

Heart Music

Musical taste in Hardy's day was what we would consider as provincial and uninformed; even that listened to by London audiences. As late as the 1890s it was freely held by European musicians that "anything was good enough for England" because the English didn't understand music. Because of a musical background too far removed from London fashionable taste to be contorted, Hardy's musicality was well in advance of most of his contemporaries. He was brought up in close touch with the primi-tive heart-music of his indigenous people, with antique strains and refrains of the kind that inspired Bach, and, in a different idiom, would inspire de Falla. There was no artificiality in Hardy's ear. We should think of the ancient carol, sung by the Mellstock quire on their Christmas rounds, "An ancient and time-worn hymn," says Hardy, "embodying a quaint Christianity in words orally transmitted from father to son through several generations down to the present characters, who sang them out right earnestly:

> Remember Adam's fall,
>   O thou Man:
> Remember Adam's fall
>   From Heaven to Hell.
> Remember Adam's fall
> How he had condemn'd all
> In Hell perpetual
>   There for to dwell…

But of course, once in London in 1862 Hardy was instantly off to Covent Garden to sample *Il Trovatore*, and when his father visited him at the close of October that year Hardy marched him off to Wallace's *Lurline*, also at Covent Garden. Indeed there seems to have been much opera-going for Hardy at that period; we find correspondence that refers confidently to Patti and Tietjens; and in later life he spoke nostalgically of those early feasts on opera.

Less sophisticated were the concerts in Westbourne Hall in Westbourne Grove, not far from where Hardy lived. To what extent he patronised the popular concerts we do not know: Saturday afternoons at the Globe Theatre, or St James's Hall, to hear Weber, Grieg, Bizet, Liszt, Glazounoff, Humperdinck, Edward German, Moussorgsky, often in the form of "selections from", rather than entireties; sopranos singing "Cherry Ripe" and "The Last Rose of Summer"; Mr Ivor McKay singing "Thou hast come"; or a solo bassoon playing "Lucy Long", or Schubert's "Serenade" – standard fare for concert-goers in the mid-Victorian period. Hardy possibly found this too refined – he is on record as saying how much he enjoyed Lottie Collin's celebrated number, "Ta-ra-ra-boom-de-ay really a very unusual performance & and not altogether as silly as people say".

The same kind of smug lethargy that gripped the mid-Victorian theatre was stifling the musical scene: a new voice was needed to shake people out of it. This was provided by George Bernard Shaw who, a few years later, would cause havoc as a theatre critic but who now, first on *The Star* newspaper, then on *The World*, sent music lovers either into convulsive spasms of horror, or else of unholy glee – the impoverished young Edward Elgar was one of the latter and when he met Shaw many years later astonished him by remembering word for word the choicest quips from Shaw's notices: "I remember a tenor who used to mark time by shooting his ears up and down … Imagine the sensation of looking at a man with his ears pulsating 116 times per minute in a quick movement from one of Verdi's operas". As Shaw ruefully remarked, the English never suppose that anything said lightheartedly can possibly be serious. Yet he was deeply serious in his determination to change the taste of the English public – and to loosen the deadly stranglehold that the writers of programme notes had on cowed concert-goers. He exposed the pretentiousness of these "experts" on music with an "analysis" of Hamlet's soliloquy on suicide in the same style:

> *Shakespeare, dispensing with the customary exordium, announces his subject at once in the infinitive, in which mood it is presently repeated after a short connecting passage in which, brief as it is, we recognise the alternative and negative forms on which so much of the significance of repetition depends. Here we reach a colon; and appointed pository phrase, in which the accent falls decisively on the relative pronoun, brings us to the first full stop.*

In 1894 the manager Robert Newman engaged a young musician and conductor named Henry Wood. Newman explained to Wood that he wanted the public to come to love great music! "I am going to run nightly concerts and train the public by easy stages," he said. "Popular at first, gradually raising the standard until I have created a public for classical and modern music."

So were born the famous Promenade Concerts – the Proms – which achieved precisely that goal, and in 1995 celebrated a glorious centenary: though Sir Henry Wood didn't quite make conducting that hundredth concert.

ADELINA PATTI, THE CELEBRATED PRIMA DONNA, WHO FIRST ENCHANTED HARDY IN THE 1860S.

Darkest London

WHEN YOUNG THOMAS HARDY, assistant architect, in his city suit and stovepipe hat, was walking daily from the pleasant middle-class suburb in Bayswater, in which he lodged, to the West End Adelphi Terrace, where he worked overlooking the Thames, a very different London was seething and stinking in horrid squalor a mile or so distant, if you took the right – or wrong – direction. This was the London that Dickens wrote about with scathing force, but which Hardy, perhaps because he never really knew it, barely touched upon.

A RAT CATCHER PLIES
HIS TRADE.

Since Tudor times London had been growing without pause: by the start of the eighteenth century all attempts to restrict the city's growth had been abandoned. During the first thirty years of the nineteenth-century the population of Greater London grew from 865,000 to 1,500,000; in the next twenty years another million persons were somehow crammed in. The conditions of overcrowding, suffering and unemployment were appalling: the gulf between rich and poor obscene, in the truest sense of that overworked word. A visitor to the London docks saw forests of masts; the cranes unloading the ships creaked endlessly; the wharves were piled with goods; the warehouses stuffed with goods: the imported wealth seemed boundless. Acres upon acres of riches; apparently sufficient to satisfy the cravings of the whole world. "And yet," wrote Henry Mayhew, in his celebrated, massive survey, *London Labour and the London Poor*, first published in 1851, "you have only to visit the hovels grouped about this amazing excess of riches to witness the same excess of poverty ... Pass from the quay and warehouses to the courts and alleys that surround them, and the mind is as bewildered with the destitution of the one place as it is with the super-abundance of the other."

The cast-offs and refuse of one class provided a means of livelihood for the class immediately beneath; and so it went, down to the depths of the dregs. The "respectably impoverished", yet still genteel, population of clerks and small employees, the lower ranks of the commercial world, gravitated to the new jerrybuilt villas swallowing up the former countryside and transforming it into suburbia, which in turn would deteriorate into mean and grimy "inner London" as newer and newer suburbs were built in their turn. The lowest and weakest of the citizens drifted into the dark central slums; the so-called "rook-

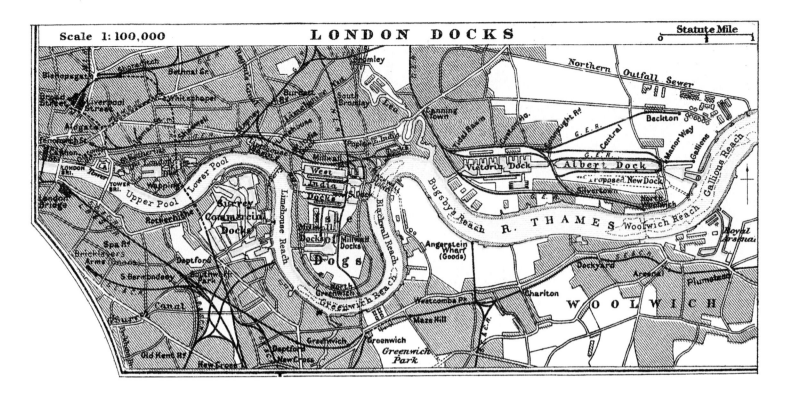

Scale 1:100,000   **LONDON DOCKS**   Statute Mile

eries" – derelict old tenements let out in lodgings or rooms and shared by so many people that it was a marvel where they all managed to sleep. It was common for an entire family with several children to live in one room. As for *how* they lived, as opposed to *where* they lived, the occupations were various: scavenging of all kinds, rag-and-bone men, totters (dealers in old clothes), pedlars, sewage scavengers, rat-catchers, traders in hare and rabbit skins, in kitchen refuse, grease and dripping; the "pure" finders (those engaged in collecting dogs' dung from the public streets), this commodity being named "pure" on account of its cleaning and purifying properties, which guaranteed it a ready market in the numerous tanyards in Bermondsey; sold by the stable-bucket full, at anything from 8d to 1s 2d a bucket, according to its quality. Earlier it had been a fairly profitable (if unpleasant) line to be in; but by the 1850's more and more people were engaged in it, "So they have pulled down the price," as one old woman complained to Mayhew, adding philosophically, "But the poor things must do something. For my part, I can't tell where all the poor creatures have come from, of late years; the world seems growing worse and worse every day."

The Mud-Larks

Perhaps the poorest of the poor were the so-called "mud-larks"; of all ages, from mere children to the aged – wading, sometimes up to the waist, at all times of the year, in the mud left by the Thames tide. They were a daily sight, crawling among the beached barges alongside the wharves, their bodies grimed with the foul soil of the river and their clothes, if such their unspeakable rags might be called, "stiffened up like boards with dirt of every description."

Some of the younger, bolder mud-larks occasionally "swept-out" an unattended coal-barge; illegal, of course. One ten year old boy told Mayhew how he had been caught doing this and given seven days detention in the House of Correction; while there he was given a coat and shoes and stockings to wear, and though there was not "overmuch" to eat, it was better than nothing, which was was quite usual. All in all, he had found the experience infinitely preferable to mud-larking and thought that he would try it again, come the winter. "It would be so comfortable to have clothes and shoes and stockings then, and not be obliged to go out into the cold wet mud of a morning."

"DARKEST LONDON" – DARKEST OF ALL THE AREA BETWEEN WHITECHAPEL AND WAPPING.

DARKEST LONDON

Voluntary Hospitals

INCE THE MIDDLE AGES the hospitals of London, had been struggling with their onerous role of attempting to succour an ever increasing tide of suffering humanity. They had their roots in the religious houses of pre-Dissolution days providing for the incurable, the maimed, the aged and the dying. Some provided shelter for travellers, particularly the many pilgrims of the times. The Priory of St Bartholomew stood in Smithfield, that of St Thomas Becket in Southwark at the start of the great pilgrim route to Canterbury and the coast road *en route* for Rome. Others were by the city gates and the Tower. Following the dissolution of the monaster-

ies by Henry VIII the hospitals shared the same fate: one by one they all went. It was not until the final year of his life that Henry refounded Bart's hospital. In the next reign, that of Edward VI, St Thomas's was reopened with 260 beds.

In 1720 the first of the "Voluntary Hospitals", was opened by public subscription; this was the Westminster Infirmary (later hospital), close to Westminster Abbey. A year later Thomas Guy built his own hospital in Southwark close to St Thomas's. 1825 saw St Thomas's moving to Lambeth; Guy's remained in Southwark. In 1733 St George's Hospital had opened at Hyde Park Corner, by public subscription. Bart's was being rebuilt, likewise by public subscription. The London Hospital was similarly

"AWAITING ADMISSION TO THE CASUAL WARD", BY SIR LUKE FILDES (1843–1927).

founded in 1740, first in Moor Field, then moving to Whitechapel. In this way came into being London's five major teaching hospitals; for each proudly boasted a medical school.

The problem besetting all hospitals at that period was finding "suitable females" as nursing staff; most nurses until then having been of the Sarah Gamp persuasion, with a bottle of gin always at the ready, "Jis' ter wet me lips." This problem was solved in the nineteenth century by Florence Nightingale's revolution in nursing practise. So were introduced upon the hospital scene those scrupulously clean and neat wards, with their endless rows of white beds and their biblical-sounding names.

Treves and Merrick

Hardy had a link with a particularly interesting character at the London: Frederick Treves, the surgeon son of Rebecca Treves, who had kept the shop in Dorchester where Hardy, aged fifteen, had bought the writing-case that he still owned at his death. In 1884, when Treves was lecturer in anatomy and assistant surgeon at the hospital, he noticed that one of the sordid shops opposite the London was exhibiting a crude painting of a man billed as the "Elephant Man". Treves entered the booth, where he saw:

> a bent figure, crouched on a stool, covered with a blanket, and huddling over a bunsen burner naked to the waist. A little man, below average height, the most curious thing about him was his enormous and misshapen head … From his forehead protruded a huge mass of bone. From the back of it great folds of spongy skin hung down, looking like a cauliflower. An osseous growth occluded one eye. Another mass of bone protruded from his mouth averting his upper lip … which had been exaggerated into an imaginary trunk… Never had I met such a degraded or perverted version of a human being.

Here was an anatomical specimen indeed! Treves, to expedite the admission of the man, handed him his card, then had him conveyed by cab to the hospital medical college,

where he identified him as "a gross case of that hereditary abnormality of bone and nervous tissue described by Von Recklinghausen." Treves learned that the man's name was Merrick. How the showman was told by the police never to exhibit such a degrading spectacle again in England, how he departed with Merrick across the Channel and exhibited the poor wretch there until the Brussels police threatened to arrest him; how he, The Elephant Man of no further use to him, bundled Merrick on to a train to London; how, at Liverpool Street station, Merrick collapsed; how the police found Treves's card and informed him; how he came at once and took Merrick to the London, smuggling him into an empty ward; how the next day Treves wrote to the *Times* describing his plight; how a public subscription was raised for Merrick to pay for his residence, for the rest of his life, at the London Hospital; how he regained powers of speech and exhibited a high intelligence, becoming the correspondent of Princess Alexandra, and how he died in his sleep when the weight of his giant head, slipping off the pillow, fractured his spine, is best told in Treves's own words. It is a deeply moving tale of asylum given to an outcast in the true spirit that inspired the creation of hospitals in the first place.

THE ELEPHANT MAN (ANTHONY HOPKINS) RECOUNTS HIS HISTORY TO FREDERICK TREVES (JOHN HURT) IN THE FAMOUS FILM DIRECTED BY DAVID LYNCH (1980).

Tess OF THE D'Urbervilles

BLANCHE SWEET AS TESS IN THE 1924 SILENT FILM VERSION OF HARDY'S MOST FAMOUS NOVEL

STONEHENGE: SYMBOLIC SITE OF PAGAN SACRIFICE.

HARDY'S YEARS OF FAME

THE ASTONISHING SUCCESS of *Tess of the D'Urbervilles* rested on several factors. Steeped in eroticism, it was written with a passion and a power that never slackened from the moment that Tess, an innocent young village lass, joined with the rest of the village maidens in a ritual springtide fertility dance, to the final page when the black flag moved slowly up the mast on the prison tower as signal that justice had been done. In between this beginning and end Hardy's genius as a story-teller bore the reader along a plot as melodramatic and objectively unconvincing as ever was penned. Yet, once embarked upon, this novel proved, still proves, impossible to put down until the reader has reached the last word in the last line. It is compulsive. In *Tess* Hardy exploited to the full the prevailing popular interest of his day in the "Woman Question", which had become all the rage with people who liked to think of themselves as progressive. In truth, his theme of the blameless maiden fallen victim to male lust and social hypocrisy had nothing new about it, but like Shakespeare Hardy knew that an oft-told tale, if good, loses nothing by retelling. With immense skill he managed to make this tale of betrayal seem to the reader to be some advanced *exposé* of male iniquity and social injustice with a liberated New Woman tearing aside the veils of conventional morality. Whereas one can only repeat that it is the stalest story in the world and Tess, as New Woman, would have been the laughing-stock – and despair – of Mary Wollstonecraft.

A Sacrifice

In the opening chapters Tess is a sacrifice to the sexual appetite of Man, then she becomes a sacrifice to social hypocrisy and bigoted convention, finally she dies as a sacrifice to what Hardy insists is perverted justice. She is presented as emancipated and free spoken; but Hardy does most of the talking for her, explaining that she only went to village school. Yet occasionally she bursts into speech,

The trees have inquisitive eyes, haven't they? … And the river says, – Why do ye trouble me with your looks? – And you seem to see numbers of tomorrows just all in a line, the first of them the biggest and clearest, the others getting smaller and smaller as they stand farther away; but they all seem very fierce and cruel and as if they said, I'm coming! Beware of me! Beware of me! …'

He [Angel] was surprised to find this young woman – who though but a milkmaid had just that touch of rarity about her … shaping such sad imaginings. She expressed in her own native phrases – assisted a little by her Sixth Standard training – feelings which might almost have been called those of the age – the ache of modernism."

The plot is unvarnished melodrama. Tess Durbyfield, a cottage girl of exceptional beauty with "a mobile peony mouth and large innocent eyes", sets out on her drunken father's behalf to establish an ancestral connection with the aristocratic d'Urbervilles. She is seduced by Alec d'Urberville, a rich bounder whose entitlement to the

D'Urberville heritage is questionable. He casts her off and she bears his child who dies soon after. Tess becomes a dairymaid and meets handsome Angel Clare – from a man with a name like that any wise woman would run like the wind – they fall deeply in love and marry. On their wedding night they confess their sins to one another. He has had a single sexual experience with a prostitute; Tess, of course, has borne an illegitimate child. She forgives him; but he abandons her, travelling to Brazil. Believing he is gone for good, Tess returns to her family and by chance meets Alec d'Urberville, who has undergone a temporary transformation and is now a preacher. Tess unwillingly becomes his mistress. Clare returns and seeks her out and, desperate not to lose him again, she disposes of the inconvenient Alec by stabbing him. She and Clare then wander into the New Forest where, for a few blissful days, they take possession of a deserted mansion. Tess seems unable to realize the gravity of her conduct; the strength of her love for Angel has "apparently extinguished her moral sense altogether." Of course they are finally discovered; flee once more, wander for miles and finally, exhausted, stumble into Stonehenge. The police arrive and arrest her. The novel ends with the black flag creeping up the prison mast, and Angel and his sister-in-law, Liza-Lu, a "spiritualized image of Tess", stumbling away hand in hand.

A Pure Woman

Hardy, as if to invite the uproar that ensued upon publication of *Tess*, affixed to it the defiant sub-title, *A Pure Woman*. Suddenly everyone was arguing about Tess; was she, or was she not, pure? Had she been justly or unjustly hanged? Did her execution imply one law for men, and another for women? Hardy was sincerely shaken when he put this question to the Lord Chief Justice who said that he would have hanged her as she had murdered Alec and would he not have hanged had he murdered her? Hardy was asking for one law for women and another for men.

Henry James described *Tess* as "chockfull of faults and falsity". He was right, of course. As a compelling, absolute-

ly stunning novel *Tess* has few rivals but as an analysis of the "Woman Question" it does not bear serious contemplation. Hardy misunderstood the issue: Tess's purity, whatever that meant, wasn't the case in point. The point was, had Tess received equal treatment at the hands of society? For the greater part of the book, she did not; but for the murder of Alec, she received, under law, the same punishment that he would have received. She was not condemned under a charge of adultery, but of murder.

The truth was that by making Tess kill Alec, Hardy gravely retarded the progress of the Women's Movement. With the thrust of that knife into Alec, Tess confirmed that Woman was as Man loved to depict her – irresponsible, instinctual and deficient in self-control and moral comprehension. Love and passion had extinguished her moral sense altogether. The old adage that when a man goes to the bad he goes to the bad, but when a woman goes to the bad she becomes infinitely more wicked than the man will ever be, seemed to be borne out by Tess. It was perceived that not only her moral sense was extinguished, but that she had *no* sense. Finding herself at last in an untenable situation, she grabbed a knife and drove it into Alec's heart. So much for the New Woman. Back to the Middle Ages.

TESS AND HER BABY, POIGNANTLY NAMED SORROW, IN A CORNFIELD: NASTASSIA KINSKI IN THE ROMAN POLANSKI DIRECTED FILM (1979).

Jude THE Obscure

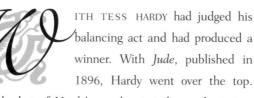

JUDE (CHRISTOPHER ECCLESTON) AND SUE (KATE WINSLET) IN THE 1996 SCREEN ADAPTATION OF HARDY'S MASTERWORK.

ITH TESS HARDY had judged his balancing act and had produced a winner. With *Jude*, published in 1896, Hardy went over the top. This, the last of Hardy's novels, started as a short story about a young man unable to go to Oxford, his subsequent despairing struggles against his lot and ultimate suicide. He would emerge as the character Jude. Though a deeply complex character, correctly defined by Hardy as "obscure", he is triumphantly brought to life, inanities and all, to hold the bewildered and finally horror-stricken reader all the way through the drama until this unlikely hero dies and the reader, exhausted, lays down the book and demands a stiff drink.

Hardy was helped in the creation of Jude by making the account of his early days and profession as a stonemason largely autobiographical. The heroine Susanna Florence Mary Bridehead (Sue for short) was less easy to capture; indeed the chief defect of the novel is that Sue is never convincing – Emma Hardy was right when she said that her husband didn't understand real women.

Hardy confessed that he had found Sue "very nebulous" at first, though gradually she had taken on "shape and reality" for him, moulding into the kind of young female he envisaged as an ideal heroine for the novel that he was determined should be his masterpiece: a girl with a mind, but who never used it because of the circumstances of life forced upon her by her sex; with healthy natural instincts, though not "impassioned". "Good, dear,

and pure … the most ethereal, least sensual woman I ever knew without inhuman sexlessness." So Jude himself would describe Sue. No wonder Hardy never really succeeded in bringing her to life for his readers! In any case he didn't like real women: in his notebook he jotted, "Real woman is abhorrent to man? Hence the failure of matrimony?"

A True Marriage

In *Jude* Hardy made clear his contempt for, and condemnation of conventional marriage. "Civilization", he once complained, "[has] never succeeded in creating that homely thing, a satisfactory scheme for the conjunction of the sexes " Romantic friendship was his ideal. Jude and Sue, in their idyllic simplicity endeavoured set up a lifestyle of their own, free from the values, conventions and constraints of the rest of society: "true" marriage. In counterpoint to this pure ideal each, through a series of blunders, had entered into wedlock with a wildly unsuitable partner, in each instance sordidly coarse and quite repugnant to Jude and Sue respectively. Ignoring all this, the pair persevered with their "true" marriage. This was an almost impossible scenario for any author to carry through successfully. Moreover Hardy was dreadfully serious in his approach. Thus, when all had fallen in ruins about the lovers Hardy made his distraught heroine exclaim:

> *"Our life has been a vain attempt at self-delight. But self-abnegation is the higher road. We should mortify the flesh – the terrible flesh – the curse of Adam! … We ought to be continually sacrificing ourselves on the altar of duty."*
> *To which Jude could only mumble the inadequate reply,*
> *"Sue! What has come over you?"*

MOUNTING TENSION
GRIPS SUE AND JUDE
AS THEY, WITH
THEIR CHILDREN,
ATTEMPT TO FIND
HAPPINESS TOGETHER.

CHRISTMINSTER
(OXFORD): THE
UNIVERSITY WHERE
IN A VISION THE
YOUNG JUDE SAW
HIMSELF AS A STUDENT.

To be sure the modern reader rather feels that he deserved all this: he had started the conversation by enquiring, "What are you thinking of, little woman?" And, when she amplified her thoughts Jude lashed out at her – insofar as he could ever lash at anything, "You dear, sad, soft, most melancholy wreck of a promising intellect it has ever been my lot to behold!' And he mused aloud, "Is a woman a thinking unit at all?" But instead of walloping him over the head with his umbrella, which she should have done, she almost agreed to run away with him all over again.

Hardy carried his strange tempting of ridicule to a point far beyond what one would suppose possible. With their three children dead, two hanged by their slightly senior step-brother, who had then gone on to hang himself, Sue gasps to Jude, "O my comrade, our perfect union – our two-in-oneness is now stained with blood" Jude corrects her, "Shadowed by death – that's all " She laments, "There is something external to us which says, 'You shan't!' First it said, 'You shan't learn! Then it said, 'You shan't labour!' Now it says, 'You shan't love!' "That's bitter of you, darling," responds Jude, as ever master of British under-

statement – three little strangled corpses lying cold in the next room. And when he wonders why the little boy turned killer Sue explains that she had told him she was expecting yet another child and he had reproached her saying there were too many of them already. "I couldn't bear deceiving him as to the facts of life … [that] all is trouble, adversity and suffering! … I said it was better to be out of life than in it at this price." To which Jude's reply is, "Your plan might have been a good one for the majority of cases; only in our case it chanced to work badly perhaps."

Easy to ridicule. And many did so when *Jude* appeared. And yet there is no other English novel to rival its morbid intensity, or equal its depths of genuine blackness, its overwhelming sense of doom. It could so easily, indeed it very nearly did, descend into the sweaty dungeon of Gothic horror, *The Castle of Otranto*, or *The Mad Monk*; but Hardy, with electrifying genius, raised it to a terrible finale akin to Greek tragedy. Our spines never cease to tingle with classic tremor when we read the words of that horrific suicide note lying on the floor of the chamber where that strangled trio dangle: "Done because we are too menny."

Hardy THE Degenerate

 UDE THE OBSCURE, for serialization purposes entitled "Hearts Insurgent", like *Tess* was subjected to a lot of watering-down for reading aloud in family circles. But, as with *Tess*, Hardy reinstated the removed material for bookform publication and, as with *Tess*, he had made up his mind that nothing would make him change this indictment of contemporary English *mores*: their inflexibility of marriage; the denial of sexual justice; the inequality of education for different social classes; indeed an indictment of English class structure itself.

Jude the Obscene

Buoyed up with the knowledge that in *Tess*, despite criticism of her, he had produced a tremendous novel he probably anticipated a similar triumph with *Jude*; aggressive as his material was and deeply depressive the mood of the story. But with *Jude* Hardy had miscalculated the reception. A storm of almost unrelieved abuse greeted it. Even those who acclaimed it as a masterpiece, among them H.G. Wells and Ellen Terry, indicated that its general tone of doom and gloom made it hard to take. The critical – and

TESS, A SYMBOL OF FEMALE SEXUALITY.

most were critical – expressed their outrage without any attempt at restraint. *The Pall Mall Gazette* reviewed it under the heading "Jude the Obscene"; the *London World* preferred "Hardy the Degenerate"; the *Guardian* reviled the novel as a "shameful nightmare"; Gosse in the *St James' Gazette* called it a "gloomy … grimy story" and told Hardy to his face that it was the most indecent novel ever written. The Bishop of Wakefield burned a copy of *Jude* in public – "Probably in despair at not being able to burn *me*," commented Hardy – and used his influence to have the work withdrawn from W.H. Smith's circulating library. Even those who, at first glance encouragingly, compared him with Zola and Tolstoy went on to add that Zola was hoggish and Tolstoy decadent. "What foul cess-pits some men's minds must be!" commented Hardy to his notebook.

Though he withdrew from novel-writing, and would win respect and renown as a poet, Hardy could never rid himself of his "sex and Wessex" reputation. Perhaps he didn't mind this as much as he sometimes suggested: in one respect it was the kind of reputation which helped to sell every word he wrote, even when unconnected with either sex or Wessex. On the other hand, it prevented some of his later work from receiving the serious criticism it merited. A case in point was his collection of short linked stories called *A Group of Noble Dames*, which Hardy sent to the *Graphic* in May 1890. They evoked the usual complaint; "Many fathers are accustomed to read or have read to their family-circles the stories in the *Graphic*; and I cannot think that they would approve for this purpose a series of tales almost every one of which turns upon questions of childbirth, and those relations between the sexes over which conventionality is accustomed (wisely or unwisely) to draw a veil". This, it should be noted, was before the publication of *Tess*.

Hardy made the desired revisions, though his anger over this is clear from the contemptuous words "the tyranny of Mrs Grundy", which he scrawled across the manuscript. In the States, where the stories were serialized in *Harper's Weekly*, much of what he had had to remove for the *Graphic* was reinserted – proof that the *Noble Dames*

were not that scandalous!. When the collected stories appeared in book-form with four additional stories included with the previous six, they were received either with half-hearted praise or open condemnation. They were considered "distasteful", "coarse" and "morbid". Only the most prejudiced Anglo-Saxon mind would read them as such, but the lack of enthusiasm seems to have stuck; to the unprejudiced reader today they seem some of the most brilliant short pieces Hardy ever wrote. Their technical mastery is superlative and they are highly entertaining.

Hardy's last published novel, *The Well-Beloved*, had been written some ten years before it appeared in book form in 1897 (it had been serialized in 1892) and Hardy recast it considerably for its 1897 reappearance. It would prove not only one of the most popular but also the best of his non-Wessex novels. It explored, with a lightish touch, the theme, said Hardy, "of the theory of the transmigration of the beloved, who only exists in the [imagination of] the lover, from material woman to material woman". His hero, Jocelyn Pierston, pursues the "elusive idealization" which he calls his "Love" through three generations of women. The novel is sexually sophisticated to a high, albeit subtle degree: Hardy enjoyed himself in applying to Pierston those famous words earlier applied to Tess; an innocent and moral character throughout. The reviews were remarkably favourable, with the exception of the *World*, which took the old predictable line: "Mr Hardy has once more afforded a dismayed and disgusted public the depressing spectacle of Genius on the down grade. Matthew Arnold once rudely referred to Burns as "a beast with splendid gleams", a description which was irresistibly called to the present writer by the perusal of *Jude the Obscure*. For in that book there were undoubtedly some splendid gleams. There are none in *The Well-Beloved*".

Following this Hardy said good-bye for good to novels (at least, his own). He was now very rich and famous. He was able to devote himself to fulfilling his dream as a nineteen year old: himself as Poet. In his poems he might be searing in his social comment and miraculous in his erotic imagery but, as he wryly murmured, nobody noticed.

ELLEN TERRY AS LADY MACBETH. SHE HAILED "JUDE" A MASTERPIECE.

Votes FOR Women

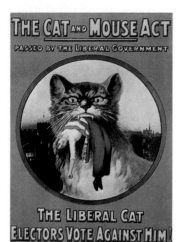

POSTER IN THE
SUFFRAGETTE COLOURS:
GREEN, WHITE AND
VIOLET, SATIRIZING
THE NOTORIOUS 1913
"CAT AND MOUSE ACT".

ecause the heroines of Hardy's novels so flagrantly flouted the social conventions of their day it was supposed by the suffragettes that he would be an influential supporter for their cause. Following the publication of *Tess* we find Emma Hardy writing to Mary Heweis, an active supporter of the Women's Suffrage Movement, to disillusion any hopes that Hardy might be a useful ally: "His interest in the Suffrage Cause is nil, in spite of 'Tess', and his opinions on the Women Question not in her favour … He only writes for Art, though ethics show up." However Emma went on to express her interest in the movement, asking for fuller details as she would like to give her support. Hardy had a rebel in his camp.

The feminists of the second half of the nineteenth century who would produce the New Woman found themselves confronted with many barriers, dating back into the distant past and generally seen as immutable. These early protagonists of the Women's Movement were often spinsters; Emily Davies spoke for many when she briskly remarked that "having a husband was the equivalent of being hamstrung." This was not sour grapes; she might have married, but refused to do so because this would have placed her in a position of total financial dependence. While women of the aristocracy and the moneyed mercantile classes received protection from the courts, the ordinary wife had no right to property of her own: indeed, except in the City of London, a married woman did not even have the right to money she earned: it had to be paid to her husband. Things began to change in 1857, when parliament first set up a court empowered to grant dissolutions of marriage and legal separations: the deserted or separated wife then gained the right to her own earnings. The wife living with her husband was not protected until the Married Women's Property Act of 1870. The 1870 Act was further strengthened and expanded by additional acts of 1882–93. Alongside these a kindred struggle took place for the right of married women to have access to their children. Under the old Common Law the father alone was parent of the child. The first mother to fight this publicly was Caroline Norton, whose battle led to the Access of Children Bill in 1838, however the most important bill on behalf of mothers' rights did not come until 1925, with the Guardianship of Infants Act. Though women might fight for these bills to be passed by Parliament, and fight they did, Parliament itself remained debarred to women; they could not even vote for parliamentary candidates. "Votes for Women!" became the battle cry.

Women's Suffrage

The first women's suffrage committee was formed in Manchester in 1865. Its honorary secretary was Mrs Elizabeth Elmy, who had served on the Married Women's Property Committee. Another member was Emmeline Gouldon, later to become the wife of Richard Marsden Pankhurst, a barrister and firm advocate of women's suffrage. Mrs Elmy was succeeded by Lydia Becker, who wished the cause of Women's Property to be dropped in favour of Women's Suffrage. In London a Suffrage Committee had been formed to back John Stuart Mill in his suffrage campaign in Parliament, he lost his seat in 1869 and devoted himself to writing his famous polemic, *On the Subjugation of Women*. The Society of Women's Suffrage was formed under Lydia Becker's influence; she insisted upon the enfranchisement of widows and spinsters only. To her, married women were a form of sub-species.

This was opposed by Pankhurst on the valid grounds that without full property rights married women would be campaigning for the vote while still in financial bondage to their husbands. Becker formed her own group, the Society for Women's Suffrage, and continued her campaign. The Pankhursts (Emmeline had now married Richard), Mrs Elmy and others of the original suffrage pioneers formed a new Women's Franchise League and by supporting the Local Government Act of 1894, which gave married women franchise in local government, cut the ground from under Becker's feet. In 1897 the various suffrage societies united within the National Union of Women's Suffrage Societies under the inspired presidency of Mrs Henry Fawcett. In 1903 Mrs Pankhurst started the Women's Social and Political Union in Manchester, thereby giving the movement a sharper political focus.

At a pre-election meeting of Liberals in 1905, in Manchester, the Pankhursts' daughter Christabel, a law graduate, and Annie Kenney, asked the speaker, Sir Edward Grey, from the public gallery what would be the Liberal policy toward women's enfranchisement should that party win the election? The two questioners were seized by stewards and they were kicked and thrown down the gallery stairs. In the street they tried to address the crowd, and were promptly arrested. Next day, in court, they were offered the choice of a fine or imprisonment and both chose the latter. It was the start of suffragette militancy.

In 1906 the Liberals came into office: the succeeding years saw the defeat of seven suffrage bills in the House, amid the mounting fury of women. A large, and peaceful, pro-suffragette meeting was held in Hyde Park in 1908; many prominent figures turned out in support of it, including Bernard Shaw, H. G. Wells and Thomas Hardy. Emma was now an active paid-up member of the London Society for Women's Suffrage. Militancy mounted. Suffragettes waylaid public figures, attacked public buildings and chained themselves to railings. When arrested and imprisoned they mounted hunger strikes; several were brought close to death in the process of forcible feeding. Under the 1913 Prisoners (Temporary Discharge for Ill-health) Act, the notorious so-called "Cat and Mouse" Act, they were released in order to recover sufficient strength to be sent back to prison; when, of course, the process began again. Despite some general indignation at this disgraceful procedure, it must be conceded that their militancy lost the suffragettes considerable public support.

In 1913, Asquith, then Prime Minister, had launched a Reform Bill to extend the male vote and announced that this would be open to women's suffrage amendments. When the bill reached the House, the Speaker ruled that such amendments would alter the nature of the bill and it was thrown out. Suffragette fury knew no bounds. At that year's Derby, Emily Davidson (*not* to be confused with Emily Davies, who had achieved her goal of admittance of women to university in 1869 with the opening of Girton College; first in Hitchin, then in 1873 in Cambridge), lost her life when she threw herself in front of the King's horse. She had not intended to martyr herself, but her death was seen as a sacrifice.

In 1914 war intervened and over the next four years the suffragettes devoted themselves to rallying round the national cause. The war over, a new Reform Bill was launched by Lloyd George and in the resulting Representation of the People Act, married women, householders and women university graduates received the franchise, the voting age being thirty and over. A further bill enabling women to become Members of Parliament was passed soon after. This was 1919. In view of the dedicated service women had given their country during the war it was impossible to deny them their democratic rights any longer.

FORCIBLY FEEDING A
SUFFRAGETTE IN
HOLLOWAY PRISON.

Birth Control

T HE CONCEPT OF "PURITY", as we have seen from Hardy's tribulations with his fiction, was of immense importance to the Victorians – it was, of course, "purity" within a specifically sexual context: in truth, synonymous with sexual ignorance. Hardy's Tess, we should remember, was depicted by him as "blank as snow"; she pleaded, in defence of her seduction by Alec D'Urberville, that she knew nothing of men – difficult to believe of a cottage girl brought up to farms and farming and surrounded by little brothers and sisters. However, this was the desired image: young women – and in many spotless middle-class households young men too – went "pure" to the matrimonial bed. Here women found themselves condemned to decades of virtually non-stop childbearing, resulting in exhaustion

FLORENCE AND THOMAS HARDY AS GUESTS OF MARIE STOPES (RIGHT) AT HER PORTLAND LIGHTHOUSE.

and chronically damaged health, though to be sure a few matrons of bisonlike stamina survived without apparent ill-effects. Premature death was a common hazard for these incessant child bearers; husbands cheerfully worked their way through a succession of wives and it was extraordinary how often these were clergymen. So long as women found themselves caught in this trap, the idea of true sexual equality remained a dream. No matter how intellectual, well educated, gifted and strong-minded a woman might be, once elevated to the status of holy matrimony she became the victim of the inexorable process of procreation. Even those who had produced the necessary quota of surviving sons enjoyed no respite. Methods of contraception *were* known and practised, but not in respectable English Victorian households. The matrons therein never associated themselves with birth-control, nor did their husbands – even if they practised it with their mistresses it could never be sanctioned in the marital bed. That was the place for begetting children, not preventing them.

The problem of over sized families apart, there was the intolerable strain that "purity" (sexual ignorance) imposed upon the marital relationship itself. Brides who knew nothing about anything, blank as snow, and young husbands who knew little, if anything, more than they did, were headed for trouble. There was a profound belief, in middle and upper class Victorian England, that women did not enjoy sex and that the orgasm was unknown to them because they were physically incapable of it. In short, the physical side of human mating was *terra incognita* so far as respectable couples were concerned. It just wasn't a subject ever discussed. Even at the North London Collegiate the girls, though expertly taught about the reproductive system of the frog, which they personally dissected in the biology lab, and perfectly

immersed in botanic structures, never heard a hint of what went on between human beings when the sexes came together. Boys were no better educated in this respect than these girls.

Marie Stopes

In December 1899 a striking-looking girl of just nineteen left the North London Collegiate with a £5 scholarship in science, worth great deal more than that today, and a place awaiting her in the Science Faculty of University College, London. Her name was Marie Charlotte Carmichael Stopes. A brilliant career was foretold for her and this she fulfilled, graduating BSc with honours, in 1902, then doing post-graduate work at University College, after which she entered the Botanical Institute of Munich University on a travelling scholarship. She was awarded her Ph.D. in 1904 and was appointed lecturer in Botany at Manchester University, the first woman on the Science staff. In 1905 she gained her D.Sc., at London, to be the youngest Doctor of Science in Britain. Backed by the Royal Society she visited Japan and, attached to the Imperial University, Tokyo, she travelled widely. In 1909, on return to England she was appointed lecturer in Paleobotany at Manchester University. In 1911 she met and married a Canadian geneticist, Reginald Gates. Five years later the marriage ended in divorce, with Marie Stopes (she always kept her own name) claiming that technically she was still a virgin. In 1918 Victor Gollancz published her book, *Married Love*, which, as she herself would say, burst upon the world like a fireball. Shortly after its publication she made a second attempt at marriage, this time to an R.A.F. pilot, H.V. Roe, backer of her book.

Married Love

Married Love, though always described as being about birth-control, is really, as Stopes's biographer June Rose puts it, a clarification of the conduct and language of sexual intercourse after the First World War. Undoubtedly

Marie Stopes was inspired to write by her own unhappy first experience of marriage. The book does contain some explicit material about contraception: however, it was in *Contraception*, published in 1923, that Stopes dealt specifically with the subject, in straightforward scientific language and manner. In *Married Love* she wrote about sex and the sexual act, which she described in full and perfect detail as none of her readers had ever found it described before. Suddenly everything was clear. The frog was swept out of view: replaced by human men and women. While some readers were shocked by her frankness and

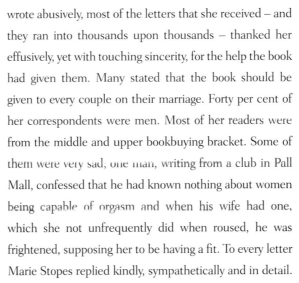

wrote abusively, most of the letters that she received – and they ran into thousands upon thousands – thanked her effusively, yet with touching sincerity, for the help the book had given them. Many stated that the book should be given to every couple on their marriage. Forty per cent of her correspondents were men. Most of her readers were from the middle and upper bookbuying bracket. Some of them were very sad, one man, writing from a club in Pall Mall, confessed that he had known nothing about women being capable of orgasm and when his wife had one, which she not unfrequently did when roused, he was frightened, supposing her to be having a fit. To every letter Marie Stopes replied kindly, sympathetically and in detail.

To spread the gospel to those not in the book-buying bracket Marie Stopes and her husband, at their own expense, opened a clinic in North London that married women, whoever they were, might attend, free of charge. Totally uninhibited and fearless in her passionate desire to help those needing advice, and sometimes merely expressing polite interest, she once gave the second Mrs Hardy, apparently over the tea-table, advice on how to use a particular kind of vaginal douche. Florence confessed that Hardy was terrified of becoming a father – at eighty-three it was understandable.

THE MALTHUSIAN TESS WITH A BROOD OF BROTHERS AND SISTERS: SHE OFTEN WISHED THAT HER MOTHER COULD CONTROL THE SIZE OF HER YOUNG FAMILY.

Animal Rights

*L*OOKING AT PICTURES of the traffic-teeming streets of Victorian cities, London above all, with the tides of horse-drawn vehicles – omnibuses, hackney cabs, vans, waggons, carriages, carts of all descriptions – jostling and cramming, it is impossible not to feel for the animals between the shafts. The horse is a sensitive creature; its memory is long; it remembers places, and associates places with frightening incidents and accident. The instincts of horses are highly developed; they are aware, as man is not, of unknown and unseen dangers. Their daily journeys through crowded, noisy city streets must have been nerve-wracking, often terrifying, as well as physically exhausting for them

Here is a philosophical London omnibus driver talking to Henry Mayhew in 1850:

It's very hard work for the horses, but I don't know that they are overworked in buses. The starting and stopping is the hardest work for them; it's such a terrible strain. I've felt for the poor things on a wet night, with a bus full of people … It's not easy to drive a bus; but I can drive, and must drive, to an inch; yes, sir, to half an inch. I know if I can get my horses' heads through a space, I can get my splinter bar through. I drive by my pole, making it my centre. If I keep it fair in the centre, a carriage must follow, unless its slippery weather, and then there's no telling. A bus changes horses four or five times a day, according to the distance. There's no cruelty to the horses, not a bit, it wouldn't be allowed. Every horse in our stables has one day's rest in four; but it's no rest for the driver except two hours, every other Sunday.

The cab horses had the toughest time, apart from the costermongers' ponies and donkeys, proverbially roughly treated. Some cabs were individually owned, but most worked for "masters"; some of whom took good care of their vehicles and horses while others didn't care what happened to them so long as they fetched home a good day's money. Few of the respectable masters worked their horses at night. According to Mayhew, of an estimated 5,000 drivers in London, very nearly half were small masters; the most respectable class and very careful of their horses because their livelihood depended on them.

The greatest cruelty to horses arose from the "bearing rein"; a short, fixed rein that bore up a horse's head, keeping it raised tight back so that the animal had its neck arched and head held high – which gave a smart and fashionable appearance, but meant that the poor creature, when pulling up hill, could not relieve the weight of its

load by stretching forward its head; and thereby throwing the weight on its collar. Thanks to public opinion, roused to indignation by protestors against what amounted to torture, and by Anna Sewell's famous best-seller and classic, *Black Beauty*, the practise was gradually dropped.

The Society for Prevention of Cruelty to Animals

Nineteenth century protests against cruelty to animals originated in eighteenth century sensitivity to the rights of all living creatures. In England this was championed by Jeremy Bentham (1748–1832), who was a strong advocate of laws to protect animals from cruel treatment. In 1822 a bill put forward by Richard Martin, MP for Galway, prohibiting the cruel and improper treatment of agricultural animals, including mules and horses, was enacted by Parliament. In the face of outstanding abuse of the law, the Society for the Prevention of Cruelty to Animals was formed in 1824 to encourage popular support for the legislation. In 1840, by order of Queen Victoria, the society was honoured with the prefix "Royal". In 1849 a further Cruelty to Animals Act was passed to buttress the previous one and yet another Act of 1854 reached the statute books containing working laws regarding the treatment of domestic animals generally. The Cruelty to Animals Act of 1876 was directed towards scientific experiments upon living creatures. In 1900 the Wild Animals in Captivity Protection Act was passed.

Both Emma and Thomas Hardy were deeply concerned about the welfare of animals. Hardy was always full of praise for the courage Emma displayed in protesting, on the spot

HORSE-DRAWN OMNIBUS
WITH CONDUCTOR
ON REAR PLATFORM
AND FEMALE
PASSENGERS INSIDE.

and in defiance of the manifest disapproval of others at her "eccentric" behaviour, whenever she saw a horse or any other creature being beaten, given tasks too great for its strength, or treated improperly in any other way – she wrote furiously to the press about the ill-treatment of a menagerie tiger. When, in the later years of their marriage sympathies between the Hardys at times became strained, their shared love of cats remained a bridge between them.

Dogs would seem not to have appealed to Emma although they did to Hardy; he had a black retriever bitch, Moss, to whom he was much attached, and, when married to Florence, allowed her infamous wire-haired terrier, Wessex, to become completely out of hand. Indeed Wessex demanded rights from his owners, such as walking about on the luncheon or dinner table snatching tid-bits from the plates of horrified guests, while he for his part reserved the right to bite anybody – apart from a mysteriously chosen few – who presented themselves at Max Gate. There were many who felt that an Act of Parliament should be passed to protect them from Wessex. Yet this did not prevent him from being, in the words of his master, "A Popular Personage at Home."

A POPULAR PERSONAGE AT HOME

"I live here: 'Wessex' is my name:
I am a dog known rather well:
I guard the house; but how that came
To be my whim I cannot tell.

"With a leap and a heart elate I go
At the end of an hour's expectancy
To take a walk of a mile or so
With the folk I let live here with me.

"Along the path, amid the grass
I sniff, and find out rarest smells
For rolling over as I pass
The open fields towards the dells.

"No doubt I shall always cross this sill,
And turn the corner, and stand steady,
Gazing back for my mistress till
She reaches where I have run already,

"And that this meadow with its brook,
And bulrush, even as it appears
As I plunge by with hasty look,
Will stay the same a thousand years."

Thus "Wessex". But a dubious ray
At times informs his steadfast eye,
Just for a trice, as though to say,
"Yet, will this pass, and pass shall I?"

THE Naughty Nineties

THE NAUGHTY NINETIES took their tone from the so-called "Marlborough House set"; that was, the circle of the Prince of Wales, later Edward VII, who, reacting against an unsympathetic mother and an unwisely restrictive education mapped out for him by Prince Albert, led the movement away from family prayers and churchgoing, toward weekend house parties, gambling, the race-course, sprees in Paris, and holidays in fashionable Continental resorts to recover from hectic London seasons. Wales's glitteringly fast set, dashingly elegant, *recherché* and effortlessly pleasure seeking, established the enormously admired and universally emulated *style Anglais*. The beautiful and coolly pensive Princess of Wales, exquisitely gowned, coiffured, and fabulously bejewelled, forever amazingly youthful,

THE ALHAMBRA CHORUS LINE: "NAUGHTINESS AND "SAUCINESS" PERSONIFIED.

partnered her husband with dazzling distinction whenever occasion demanded and then quietly left him to his friends and mistresses. Nonetheless beneath his flamboyant exterior there developed an increasingly serious and statesmanlike character, through no fault of his own a distinctly late-developer: but of this the world at large knew little, if anything.

The *style Anglais* demanded a prodigious amount of capital to carry it off properly: everything of the finest quality possible and therefore vastly expensive; everything done with that easy dash which proclaims that money is no object. Despite this it was copied by everyone, everywhere: from those who really could afford Cowes and Le Touquet, to those who only afford a week at Broadstairs. The immortal Lupin Pooter survives to give us a perfect idea of the 'nineties image balanced between Holloway,

where he lives, and Bayswater where he intends shortly to take up residence in furnished apartments at two guineas a week; half his salary. An ingenuous expression; a loud checked suit; "Murray Posh 'one-price' [three shilling] hat"; hired pony and trap; his dubious stocks and shares; his "fast" cigarette smoking fiancee, "Lily Girl"; "a little painted round the eyes", as her prospective father-in-law, the even more immortal Charles Pooter, sighs to his *Diary of a Nobody* – that work of genius bequeathed to us by George and Weedon Grossmith.

How naughty you were in the Naughty 'Nineties and the sort of naughtiness it was, depended, therefore, on the social class to which you belonged and how much money you had at your disposal. And also, precisely what standard of behaviour you were taking as your yard-stick when you labelled the goings-on around as you as "naughty"; what some found iniquitous others were no doubt ready to call amusing, or good fun. Part of the aristocracy had been "very naughty", what others called "depraved", long before Victoria came to the throne and continued to be so throughout her reign: had there been no "wicked" social sphere for the Prince of Wales to join, then he would have had no one to be wicked with in the first place and so would not have driven his, genuinely very good, father to his grave, as the unhappy Queen believed to be the case.

An Explosion of Fizz!

But the English middle-classes were not depraved; they had simply been bottled up under Victoria for half a century and now, when the cork relaxed a little, as the national economy put more money in their pockets and the laxity of Marlborough House filtered down, there was an explosion of fizz!! – probably, in most cases, more gas than reality, but nonetheless eyebrow raising to those who had grown up within the shadow of "our own dear Queen".

Furthermore, Victorian prosperity and Victorian civilization, in both their grosser and higher aspects, were the result of a hundred years immunity from great wars and any serious national danger: secure in the knowledge that

they had the protection of the world's largest, and best, navy the English had come to see their peace and prosperity as part of nature's natural law. This attitude greatly contributed to their *fin de siècle* laxity.

The many and complex graduations of English society make it impossible, here, to attempt to define which area of entertainment and naughtiness belonged to which. Obviously some had suppers with actresses in private rooms and drank champagne out of slippers, while others were enjoying an evening at the Alhambra music-hall in Leicester Square followed by supper at Gatti's in Charing Cross; by no manner of means a cheap evening, but not Romano's; or, facing in the other direction, not the Metropolitan in the Edgware Road, which opened in 1867 with a variety programme including Tom Costello, Kate Carney, Fred Russell and Alexander Dagmar, under the management of Henri Gros. Or the Palladium,

formerly Hengler's circus; in 1895 the ring was turned into the National Skating Palace, with real ice, for a while becoming all the rage. The Palace Theatre, Cambridge Circus, had opened in 1891 with Sullivan's opera, *Ivanhoe*, and calling itself the Royal English Opera House; in December 1892 it became the Palace Theatre of Varieties and put on top-bracket music-hall. All this was good light-hearted entertainment, but none of it might be described as naughty – the music-hall stars were fond of calling themselves and their acts "saucy", and saucy sometimes, indeed frequently, veered "very near the knuckle", but none of this was in the same social league as Wodehouse's famous Hon. Galahad Threepwood: "a notable lad about town, a *beau sabreur* of Romano's. A Pink 'Un. A Pelican, ... when he had looked in at the old Gardenia, commissionaires had fought for the privilege of throwing him out." Obviously the *real* thing.

POSTER STRONGLY INFLUENCED BY TOULOUSE-LAUTREC; PARIS IN THE NINETIES WAS RECKONED FAR NAUGHTIER THAN LONDON, AND HERE WE ARE GIVEN A WHIFF OF THE MOULIN ROUGE.

THE NAUGHTY NINETIES

WITH FINE COLOURED PORTRAIT OF THE QUEEN.

THE PENNY ILLUSTRATED PAPER QUEEN'S DIAMOND JUBILEE NUMBER, JUNE 2, 1897.

DIAMOND JUBILEE LIFE of QUEEN VICTORIA

DUDLEY CLEAVER /97.

ISSUED FROM THE PENNY ILLUSTRATED PAPER OFFICE 1897.

PRICE SIXPENCE.

10, MILFORD LANE, STRAND, W.C.

ISLAND POSTAGE, ONE HALFPENNY.

By permission of W. and D. Downey, 57 and 61 Ebury Street, London, S.W.

Copyright.

HER MAJESTY QUEEN VICTORIA.

5 A New Century

THE DEATH OF QUEEN VICTORIA, coinciding as it did with the arrival of the new century, gave the nation the sensation of having crossed a truly momentous threshold. Moreover, this sense of history in the making was further heightened by the fact that the new reign was the first for sixty-five years.

As it turned out, the transition from Victoria to Edward VII was a smooth one. His easy charm and extrovert personality rapidly won people to him and, perhaps unexpectedly, he revealed a perceptive understanding of what a constitutional monarchy meant in the twentieth century. Queen Alexandra had long since, as Princess of Wales, endeared herself to the nation by her charm and beauty combined with the dedicated spirit in which she approached her role as Royal Consort; hers had not been an easy life, as was well known, and she was admired for the self-possessed way in which she had handled the situation.

The twentieth century would see the arrival of the age of the automobile; though, at the start, nobody guessed the brief extent to which the days of steam were numbered. The telephone had been well-established by the close of the nineteenth century – by 1891 it had been possible to speak to Paris from London. Wireless telegraphy received an enormous public boost when, in 1910, the murderer Crippen was identified as a trans-Atlantic passenger and arrested at the moment when he landed ashore; the whole operation having been made possible by wireless. 1905 had seen the advent of the famous HMV gramophone. The first motion pictures had been seen in London in 1896 and the new century saw them being shown as part of the variety bill at the Empire Theatre.

Britannia, with fierce determination, continued to rule the waves. The steam turbine made rapid progress. The Royal Navy's first submarine entered the water in 1901, triggering a Britain versus Germany contest in submarine building. The mounting threat of German seapower resulted in the British Dreadnought; a remarkable vessel which instantly made every other battleship obsolete. This was launched in 1906. Germany quickly proved that she could build

Dreadnoughts too. A desperate and ever mounting naval race was the result; with a noisy public response, "jingoism", sweeping the country.

The Boer War (1899–1902) in part sobered and depressed people, for not all were in favour of the British fighting the Boers, but it also helped fan the jingoistic spirit among the less thoughtful. In a number of ways the warfare in South Africa was a prologue to the far greater, and infinitely more terrible war which lay a mere twelve years distant in time – but which was anticipated by so few.

Following the defeat of the Boers the twentieth century seemed to recover itself: Britannia continued to rule the waves, with Germany insistently on her heels; wealth accrued, the sun shone. Edward VII, scenting trouble ahead, and increasingly distrusting his nephew, the Kaiser, worked hard at the *Entente Cordiale* with France. Edward's death in 1910 brought George V to the throne; he had little time to settle into his reign before the outbreak of the Great War in 1914. The twentieth century was doomed almost before it had begun – nothing would ever be the same again.

THE End OF AN Era

QUEEN VICTORIA'S Golden Jubilee in 1887 was a magnificent occasion, accompanied by demonstrations of enthusiasm from her subjects which astonished her as much as they deeply touched her. This Jubilee was the crowning triumph of her reign. Ten years later Victoria was still on the throne; her reign the longest in British history. The task of organizing her Diamond Jubilee was entrusted to the Prince of Wales and he made a splendid job of it.

The Thanksgiving Service for the Golden Jubilee had been held in Westminster Abbey; a long service, in the presence of a congregation of notables drawn from the nobility, the sciences, arts, and professions, with a choir three hundred strong singing music composed by Prince Albert; the Queen, a tiny figure, had sat throughout uncomfortably perched on the Coronation Chair. It was felt that, ten years on, a repeat of this would be too much of an ordeal for her. The Prince of Wales, always a gambler, decided to put his money on fine weather and hold an open air service on the steps of St Paul's Cathedral.

GOLDEN JUBILEE COMMEMORATIVE MUG.

The great day, June 22, 1897, threatened rain until the moment when the Queen was assisted into her carriage to be conveyed to St Paul's as star piece of the largest triumphal procession ever to have been witnessed in history. The instant she entered her carriage the sun appeared from behind the dark clouds gathered over Buckingham Palace, and continued to blaze forth for the rest of the day. Vast throngs of people lined the route leading to St Paul's. Before the procession started out the Queen sent a telegraphic message across the world: "From my heart I thank my beloved people. May God bless them."

The *motif* of the occasion was The Empire and the bonds which held it together. All the leaders of the Empire nations were present; representatives of the Colonial forces and of all the nationalities subject to the Crown: "Chinese from Hong Kong; Hausas from the Niger and the Gold Coast; Dyaks from North Borneo; Zaptiehs from Cyprus mounted on little ponies; Zouaves from the West Indies; Malays from the Straits-Settlements" to quote from one report. But the finest sight of all were the Imperial Service troops from India. Then, the Indian Princes, "mounted on splendid warhorses and arrayed in gorgeous attire, excited the loud enthusiasm of the multitude of spectators." Behind them was a long *cortège* in which were seated envoys from the great Powers of the world: "The Papal Nuncio in his purple robes sat by the envoy of the Emperor of China, who was clad in gorgeous oriental costume, and further distinguished by his fan."

These were followed by the Queen's numerous grandchildren and great-grandchildren. Other carriages conveyed older relatives of the Sovereign, next came Prince George – the future George V – and "a glittering troop of princely men" – Persian, Egyptian, Siamese and Japanese, with the Crown Princes and Grand Dukes of the reigning families of Europe. Then, an escort from the regular Indian Army. Lord Wolsely rode in their rear and immediately behind him, in a carriage drawn by eight cream coloured horses, came the Queen.

The Prince of Wales rode on a charger alongside her carriage. "Every now and then he bent from his saddle and called the attention of his mother to some object of interest. It was clear that he was exceedingly delighted at the extraordinary success of the marvellous pageant which he had spent months in arranging." From the first, he had been determined that the people themselves should have the feeling of being part of it all. Now, "It was the turn of the swarming millions of London to co-operate with him, and it was clear that they were carrying out their part of the work with an unparalleled depth and force of passionate feeling. The streets of London that day rocked with the thunder of their cheers. At times the conclamation of the incomparable multitude seemed to be so physically overpowering, that the Prince tenderly bent down, solicitous for his aged mother." And now the miracle occurred; for miracle all who witnessed that extraordinary occasion agreed it to have been.

Far, however, from being overcome by the sonorous and vehement greeting of her subjects, Queen Victoria seemed to draw new life from the frenzy of affection through which she moved, Her grave, calm face now twitched with suppressed emotion, and now flashed out in smiles; and in some strange, unconscious way she seemed to exercise a hypnotic influence on the largest crowd ever seen in the history of the world. Her womanliness, her extreme age, the sense of terrific power resting in her venerable hands, endowed her with a mystic, wonderful air. She seemed, indeed, a consecrated figure, reigning over three hundred and fifty million people by something more than constitutional right.

At Temple Bar the Lord Mayor, in his robes of state, met the Queen at the gate to his city and presented to her the pearl-handled sword, symbolical of peaceful entry into the capital of the Kingdom. The Royal procession then resumed its way to St Paul's. On arrival of the Queen at the cathedral steps the thunderous cheers of the crowd suddenly hushed. The great massed choirs and bands rendered the "Te Deum" and the Bishop of London intoned the special Thanksgiving prayer. At the close of this, the Archbishop of Canterbury pronounced the Benediction and then, as if by common consent, the multitude around the cathedral started to sing the National Anthem. It was taken up by the vast crowds thronging the neighbouring streets: London became one vast chorus. The effect was

stupendous, not least upon the Archbishop of Canterbury. He stepped forward and cried, "Three cheers for the Queen!" As with the National Anthem, this was not organized, but he had voiced the wishes of the people: "They gave vent to the enthusiasm which had been working in them in explosion after explosion of sound, reverberating like the roll of thunder, far away into the distance."

Four years later, on February 2, 1901, the people of London once more turned out to watch another great procession; that of Queen Victoria's coffin conveyed on a gun carriage, followed by the new monarch, Edward VII, on his charger; the German Kaiser, riding on his right, and the King's brother, the Duke of Connaught, on his left. A vast concourse of royalties and heads of state followed behind, a blurred flow of blue and black as the procession made its way to Paddington Station, where the Royal Train was waiting to take the Queen's body to Windsor. "Not a sound came from the people to betray their presence or emotion. An intense and solemn hush brooded over the closely packed streets; nothing was heard but the tramp of horses' feet and the wailing music of the funeral march as the bier was slowly drawn into the station."

VICTORIA'S FUNERAL CAVALCADE.

THE
Dynasts

T HE DYNASTS, a verse drama, was published in three parts: appearing in 1904, 1906 and 1908 respectively. The action covers the Napoleonic campaigns of 1805–1815. Hardy had carried the idea for this work within him for many years before he at last began to write it in earnest in 1902. It was in 1868, when in London as a young architect, that he had recorded at some length the outline of a narrative poem based on the Battle of the Nile. He put this aside while he tried his hand at the more lucrative business of writing novels; though not entirely abandoning poetry, inasmuch as he envisaged his first novel, *The Poor Man and the Lady*, as "a novel without a plot, containing some verses." This did not work and, as we have seen, was not only abandoned but also pillaged to provide material for other books by the aspiring author. There followed a full quarter of a century of professional prose fiction, though the shade of Napoleon still hovered

A 1914 PERFORMANCE OF "THE DYNASTS" AT THE KINGSWAY THEATRE, LONDON.

over Hardy: in 1875 he is found jotting a note, "Memo. A Ballad of the Hundred Days. Then another of Moscow. Others of earlier campaigns – forming altogether an Iliad of Europe from 1789–1815." In 1891 we find him jotting another note: "A Bird's-Eye View of Europe at the beginning of the Nineteenth Century … It may be called 'A Dream of the Times of the First Napoleon.' "

Taking Shape

Gradually Hardy edged toward this epic, as if under a spell. Things fell mysteriously into shape. In 1879 he had a fortunate, and wholly unpremeditated glimpse of Napoleon's nephew, "Plon-plon", said to bear an uncanny resemblance to the Emperor. Hardy later said that this had been of enormous help to him when visualizing Napoleon while writing *The Dynasts*. On another occasion he was in Paris when the French Crown Jewels came up for sale and were placed on view in the saleroom; Hardy went to see these. In 1876 he paid his first visit to the battlefield of Waterloo. In 1887 he visited Milan cathedral during a holiday in Italy. In 1896, with *The Dynasts* "bee-hiving" in his head, as he would have put it, he again visited Waterloo; it was October and he had it to himself, apart from some ploughmen and a flock of sheep, and walked the length of the English line. In Brussels he made notes, "Europe in Throes / Three Parts. Five Acts Each / *Characters*: Burke, Pitt, Napoleon, George III, Wellington … and many others." Another note in his memo book ruminates upon how, for the coming drama, he plans to use the "cinematic" technique of *Lear* and *Anthony and Cleopatra,* what Eisenstein would later make famous as the technique of *montage*. He paid several visits to Chelsea Hospital to talk with Waterloo

veterans. He read long hours at the British Museum. So he prepared himself for the work which had now taken complete possession of him. Such obsession can only have deep roots. Hardy had first come under the spell of "Boney", as he called him in the traditional English manner, while seated at his grandmother's knee by firelight, listening to her as she recounted memories of the tyrant who threatened England with his arrogance and pride and how defences were built along the Wessex coast and people went to bed at night with "tremors and trepidations" lest in the morning they should wake up to find that he had landed.

Although intended to be read and not acted, it is clear from what Hardy himself said about *The Dynasts* that he thought of it as ancient-style recitation, so vivid and compelling that it prompted pictures in the minds of the listeners. Its shape, he explained, was essentially "the instinctive, primitive, narrative shape. In legends and old ballads, in the telling of 'an owre true tale by country folks on winter nights over a dying fire' the story unfolds under its own traditional impetus of "what he said, and what she said, the action often being suggested by the speeches alone." The pictures forming in the mind's eye should comprise a "panoramic show, a series of historical 'ordinates' [using a geometrical analogy]. The subject is familiar to us all," continued Hardy, "and foreknowledge is assumed to fill in the curves required to combine the whole gaunt framework into an artistic unity. The spectator, in thought, becomes a performer whenever called upon, and cheerfully makes himself the utility man of the gaps." To further aid the spectator a chorus of "phantasmal Intelligences" comments upon the unfolding action in delphic utterances, while behind the entire thing is that blind, amorphous force, apparently without reason or motive, the presence of which is at work in everything that Hardy wrote: "God, or The Will, or The Absolute,"intoned Hardy, "contracting himself to make way for the world." In *The Dynasts* Hardy was at his most elusively gnostic. Nobody really knew what to make of it; to be honest they still don't. Max Beerbohm decided to enter into the fun, with his review, "Thomas Hardy as Panoramatist" in the *Saturday Review*, 30 January 1904,

I confess that I, reading here the scene of the death of Nelson, was irresistibly reminded of the same scene as erst beheld by me, at Brighton, through the eyelet of a peep-show, whose proprietor strove to make it more realistic for me by saying in a confidential tone," Ardy, 'Ardy, I am wounded, 'Ardy. – Not mortially, I 'ope, my lord? – Mortially, I fear, 'Ardy.' The dialogue here is of a different and much worthier kind: yet the figures seem hardly less tiny and unreal. How could they be life-sized and alive, wedged into so small a compass between so remote and diverse scenes?.

"NAPOLEON CROSSING THE ALPS", PAINTED BY JACQUES-LOUIS DAVID (1748–1825).

Max made amends by adding that despite reservations, *The Dynasts* was still a great book. He thought it would have been better in prose, but … Still a great book.

Crippen AND Spilsbury

N NOVEMBER 1910 Florence Dugdale was startled to have Emma Hardy ask her did she not think that Mr Hardy bore a striking resemblance to Dr Crippen? Emma added, darkly, that she would never be surprised to wake up one morning and find herself buried under the cellar floor – which was where Mrs Crippen had recently been discovered. Florence, now well into an affair with Hardy, thought it best to hurry away before she was further asked if she didn't think that she herself resembled Ethel le Neve, Crippen's mistress.

Hardy biographers spend much time surmising whether or not Emma knew of Hardy's infatuation with Florence. Of course Emma knew. She made this comparison of Hardy and Crippen – and was silently hinting at Ethel le Neve – because she was perfectly aware of what was happening, and indulging her always rather freaky humour at Florence's expense, while making it perfectly clear that no wool was being pulled over her eyes. But Florence, though in some ways intelligent enough, in others was startlingly obtuse; she Emma's comparison of Hardy with Crippen as yet more proof that Emma was "queerer than ever" – meaning, growing dottier every day. A comforting thought to one intent on deluding her.

The Protagonists

During Hardy's lifetime, from October 1910 onward, two men truly qualified to be known as "household names". The first was Crippen; the second was Spilsbury. To call anyone "Crippen" was abusive indeed. And when the posters on news-vendors'

stands read the simple announcement, SPILSBURY CALLED, the world knew that a first-rate murder investigation was afoot.

Hawley Harvey Crippen, "Dr" Crippen (American medical qualifications were viewed askance in England in those days and the Michigan-born Crippen had trained and qualified in the States) was one of the most famous murderers of the twentieth century – or any other century, though in retrospect it is a little difficult to say why. Spilsbury was the pathologist who, with his microscope, produced the conclusive evidence that sent Crippen to the gallows. The case fascinated the public from the first and still does. It seems that Spilsbury himself felt the spell, and not simply because the case was the turning-point in his career. His own volume in the "Notable British Trials" series, *The Trial of H.H. Crippen*, he read throughout his long life again and again, as his markings and marginal comments reveal. Clearly there was always more to learn from Rex *v.* Crippen.

Dr Bernard Spilsbury, as he then was (he was knighted in 1922) was thirty-three at the time of the Crippen case; his first big case, and a landmark in the history of forensic medicine. Spilsbury went on to become what was known, in popular terminology, as "the leading medical detective of the day." Asked why he had taken up such a strange branch of medicine in the first place, spent entirely in the mortuaries, criminal courts, and his laboratory, he replied, "I have always had an insatiable interest in villainy."

The Crippens lived in Camden Town, Number 39 Hilldrop Crescent, of hideous memory. Mrs Crippen, née Kunigunde Mackamotski (half American-

SPILSBURY IN THE
EARLY DAYS OF
HIS CAREER.

A SHUDDERSOME RELIC!

German and half Polish), was dark, vivacious, fond of clothes, jewelry, dining out, having fun; all the things her husband couldn't afford on a salary of £3 a week. However, that he did afford them suggests that the side deals he engaged in, and which the police described as "shady", must have been more than a little dubious. Mrs Crippen, who had a small talent as a singer, which she had convinced herself was a large one unfairly ignored by talent spotters, tried her luck in the music-halls but made little headway. For two years before her death she was honorary treasurer of the Music Hall Ladies Guild, and earned a certain popularity at amateur charity performances and the like. She was popular and charming in her "theatrical" circles, overbearing and bad-tempered at home. It was a childless marriage and held no compensations of any kind for Crippen. Although an exceptionally small, quiet man, with the protuberant eyes of the thyroid sufferer, bespectacled, balding, altogether inconspicuous apart from a sandy walrus moustache, Crippen had managed to obtain consolation with a young typist, Miss Ethel le Neve; as quiet and inconspicuous as he was himself.

The Crime

When at last he could stand Mrs Crippen no longer and she, being equally tired of him and knowing about Miss le Neve, decided to leave him, taking all their joint savings with her, he ordered five grains of hyoscin hydrobromide from a New Oxford Street chemist's shop and, having administered it to her after a small dinner-party, on January 31, 1910, sat back and awaited the desired effect. Mrs Crippen was dead by midday next day. Thereafter Crippen pawned his wife's jewelry, told her friends that she had been summoned to a sick relative in America, and Miss le Neve moved into Hilldrop Crescent. Crippen then told his wife's friends that she had died in Los Angeles. He explained everything so well, and carried on so normally, that no questions were asked. The police were finally alerted when a friend of Mrs Crippen, trying to trace her during a visit to the States, had his suspicions roused. After

the police called at Hilldrop Crescent, Crippen at last lost his nerve and fled across the Atlantic with le Neve disguised as a boy. At Hilldrop Crescent, the police found headless and limbless human remains under the cellar floor. A team of medical experts got to work and traced hyoscine in the organs. Spilsbury, with his microscope, identified an abdominal scar that linked the remains with Cora Crippen. Crippen and le Neve were detected on board ship and arrested, thanks to wireless telegraph. A sensational trial followed, during which Spilsbury put up a star performance in the witness box, emerging unscathed from vicious cross-questioning. He furthermore sent for his microscope and, in a room adjoining the Old Bailey's famous Court Number one the young pathologist demonstrated to the jury the existence of the scar, which defending counsel had suggested was no more than a fold of skin.

The newspapers, of course, had a field-day. Crippen, with his packet of poison, his skilled dismembering of his wife's body, his cool behaviour following the murder, and his subsequent flight with his young mistress disguised as a boy; Chief Inspector Dew prizing up the cellar floor, Splisbury with his microscope – all passed into folklore.

CRIPPEN IN THE DOCK AT BOW STREET, PRIOR TO TRIAL AT THE OLD BAILEY.

Honours

THE WRITER Somerset Maugham once remarked that, in order to be accorded true literary fame in England, it was necessary to live to be old. Hardy was a good example of this – the older he grew, the more famous he became.

He seems always to have looked upon official honours with a degree of scepticism. He quietly declined a knighthood on more than one occasion, convinced that "Sir Thomas Hardy" would not be right for him. In 1905 he received his first honorary doctorate; Doctorate of Laws from the University of Aberdeen. In 1913 he received the D. Litt. (Doctorate of Letters) from Cambridge University, and five months later Cambridge again paid him tribute when he was made an Honorory Fellow of Magdalene College. These university honours particularly pleased him because he saw them as gestures from that academic world after which he had so aspired when a young man, but had never actually reached.

In June 1910 his name appeared in the first Birthday Honours List of George V as a recipient of the Order of Merit. This, of course, was an honour that could not be refused; Hardy duly presented himself to receive the honour at Buckingham Palace. His wife did not accompany him but instead sent his secretary, Florence Dugdale, along with him; to ensure – said

Emma – that he behaved himself and was properly dressed. Four months after he received the O.M., Hardy was given the freedom of the Borough of Dorchester; for personal reasons this, we are told, pleased him most of all the honours heaped upon him. His wife accompanied him on this occasion; in full evening dress, as was he. She looked as delighted on his behalf as he so obviously was.

The Gold Medal

In 1912 the Royal Society of Literature presented him with its Gold Medal on the occasion of his seventy-second birthday. It was Hardy's wish that the ceremony should be private; Henry Newbolt and W.B.Yeats journeyed to Max Gate to make the presentation upon the Society's behalf. They found themselves the only guests, apart from two cats who sat on the table beside Emma's plate during luncheon. The meal was followed by the ceremony; Hardy insisted that his wife should not be present at this. Newbolt and Yeats protested; but Hardy refused to change his mind.

Accordingly Emma quietly left the room and the presentation went ahead, with all the formality of a public occasion. Hardy read a very long speech that was devoted to warning against the increasing corruption of the English language.

HARDY'S STATUE IN DORCHESTER, T.E LAWRENCE THOUGHT IT CAPTURED HARDY'S "EFFECT OF LIVING WITHIN HIMSELF."

He explained that he had already sent copies of the speech to the London papers as being that with which he had addressed the deputation and addressed with the said speech the deputation must therefore be. The reason why Emma was made to leave the room was because females were not allowed to become members of the Royal Society of Literature and so she would not have been present had it been a public occasion.

Poets' Tribute

In 1913 Hardy was passed over as Poet Laureate in favour of Robert Bridges; this was scarcely surprising. Tennyson was the last Poet Laureate of the old school and Hardy was perfectly correct when he observed that he himself would have been wholly unsuitable: "Bridges is a safe choice". True poets are not safe people.

Hardy's fellow poets acknowledged his worth in October 1919, when Siegfried Sassoon arrived at Max Gate with the "Poets' Tribute": a handsomely bound volume containing forty-three poems by forty-three living poets, including Bridges, Kipling, Yeats, Sassoon, Graves and D.H.Lawrence. Each poet had inscribed in Hardy's honour a copy of one of his own poems. Hardy, deeply touched, wrote personally to each of the poets. And yet more local recognition – this always being slower to arrive than national, or even international, recognition. On December 2 of that same year Hardy opened the Bockhampton Reading Room and Club, erected as a local war memorial. This again touched him deeply. 1922 found him receiving an honorary Fellowship from Queen's College Oxford, and being comtemptuous of Harley Granville Barker and his wife for their decision to winter in Italy. G.B., said Hardy, had evidently abandoned his writing: "For it is impossible to write, & have other interests. In writing, as in all work, there is only one way – to stick to it."

1925 saw more poems. *Human Shows, Far Phantasies, Songs, and Trifles.* Two years before that Hardy had shown Granville Barker what he had meant about "sticking to it" by writing a poetic drama, *The Famous Tragedy of the*

Queen of Cornwall, which he sent to Granville Barker for criticism and comments, before making it available for production by the Hardy Players in Dorchester; a production which Hardy was actively engaged in. In July 1927 Hardy made his last public appearance when he laid the foundation stone of a new building for the Dorchester Grammar School, which was moving to a site not far from Max Gate, The day was wet and gusty and the party of dignitaries, wearing overcoats, marched across the muddy building site, led by a determined-looking Hardy. For the last time in his life he wielded a mason's trowel.

HARDY RECEIVING THE D.LITT. CAMBRIDGE UNIVERSITY, 1913.

THE Titanic

ON THE NIGHT OF April 14, 1912, the White Star liner *Titanic* struck an iceberg on her maiden voyage and sank with the loss of 1,513 lives. The largest, most luxurious vessel afloat, the *Titanic* had a double-bottomed hull divided into sixteen watertight compartments and, since four of these could be flooded without endangering the ship's buoyancy, she was considered unsinkable. The result of this was that the *Titanic* had only

1,178 boat places for the 2,224 persons aboard and it was deemed unnecessary to hold any lifeboat drills during the voyage. This hubris, which so many subsequently perceived, with hindsight, as symptomatic of a doom-laden era, bore the *Titanic*, "gaily great", across the waves toward the *Nemesis* awaiting her, a "Shape of Ice".

Steaming at twenty-two knots, too fast for the prevailing conditions, the *Titanic* collided with the iceberg, ripping a three hundred foot gash in the liner's port side and rupturing five of her watertight compartments. This was

shortly before midnight, off the Grand Banks of Newfoundland. The *Titanic* sank at 2.20 the following morning, after indescribable scenes of confusion, in no small measure due to the lack of lifeboat drills during the journey. Moreover there was a strange lack of urgency about the way things were conducted, as if Hardy's "Hopeless Hand of Fate" were at the helm. Everything was against survival. The Leyland liner *Californian* was less than twenty miles away all night, but its radio operator was asleep and so the *Titanic*'s signals for help went unheard. Only the arrival of the Cunard liner *Carpathia*, twenty minutes after the *Titanic* went down, prevented further lives being lost in the icy waters.

The White Star Line was founded by Thomas Henry Ismay of Maryport, Cumberland, in 1867, when he acquired the name and flag of the White Star Line of Australian clippers, a line which a fellow Cumbrian, John Chambers of Ullcoates, had founded. After taking over the White Star Line Ismay introduced iron ships instead of the wooden vessels used in the Australian trade and then went on to form the Oceanic Steam Navigation Company, introducing a new high class passenger service into the Liverpool and New York trade. The first ship of the company, *Oceanic*, was built by Harland and Wolff of Belfast; it was said of her that she was "more like an imperial yacht than a passenger steamer." Over 50,000 people went to see her when she arrived in New York after her first passage our from Liverpool. By 1874 the White Star Fleet was already one of the best and by 1888 was covering the American Service, the Colonial Services (New Zealand and Australia) and the Pacific Service. The first Mercantile Armed Cruisers were the *Teutonic* and *Majestic*; the *Teutonic* took part in the Naval Review, Spithead, June 1897, for Queen Victoria's Diamond Jubilee.

Steamer after steamer of increasing tonnage was added to the fleet; a new *Oceanic* replaced the original pioneer ship in 1899. This fleet resounded with names suggestive of a school of whales all suffering from the hiccups – *Oceanic, Majestic, Teutonic, Germanic, Britannic* ... there was no end to them; but they were wonderful ships. The *Titanic* was a magnificent leviathan with which to cap them.

Joseph Bruce Ismay, eldest son of founder Thomas, sailed aboard her on her maiden voyage. Of the 705 people rescued, Joseph Ismay was in the last lifeboat. It would have been better had he gone down with the ship. Thereafter his life was ruined; he became a near recluse suffering incurable depression and remorse. He died in 1937, aged seventy-five: after a quarter of a century of reliving that terrible night over and over again.

Hardy's poem, "The Converging of the Twain: Lines on the loss of the 'Titanic'", was finished just over a week after the disaster and was first printed in the programme of the Dramatic and Operatic Matinee in Aid of the *Titanic* Disaster Fund, held at Covent Garden on May 14, for which it had been commissioned.

THE CONVERGENCE OF THE TWAIN
(Lines on the Loss of the 'Titanic')

I

*In the solitude of the sea
Deep from Human vanity,
And the Pride of Life that planned her, stilly couches she.*

II

*Steel chambers, late the pyres
Of her salamandrine fires,
Cold currents third, and turn to rhythmic tidal lyres.*

III

*Over the mirrors meant
To glass the opulent
The sea-worm crawls—grotesque, slimed, dumb, indifferent.*

IV

*Jewels in joy designed
To ravish the sensuous mind
Lie lightless, all their sparkles bleared and black and blind.*

V

*Dim moon-eyed fishes
Gaze at the gilded gear
And query: "What does this vaingloriousness down here?"*

VI

*Well: while was fashioning
This creature of cleaving wing,
The Immanent Will that stirs and urges everything.*

VII

*Prepared a sinister mate
For her—so gaily great—
A Shape of Ice, for the time far and dissociate.*

VIII

*And as the smart ship grew
In stature, grace and hue,
In shadowy silent distance grew the Iceberg too.*

IX

*Alien they seemed to be:
No mortal eye could see
The intimate welding of their later history,*

X

*Or sign that they were bent
By paths coincident
Of being anon twin halves of one august event.*

XI

*Till the Spinner of the Years
Said "Now!" And each one hears,
And consummation comes, and jars two hemispheres.*

AN ARTIST'S IMPRESSION OF "THE MOMENT OF CONSUMMATION": THE SHIP COLLIDES WITH THE ICEBERG.

THE TITANIC

Emma's
LAST Years

*L*ITERARY GOSSIP is seldom kind to the wives of literary lions. Biographers turn to gossip as a legitimate source and from such portraiture distorted portraits find their way into print, to be quoted as true likenesses. Unless some further biographer is prompted to turn a more sympathetic eye upon the alleged wifely spanner-in-the-works of the great man, she will pass down to posterity for ever bearing little resemblance to her true self.

EMMA HARDY WITH HER COMPANION, FLORENCE DUGDALE, ON THE BEACH AT WORTHING, JULY 1911.

Emma Hardy is a case in point. She and Hardy were genuinely in love when they married and, though never blessed with the children they both so much wanted, they remained devoted to one another until the final years of their thirty-eight years of marriage. Even at the last they continued to domicile together and find occasional tolerable company in one another. It was true that Hardy was then conducting an affair with Florence Dugdale, but he was seventy and Emma was wise enough to see that he was being old and silly. She herself took advantage of Florence by using her as a typist and and useful companion. Why not? Florence had attached herself like a limpet to Hardy, which meant that Emma saw a good deal of her too, and she might as well be made use of. So Florence found herself reading and typing Emma Hardy's mostly unpublished manuscripts, and making enthusiastic noises over them, and going on little jaunts with Emma. And behind Emma's back Florence laughed at her and jeered at her, and because anything and everything is avidly seized upon in the interests of biography, the distorted portrait that Florence drew of her rival has been taken as a serious contribution to Hardy biographical material. What it does tell us, in all seriousness, is what Florence Dugdale was like, but it badly misleads us about Emma Hardy.

A Baffling Personality

Intelligent, well read, spirited and vibrant (unlike Florence), refined, energetic and enthusiastic, genuinely very kind, dependable, and at moments completely childish, Emma's was a baffling personality. She was a natural eccentric, perfectly unselfconscious and spontaneous. That Hardy adored her is really no surprise; she was Eustacia Vye without the cruel single-mindedness of purpose; she possessed Bathsheba's wonderful current of impulse, and if Tess may be said to be drawn from any real woman, then that woman was the young Emma, with her forthright approach and courage. She could never have been really beautiful, but undoubtedly she was visionary for Hardy. As she aged she lost her physical charms, while her mental instability was distressing; but despite this, underneath there was always, for Hardy, his original well-beloved Em.

Of course, when he found himself a famous man whose company was sought by society hostesses, he naturally hoped to take sexual advantage of the situation. But he was not, physically speaking, a man likely to put temptation in the way of women; he was no H.G. Wells, bursting with sexuality and magnetism. Hardy could be charming when he chose, he had infectious laughter and social zest once he got going, but none of this made him the kind of man he would have liked to have been when he found himself, in late middle-age, courted by ladies whose only reason for making themselves delightful to him was that they hoped he would use his literary influence on their behalf. All Hardy wanted to do was to get into bed with them. On first meeting them, he eyed them appraisingly. were they *really* emancipated? Emancipation meaning, to Hardy, and indeed to most men, just one thing. No, they were not. None of them would risk losing their social position for Hardy.

Meantime Emma, who was far from being an unsophisticated observer, watched her husband with a remarkably objective eye. When the highly intelligent and newly-wed Elspeth Grahame turned to Emma for advice upon how to deal with a wayward husband Emma proved very much up to the mark in what she had to say, "Characters change so greatly with time, and circumstances. I can scarcely think that love proper, and enduring, is in the nature of Man [and] perhaps there is no woman whom 'custom will not stale'." Emma advised "keeping separate

a good deal" as a wise plan in a crisis. And being both free; and expecting little; not "anything you may set your heart on."She is not complaining merely stating what experience has taught her. "Love interest, adoration, and all that kind of thing is usually a failure ... If he belongs to the public in any way, years of devotion count for nothing ... It is really a pity to have any ideals in the first place.This is gruesome, horrid, you will say ... but you have asked me."

That something went seriously amiss with the Hardy marriage in the 1890s is clear. It is easy to point at Florence as the chief cause, but Emma would have been able to handle that. Her real distress came from the fact that Hardy refused to recognize that she had played any part in his success; the support she had given him when he had been so ill with *A Laodicean*; the years of effort she had put into making theirs a happy marriage. Now he wrote books, like *Jude the Obscure*, in which he attempted to expose marriage as a social evil; or, in *The Well-Beloved*, derided it. How could she expect the world to believe that theirs had been a satisfying marriage, that she had made him happy, when Hardy wrote like that? At the close of her life she was obliged to see everything as having been a total waste of effort, of time, of love.

She followed her own advice of keeping separate. A study was built for her and here she wrote, read, kept up a correspondence centred upon her interests; suffrage, hospitals, Zionism, prevention of cruelty to animals. In London she joined a women's club, the Alexandra, so that she might spend time in Town without Hardy. An article in the magazine *Black and White*, in 1892, described her as "so particularly bright, so thoroughly *au courant du jour*, so evidently a citizen of the wide world". And this, when you read her letters, her journal, and follow her in her unflagging full-blooded lifestyle is what you feel her to have been. In her diaries, which Hardy read after her death, were some hard things about him. "Sheer hallucination in her, poor thing," he murmured tenderly.

EMMA PHOTOGRAPHED FOR "THE TATLER" IN 1904.

Florence

LORENCE EMILY DUGDALE was born in 1879, second of the five daughters of a schoolmaster and his wife, a former governess, who suffered severely from recurrent depressions. Florence had always wanted to be a writer, but trained as a pupil teacher. She got her teaching certificate, but could not continue in the profession because of her chronic state of poor health. Like her mother she suffered from recurrent depression, and when not depressed she was melancholy and complaining. To be sure she had plenty to complain about; dreadful headaches, poor digestion, anaemia, exhaustion, frightful colds in the head, equally frightful sore throats – all these afflictions were real. Real, too, was the almost constant spectre of cancer which involved her, from early middle age onward, in successive painful operations and at last, in her lonely widowhood at Max Gate, killed her in 1937.

The desire for power was the propelling force of Florence's life. She was small, frail and debilitated; but throughout her life she possessed, and exercised, a frightful kind of power; tough as old boots, when she chose or needed to be; exhibiting a terrifying tenacity of purpose; thick as three, rather than the proverbial two, planks when it was essential for her that she should misunderstand a thing. She early discovered that

FLORENCE HARDY – A GREAT LITTLE COMPLAINER.

her gift for writing was small and looked around for a literary man to boost her, and so aimed for Thomas Hardy. If her own writing would never make her famous, being Mrs Thomas Hardy would invest her with a certain literary fame. She first met Hardy in 1905 and according to one keen observer she was determined to marry him, "by fair means or foul", from the first.

Of course, when Florence first met Hardy he still had a wife; but he was already well infected by the harem syndrome, even if only able to indulge it in his imagination. Pretty little Miss Dugdale – in her early youth she was rather beautiful, with enormous, lustrous eyes – with her "sweet" little gifts of flowers and birdlike twitterings hoping that she hadn't outstayed her welcome when she came to tea ("I do not think you stayed at all too long, & hope you will come again", was the response of Hardy), saw which way the wind blew. Hardy did not understand women, except those he invented, as Emma had observed. He was quite out of his depth with Florence. She became his mistress and made herself appear as a bright and chipper little creature, always ready to "romp" with him, as she put it, Hardy smugly assumed that at seventy he still held charms for the opposite sex. A recent rebuff from the socially distinguished, beautiful Mrs Florence Henniker had shaken his confidence, but Florence Dugdale restored it.

The Second Mrs Hardy

By the summer of 1910 Florence began cultivating friendship with Emma. They seemed to become quite attached to one another; though Florence lost no opportunities of laughing at Emma. Both Hardy and Florence seemed certain that Emma had no idea she was being deceived; however, Emma's well aimed remarks about Crippen undoubtedly had the effect of discouraging Florence from visiting Max Gate: she put in no further appearances there until Emma's death, when, to the high indignation of the Max Gate servants and the scandalization of Dorchester, Florence installed herself as Hardy's "housekeeper". In early March, 1913, three months after Emma's death, Hardy, with his brother, Henry, made a pilgrimage to St Juliot. Hardy arranged it so that he was there on March 7, the forty-third anniversary of his first meeting with Emma. Florence, resentful at being left behind, moaned, "All I hope is that I may not, for the rest of my life, have to sit and listen humbly to an account of her virtues and graces."

She would appear to be taking it very much for granted that she would be spending the rest of her life with Hardy. But he had not proposed to her, and Emma's niece, Lilian Gifford, was now at Max Gate as "housekeeper". This rather fraught state of affairs lasted for another year; with Hardy showing himself as not over keen to marry Florence. Finally she seems to have issued an ultimatum; either Lilian left, or Florence did. Lilian left. Hardy and Florence were married on April 10, 1914. Hardy, when breaking the news referred to it as a "trifling incident." Her father, on hearing that a special licence had been applied for, exclaimed,"She's pulled it off!"

In a way Florence had pulled it off, but in a way she had not. Being married to Hardy meant that she had a man in his seventies to care for: she was housekeeper, nurse, guardian, companion. At first she wondered whether they might have a child, but she gave up this idea and installed her dog Wessex instead; he enlivened the literary scene by chewing Galsworthy's trousers to shreds and holding Barrie to ransom on the doorstep.

Florence's favourite lament was that by marrying, at the age of thirty-two, a man more than twice her own age, she had in one step transferred from youth into her own, dreary, middle-age. It was a fate of her own contrivance.

What she had never anticipated was that Hardy would recapture the voice of an impassioned younger man and write a series of famous love poems, not about his new bride, but addressed to his first wife. This unexpected blow all but destroyed her. Yet not everything was lost. Social life became frenetic; streams of people appeared, all come to meet Thomas Hardy. Her finest hour was when the Prince of Wales lunched at Max Gate. Hardy wore his formal best, the Prince sported elegant tweeds. Florence wore an obviously very expensive, becoming silk two-piece and an extraordinary befeathered hat. HRH had been briefed for the occasion by no less a person than Queen Mary herself. Turning to his host the Prince said politely, "My mother tells me you have written a book called 'Tess of the D'Urbervilles'. I must read it some time."

FLORENCE AND HARDY AT ALDEBURGH IN THE EARLY DAYS OF THEIR LIAISON.

THE Great War

HE 1914–18 War, the "Great War", was always seen by those who lived through it as an enormous barrier cutting history in two; pre-war, and post-war; a world in which everything had had shape, meaning and purpose, and another world in which, in the popular phrase,"everything was gone to pot." Among the British alone, three quarters of a million men died on active service; over one and a half million were wounded. The daily slaughter on the Western Front was, to quote the poet Wilfred Owen, "Carnage incomparable." When we gaze around us at the troubled and often hopelessly inhuman world in which we live today and ask, "Why?" we have only to look back at the Great War for the answer. Darkness fell in the high summer of 1914 and it has been dark ever since. Again to quote Owen,

War broke. And now the winter of the world
With perishing great darkness closes in.

The Great War, although it demanded vast national effort to win victory, or what at the time was seen as victory, for Britain and the Allies, did not involve the bulk of the population in the struggle as did the Second World War. The

Service casualties of the Great War and the ever-lengthening casualty lists plunged the countries of Western Europe into a grief and sorrow that had barely begun to lift its pall before the 1939–45 war started. But the truths of the terrible slaughter were only known to those who were present on the actual battle-fronts. There was no way in which British civilians could have any idea of what their troops were really experiencing. There was no television: not that this would have revealed much, censorship of the news being stringent and deluding the public being the chief object of the wartime journalism. The newspapers were packed with lies and jingoistic nonsense. Radio broadcasting didn't exist. People writing home from the Front naturally shielded their friends and loved ones from the stark truth; in any case the letters of the troops were censored. On the Home Front there was little actual hardship; there were food and fuel shortages, but no rationing of the kind experienced in the Second World War. Women came forward without hesitation to "do their bit", but the conscription of women had to wait until 1941, two years after the start of World War Two.

Resultantly, the population was divided between those who crossed the Channel to fight – and discovered what the war was really like – and the civilians who remained at

A NEW CENTURY

home in almost total ignorance of what the "boys at the Front" were experiencing. It is generally supposed that Hardy was violently opposed to the war; but he was not. He saw it as a necessary evil and it was not until he came into contact with the young soldier-poets of the war, particularly Siegfried Sassoon, that he had any better notion of what was happening than any of the other old men he met. The difference between Hardy and the civilians around him was that, unlike them, when war broke out he didn't think that "it would be over by Christmas"; he thought that it might well be "a matter of years and untold disaster" and moreover he never indulged in jingoism and unthinking hatred of the Germans.

On September 3, 1914, Hardy attended a conference in London of writers concerned with "the organization of public statements [to neutral countries, publicising] the strength of the British case." Two days later he wrote his famous poem, "Men Who March Away"; one of the most popular poems to come out of the war but not of the genre of poetry written by the soldiers; it was a moving, but bland, composition. He wrote other war poems, but his heart was not in them and he was never able to give them the "reality" that imbues so much of the rest of his poetry. Florence, meanwhile, took to her pen with a patriotic tale which appeared in the *Sunday Pictorial* for June 13, 1915, called "Greater Love Hath no Man … The Story of a Village Ne'er-Do-Weel" by "Mrs Thomas Hardy". Painful in its jingoistic patriotism, it flooded Hardy with horrified embarrassment. Emma with her dancing daffodils had never brought him such blushes. He expressed his displeasure in no mean terms. To a friend, Lady Hoare, Florence sighed that Hardy disliked her being "a scribbling woman."

In October 1915 British sentiment against the Germans mounted, with the execution of the nurse Edith Cavell in German occupied Brussels. Miss Cavell had helped some two hundred and fifty British and French soldiers and many Belgians and French escape into Holland. She was shot under the orders of the Military Governor of Brussels. Before she died she uttered the celebrated words, "Patriotism is not enough. I must have no hatred or bitter-

ness to anybody." In these words she clarified her motive in acting as she had done, and at the same time forgave her enemies. Her execution is generally regarded as judicial murder. At the time it was a major political blunder which played an undoubted part in creating the popular demand in Britain for the harshest possible reparations from Germany following the Armistice in 1918. Hardy, in concluding *The Dynasts* in 1908, had allowed himself, for once, to sound an optimistic note about the future:

> But – a stirring thrills the air
> Like to sounds of joyance there
> That the rages
> Of the ages
> Shall be cancelled, and deliverance
> offered from the darts that were,
> Consciousness the Will informing, till
> it fashion all things fair!

After the war and the resultant Treaty of Versailles with its unforgiving terms for the German people, Hardy said that he would not strike that note of hope in these lines were he presently writing them, because of the nature of the treaty. In fact by now Hardy had come to believe in his heart that war was caused by "supernatural agencies over which mankind as a whole had no control".

"THE MENIN ROAD", BY PAUL NASH (1889–1946) ONE OF THE PRIMARY ARTISTS OF THE FIRST WORLD WAR.

THE War Poets

HE POETS OF THE GREAT WAR were, and remain, a group apart. Their talent was forced into precocity by the knowledge of how little time might be theirs, their maturity was born of suffering. Without exception, these young men were all in revolt against the brutality of their experience and the utter pointlessness of the war.

Hatred of their fellow men was not a word the War Poets knew; that is, unless it was a hatred of the smug civilians at home, a feeling which sometimes burst bitterly from them, as in Siegfried Sassoon's 1916 poem entitled "Blighters":

The House is crammed: tier beyond tier they grin
And cackle at the Show, while prancing ranks
Of harlots shrill the chorus, drunk with din;
"We're sure the Kaiser loves the dear old Tanks!"

I'd like to see a Tank come down the stalls,
Lurching to rag-time tunes, or "Home, sweet Home," –
And there'd be no more jokes in music-halls
To mock the riddled corpses round Bapaume.

Historically, poetry and soldiers have gone together. Perhaps it is not surprising; poetry arises from intensity of emotion, and emotion, when it is not stunned by war, is

"MY MEN, MY MODERN CHRISTS", JOHN SINGER SARGENT'S 1917 PAINTING "TWO SOLDIERS OF ARRAS".

roused to a pitch of pity, shock and indignation, as well as stimulated to a new and unexpected capacity for appreciation of beauty, which needs to be experienced to be believed. The packed audiences at the lunch-time concerts at the National Gallery during the London blitz were a case in point: and the music played was of what might fairly be described as a high intellectual standard. That great young poets sprang up on battlefields of the Great War should really be no surprise; whereas it would have been surprising had they come from the civilian population of Britain. A suggestion, in 1917, that the No Man's Land of the Western Front should be called "England", because "we keep supremacy there", brought from Wilfred Owen a blast of ironical invective: "It is pock-marked like a body of foulest disease, and its odour is the breath of cancer. I have not seen any dead. I have done worse. In the dank air I have *perceived* it, and in the darkness, *felt…* No Man's Land … is like the face of the moon, chaotic, crater-ridden, uninhabitable, awful, the abode of madness. To call it 'England'! I would as soon call my House Krupp Villa, or my child Chlorina-Phosgena".

Julian Grenfell (killed 1915), Robert Graves, Robert Nichols, Wilfred Owen (killed 1918), Edmund Blunden, Siegfried Sassoon, Charles Hamilton Sorley (killed 1915), Herbert Read, Isaac Rosenberg (killed 1918) … these names are but a few. They were not extolled at home at the time that they were writing; their sentiments about the war they were fighting were at complete variance from the official, and acceptable, way of thinking. Wilfred Owen again, writing from hospital on the Somme, "I have comprehended a light which never will filter into the dogma of any national church: namely … pure Christianity will not fit in with pure patriotism." He himself was, he said, "A conscientious objector with a very seared conscience … Christ is literally in 'no man's land'". It is always dangerous to draw comparisons and say who will live as poets for posterity and who will not, but it seems safe to say that among the Great War poets Sassoon and Owen will surely be remembered in years to come. The former was notable for his concentrated and bitterly realistic verses; the irony of

his short, tense pieces. The nephew and ward of Hardy's old friend, Hamo Thorneycroft, Siegfried Sassoon came to know Hardy through correspondence in 1916; in 1917 Sassoon dedicated his first volume of poetry, *The Old Hunstsman and Other Poems*, to Hardy. It contained some bitter war poems; a year later Sassoon presented Hardy with his second searing collection of poetry, *Counterattack*. Sassoon, who was awarded the MC and recommended for the DSO for his bravery in battle, was invalided home in 1917, having been wounded; sickened and revolted by all that he had seen on the Western Front he repudiated the war and all it stood for and returned his MC. Greatly respected by brother soldiers, and already a legend for his war poems, the army thought it best not to make a martyr of him and invalided him out, as mentally unstable due to shell-shock. "Does it Matter?" suggests why his was a voice his seniors feared,

SIEGFRIED SASSOON
IN 1915.

> Does it matter? – losing your legs?…
> For people will always be kind,
> And you need not show that you mind
> When the others come in after football
> To gobble their muffins and eggs…

In November 1918 Sassoon called upon Hardy at Max Gate and thereafter the young man and the revered Master became close friends.

Wilfred Owen is seen as having promised to belong to the great poetic tradition of Keats. His brief, forceful phrasing and his experiments with a new metrical scheme, that of assonances, made him a salient influence upon the poets of the "modern movement". Above all, he captured the pity and waste of the war; the grief and mourning which would linger long after the guns were silenced. His "Anthem for Doomed Youth" says it all,

> What passing-bells for those who die as cattle?
> Only the monstrous anger of the guns,
> Only the stuttering rifles' rapid rattle
> Can patter out their hasty orison…

Moments OF Vision

STINSFORD CHURCH,
WHICH APPEARED IN
THE FRONTISPIECE OF
HARDY'S FIRST VOLUME
OF POETRY (1928).

I̶N MAY 1917, in his letter thanking Sassoon for *The Old Huntsman*, Hardy said that he did not know how he could "stand the suspense of this evil time were it not for the sustaining power of poetry." Poetry had been sustaining Hardy for over fifty-eight years.

In that dark year when Sassoon dedicated his first poems to Hardy, the seventy-seven year old veteran published his fourth volume of poetry, *Moments of Vision*. Include in this were the "Poems of War and Patriotism", which paled in comparison with Sassoon's poems. Hardy had not been born into a world that put him into soldiers' dress; the garb he had adopted had been the cloak, staff and hat of the pilgrim that he saw himself to be. Hardy had never been a great one for lengthy narrative, or philosophical poems such as Wordsworth had written, profoundly influenced as he had been by Wordsworth. In *The Dynasts* Hardy had worked all, or almost all, of his Tennysonian inclinations out of his system. Except when training himself for poetry, during his period of apprenticeship, when he had exercised for hours on end disciplining himself in the techniques and styles of Spenser, Shakespeare, Milton, Wordsworth, traditional ballads, popular old songs – anything he felt would assist his development – he had always used his own voice; his visions, which had inspired his poems, thanks to his extraordinary eye linked with his equally extraordinary imagination, had produced a poetry unique to himself. Here is "In the British Museum",

"What do you see in that time-touched stone,
  When nothing is there
But ashen blankness, although you give it
  A rigid stare?

"You look not quite as if you saw,
  But as if you heard,
Parting your lips, and treading softly
  As mouse or bird.

"It is only the base of a pillar, they'll tell you,
  That came to us
From a far old hill men used to name
  Areopagus.

—"I know no art, and I only view
    A stone from a wall,
But I am thinking that stone has echoed
    The voice of Paul;

"Paul as he stood and preached beside it
    Facing the crowd,
A small gaunt figure with wasted features,
    Calling out loud

"Words that in all their intimate accents
    Pattered upon
That marble front, and were wide reflected,
    And then were gone.

"I'm a labouring man, and know but little,
    Or nothing at all;
But I can't help thinking that stone once echoed
    The voice of Paul."

⟨⟩

Hardy once confessed, "Half the time (particularly when I write verse) I believe … in spectres, mysterious voices, omens, dreams." Because he wrote with such conviction of these things we believe in them too when we meet them in his poems. "Who's in the Next Room", "The Clock of the Years", "The Shadow on the Stone", or the haunting poem of omen, "Near Lanivet, 1872", all from *Moments of Vision*, are unforgettable pieces in this mystic vein.

But of all such poems it is surely "Voices of Things Growing in a Churchyard" (from *Late Lyrics and Earlier*,(1922), which is most quirkily and inimitably Hardy in its imagery, its spooky oddity of tone; nobody else but Thomas Hardy could have conjured this one:

"These flowers are I, poor Fanny Hurd,
    Sir or Madam,
A little girl here sepultured.
Once I flit-fluttered like a bird
Above the grass, as now I wave
In daisy shapes above my grave,
    All day cheerily,
    All night eerily !

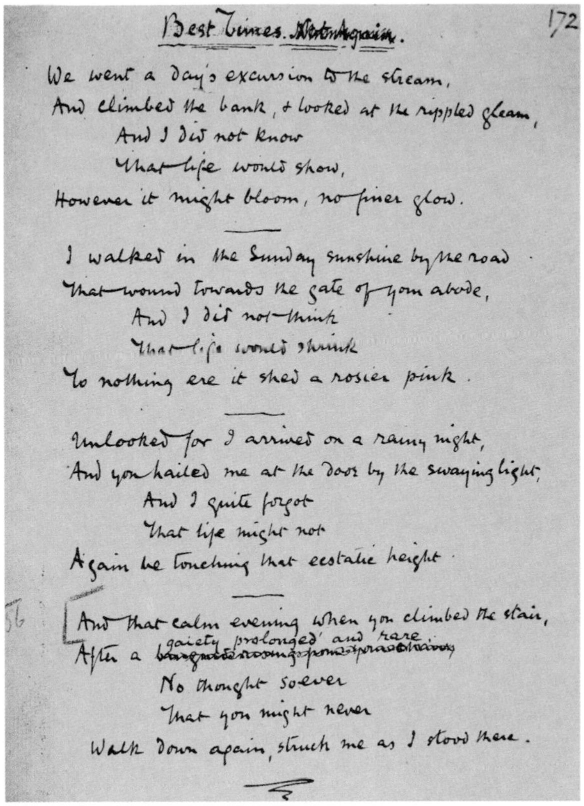

MANUSCRIPT OF HARDY'S POEM "BEST TIMES", REWRITTEN FROM AN EARLY DRAFT.

—I am one Bachelor Bowring, "Gent,"
    Sir or Madam;
In shingled oak my bones were pent;
Hence more than a hundred years I spent
In my feat of change from a coffin-thrall
To a dancer in green as leaves on a wall,
    All day cheerily,
    All night eerily !

⟨⟩

To a child who remarked of Max Gate in later years, "That is a quiet place – That house in the trees with the shady lawn", Hardy replied,

"It is a poet's bower,
Through which there pass, in fleet arrays,
Long teams of all the years and days,
Of joys and sorrows, of earth and heaven,
That meet mankind in its ages seven,
    An aion in an hour."

⟨⟩

THE Arts IN THE Twenties

 HILE HARDY wrote his *Satires of Circumstance*, a new artistic movement was beginning to emerge in London. The launch-pad for "Bloomsbury" is generally recognized as having been Roger Fry's first post-Impressionist exhibition in London in 1910. Fry, a painter and critic, launched a second exhibition, also post-Impressionist, in 1912; these two exhibitions, particularly the first, caused uproar and scandal of an epoch-making order. They may correctly be said to have inspired an English revolution in the Arts. Another vital influence was Serge Diaghilev's *Ballets Russes*, first seen by London in 1911, after having already taken Europe by storm. The *Ballets Russes* synthesized all that was modern and progressive in the Arts: Picasso, Derain, Cocteau, Ravel, Stravinski – all contributed to the *Ballets Russes*, which together with dancers like Tamara Karsavina and Vaslav Nijinski, had an unprecedented effect: it was, as Osbert Sitwell wrote, the flowering of an art form, witnessed perhaps once in a century.

BAKST DESIGN FOR A COSTUME FOR "NARCISSE"; BALLETS RUSSES, 1911.

The Sitwells

The Sitwells, Edith, Osbert and the somewhat younger and less prominent Sacheverell, played, cheek by jowl with Bloomsbury, a leading role in the Arts of the 1920s and 1930s; indeed, they were described by one eminent critic as "the major preceptors of the post-war generation." There has been a tendency, over the past years, to discount them; partly because, with their aristocratic background, they have been seen as élitist, and partly because, with their remarkable gifts and style, they made many enemies. But Bloomsbury itself was equally essentially élitist, yet does not cease to exert influence and fascination. In any case, the enormous success of the exhibition, *The Sitwells and the Arts of the 1920s and 1930s*, held at the National Portrait Gallery, October – January 1995, confirmed their continuing importance.

Edith, poet, critic, biographer and novelist, escaped from the Sitwells' ancestral home, Renishaw, in 1913 and settled in a shabby flat in London where she lived a frugal existence, being allowed only a small allowance from her father, Sir George Sitwell, supplemented by working in the pensions office in Chelsea at the outbreak of war in 1914, earning £1 30 shillings a week. To her dingy Bayswater abode came poets such as Yeats, Graves, Eliot, and Ezra Pound. They drank tea and consumed penny buns with treacle; the only refreshment offered.

Intensely dismissive of the Georgian school of poets and of Edward Marsh, editor of *Georgian Poetry*, Edith, together with her friend Nancy Cunard, founded a periodical anthology, *Wheels*, to promote an alternative, "modernist", approach. Osbert Sitwell, whose reputation like Edith's started with poetry, had been sent home from active service in France with a septic foot. He met Wilfred Owen through a mutual friend, Robert Ross, who had been asked by Siegfried Sassoon to keep an eye on Owen, then home on sick leave. Osbert Sitwell and Owen continued to stay in touch through correspondence and poems. The latter returned to the Front saying he preferred its horrors to the war-profiteering civilians of

England. Owen was killed in action a week before the Armistice; in London he had been invited to contribute to the 1918 edition of *Wheels*; his poems were published posthumously in the following, fourth, "cycle" of the anthology, which was dedicated to his memory. Sassoon went on to edit a collection of Owen's poems, first published in 1920.

The Bloomsbury Junta

The Sitwells were closely associated with Bloomsbury for reasons social and professional, but were never of it; just the reverse, they declared war on it, seeing it as a "junta". They were well placed to be able to present an alternative influence to Bloomsbury, Edith having *Wheels* and Osbert, with the financial aid of Arnold Bennett, having in 1918 bought into the publication, *Art and Letters*. But this said, links with Bloomsbury were maintained; indeed cordial social relationships existed between the Sitwells and Bloomsbury names such as Clive Bell, Roger Fry, Virginia Woolf, Maynard Keynes and Lydia Lopokova and Harold Acton, not to mention T.S. Eliot and William Walton. Edith would have her portrait painted by Roger Fry, as well as by the famous South American artist, Alvaro Guevara.

Wit, in the 1920s and 1930s, was not expected to be kind; we should see Edith's famous dismissal of Virginia Woolf as a novelist, "She's a beautiful little knitter", and Woolf's obervation to Edith, "Of course you're a good poet, but I can't think why", as a species of neighbourly sparring.

Façade brought true fame to the Sitwells, and especially Edith, in 1923. The first performance took place in Osbert's drawing room at Carlyle Square. Edith's poems, partnered by Walton's music, with Edith declaiming the poems through a megaphone simultaneously with the music, caused a sensation. Later the young Constant Lambert took over the megaphone. He subsequently became the conductor and Director of Music at the Vic-Wells ballet. In his earlier, *Façade* days, he was responsi-

ble for spreading the outrageous, but delectable, rumour that William Walton was the illegitimate child of Dame Edith Smythe by Sir George Sitwell.

Predictably *Façade* resulted in the Sitwells becoming the butt for the popular Press and the non-intellectual public in general. But voices which counted were raised in their praise: Kenneth Clark declared it was wonderful to find people so liberated from accepted thought and values – particularly from Bloomsbury and Roger Fry. Evelyn Waugh once called them "life-enhancing". While Cyril Connolly remarked of them that, despite their many faults, the Sitwells were "a dazzling monument to the English scene."

In due course, between 1945 and 1950, Osbert Sitwell would publish his five volumes of autobiography and memoirs, which are recognized as one of this century's major contributions to both literature and social history. Edith, besides her poetry, produced some outstanding prose, including *Victoria of England* (1936), *I Live Under a Black Sun* (1937), and a notable volume of criticism, *Aspects of Poetry* (1934).

EDITH AND OSBERT SITWELL IN THE DRAWING-ROOM, CARLYLE SQUARE, c.1926.

THE ARTS IN THE TWENTIES

Cars, Planes AND Camels

HE AGE OF THE motor-car had arrived in Britain with the new century. A series of motoring events, collectively named as "The Thousand Miles Trial", took place in the spring of 1900, receiving publicity in the *Daily Mail*; Alfred Harmsworth, the proprietor of that paper, being himself an enthusiast of the motor-car. The public responded. In 1904 there were 8,000 private cars in Britain; ten years later there were 132,000. The motor-cycle was the poor man's motor vehicle: by 1914 there were 120,000 on the roads of Britain. Public and business transport similarly exchanged the horse for the engine; motor-buses and taxis increased from 5,000 in 1904 to 51,000 in 1914. The number of motorized goods vehicles rose in that same period from 4,000 to 82,000.

Motor manufacturing before the 1914 war was a risky and highly competitive enterprise. British car firms concentrated on making expensive cars for a luxury market. By contrast, in the United States car manufacturers were already aiming for mass production in a large market, with vehicles at realistic prices. By 1912 the US output was already 500,000 vehicles – a figure not reached in Britain until the 1920s. An Act of 1865 – admittedly with heavy agricultural traction engines in mind – limited the speed of a motorized vehicle on a public highway to 4 mph; in 1896 this was raised to 12 mph; in 1903 it was raised to 20 mph, at which level it remained until 1930.

Motoring in the Edwardian era was uncomfortably bumpy; solid rubber tyres were not exchanged for pneumatic ones until early in the 1900s. Roads in towns were often made of wooden blocks which grew slippery in wet weather, brakes were still far from satisfactory.

Post-war Britain saw the gradual growth of a car industry using mass production methods and reflecting middle class affluence and new styles of living. Hardy enterprisingly bought Florence a small car and this changed their social life radically; they jaunted about the county visiting friends and going on sightseeing trips. We find them motoring over to lunch with Marie Stopes at her lighthouse on Portland, for instance, or making a tour of cathedral cities and cathedrals. More and more people came to Max Gate, some invited, some not; the Max Gate tea-parties became sought-after literary occasions. Hardy was not fond of entertaining people to luncheon because that cut into his working day; but we find H.G.Wells and Rebecca West lunching at Max Gate on one occasion, and Shaw and T.E. Lawrence enjoying a lunch-party on another.

The aeroplane (not yet the airplane) had arrived but civil passenger flying was still little known. 1924 saw the creation of Imperial Airways, a government-subsidised monopoly-operating company. Hardy did not live to see the airminded age in the popular sense. An aeroplane in the sky was a wonder for him.

A NEW CENTURY

Lawrence of Arabia

It was through the poet Robert Graves that Hardy met T.E. Lawrence ("Lawrence of Arabia") in 1923. Lawrence was then thirty-five years of age, and a war hero in a style which was quite unique. He appealed strongly to the romantic imagination of the country; he was internationally famous; he was spoken of in confidential tones as having been a spy; and there was something odd about him which gave him enormous glamour for the many, and made him suspect as a character to the few, who, from the corner of their eye, thought they detected a phoney. His passionate desire in life, he said, was for anonymity; this was impossible because, as has been often said, he possessed a genius for backing into the limelight.

In 1910 he took a first in modern history at Oxford, then spent a year touring Syria on foot, studying Crusading architecture and picking up colloquial Arabic. In 1911 he accompanied an archaeological expedition to the Euphrates to excavate the ruins of Carchemish. There he remained until 1914; further exploring Syria, and Mesopotamia. On the outbreak of war he was sent to Egypt attached to a rudimentary Military Intelligence unit and was a leading spirit in in the negotiations leading to the Arab revolt and in organizing the Arab Bureau. How he won the confidence of Faisal and took part in the desert revolt, pushed behind the enemy lines in Syria, and, joined forces with the famous raider, Auda Abu Tayyi, routed a Turkish battalion, and drove a passage to Aqaba, has become desert history and been the stuff of a famous film. He led a battle in Wadi el-Hesa, in which the enemy suffered a decisive defeat, then he turned his attention to train wrecking with such success that a large reward was offered for "El-Orens, destroyer of engines." Early in 1918 he failed by a hair's breadth to cut the railway connection with Damascus. In that autumn Faisal and Lawrence, in conjunction with General Allenby, organized a new advance on Damascus. Faisal and Lawrence captured Damascus several hours ahead of the British and Lawrence took charge of the city until Allenby arrived.

Lawrence played an active part in the peace conference of 1919, until at length, disgusted by what he saw as a failure on the part of the Allies to fulfil their obligations to the Arabs, he quit government service in 1922 and enlisted as a mechanic in the Tank Corps, taking the pseudonym of Private Shaw. He was stationed at Bovington Camp, close to Max Gate, where he was soon spending as much of his off-duty time as he could manage. Hardy regarded him as almost a son, while Florence extolled him as "one of the few entirely satisfactory people in the world." Like the Bernard Shaws, with whom Lawrence placed himself on similar family terms, the Hardys called him "the Prince of Damascus."

He was transferred to the RAF in 1925, and departed to serve on the northwest frontier of India. Called away suddenly, he had no opportunity to say good-bye to Hardy, which both found distressing. Lawrence was recalled to England in April 1928; but Hardy had died in January.

Lawrence's famous account of his desert adventures, *The Seven Pillars of Wisdom*, saw first publication in 1926, in a thirty guinea subscribers' edition, with illustrations by Eric Kennington. An edition for general circulation appeared in 1935. *The Seven Pillars of Wisdom* lives on as a classic contribution to desert literature.

PETER O'TOOLE AS LAWRENCE IN THE DAVID LEAN FILM OF HIS LIFE.

THE REAL LAWRENCE: HE WAS KILLED IN A MOTORCYCLE ACCIDENT, IN 1936.

CARS, PLANES AND CAMELS

6 THE IMMORTAL
Thomas Hardy

HARDY'S ASHES LIE IN Poets' Corner, Westminster Abbey. Nobody, it might be thought, could hope for a better guarantee of immortality than this. In due course, as a further gesture to his lasting fame, a statue was erected to his memory in Dorchester. Eric Kennington made the statue; Sir James Barrie unveiled it. So there sits Hardy, very much in the attitude of one who picnics in solitude on top of a white stone plinth. T. E Lawrence liked it: "It holds somehow that strange effect of living within himself that always Hardy gave me." A rather large notice was placed beside the statue; PLEASE DO NOT WALK ON THE GRASS.

Seventy years after his death, thanks to films, television and radio, and to a lesser degree his books, Hardy is still surprisingly to the popular forefront. Miraculously all his novels are still in print; are on the shelves of bookshops, as is also his collected poetry. In the world of today, in which books and reading are believed by many to be becoming obsolete, this is a marvellous tribute to Hardy.

It is also a sobering thought, or should be, that his novels were written to make money, not to produce great literature, or anything of that sort. When, in 1920, Hardy went to Oxford at the invitation of the Oxford University Dramatic Society to see their performance of *The Dynasts*, the Society's first production since the end of the war, their first annual play in this first post-war series, not only did he give the OUDS permission to perform the play – of which, of course, he held the copyright – but he gave them the play. Charles Morgan, who later became dramatic critic of *The Times*, was then manager of the OUDS; in conversation with Hardy, while making a little tour of Oxford prior to the performance, Morgan ventured to ask him if he would ever write another novel? Hardy replied that he had given it up long ago: "I wanted to write poetry in the beginning; now I can … my stories are written." The novels had served their purpose: had bought him his freedom; the novels were the ransom fee of the poet. Hardy wrote poetry to the end. His last volume of poems, *Winter Words*, was published posthumously. The final poem of all is called "He Resolves to Say No More".

HE RESOLVES TO SAY NO MORE

O My soul, keep the rest unknown!
It is too like a sound of moan
When the charnel-eyed
Pale Horse has nighed;
Yea, none shall gather what I hide!

Why load men's minds with more to bear
That bear already ails to spare?
From now alway
Till my last day
What I discern I will not say.

Let Time roll backward if it will;
(Magians who drive the midnight quill
With brain aglow
Can see it so,)
What I have learnt no man shall know.

And if my vision range beyond
The blinkered sight of souls in bond,
– By truth made free –
I'll let all be,
And show to no man what I see.

THE Hardy Players

ARDY NOTED in his diary that to dramatize a novel was a mistake in art; the play ruined the novel and the novel the play. In spite of this aura of reproof from the novelist himself, adaptations of Hardy for the stage have always held appeal for the theatrical; doubtless principally because of the essentially stagey plots and, with a few honourable exceptions, cardboard characters. Dramatic high-spots and tableaux present themselves to the would-be producer's inner eye, while the actor or actress scents wonderful possibilities of "building-up" a character specifically designed, for serialization purposes, to be trapped in cliff-hanging situations at regular intervals; perfect for memorable exits to stunning applause. Hardy's novels, perhaps more than most, are pre-eminently for reading; their power and haunting qualities lie in the writing. *Tess* remains an outstanding

work because of Hardy's experiments therein with seasonal moods, scenery, climate, hour of day or night, the accompanying sexual response, even when unconscious, to these stimuli, and above all his use of an exceptionally subtle erotic symbolism.

However, as we have learned, Hardy from the first wrote his novels to make money, and if adaptation of them for the stage increased their earnings, then he would adapt. Accordingly, following the success of *Far From the Madding Crowd* as a novel, Hardy prepared a stage version, *The Mistress of the Farm: A Pastoral Drama*, assisted by J. Comyns Carr, the dramatist and critic. This was submitted to John Hare and William Kendal, the managers of the St James's Theatre. They provisionally accepted the play and tentatively put it into rehearsal, before deciding against it, in November 1880. Toward the end of 1881, while Hardy was writing his new story, *Two on a Tower*, his

attention was distracted by the opening, at the St James's, on December 29, 1881, a new play, *The Squire*, by Arthur Pinero, no less. The "squire" of the piece was a woman farmer, and it was only too obvious that Pinero had drawn heavily on *Far From the Madding Crowd* for so-called inspiration. Indeed, it later transpired that Kendal's wife, Madge Kendal the actress, had retailed the plot of *The Mistress of the Farm* to Pinero, with results which now sent Hardy into a frenzied session of defending his professional interests. A heated theatrical controversy broke out, which Hardy found most distressing. On the other hand Comyns Carr, hardened to the ways of the commercial theatre did a thorough overhall of *The Mistress of the Farm*, got a company together, and presented the play as *Far From the Madding Crowd* at the Prince of Wales Theatre, Liverpool, on February 22, 1882, with Marion Terry as Bathsheba. On April 29 the play transferred to London's Globe Theatre where it ran for just over ten weeks.

Despite the theatre's lifelong fascination for Hardy he never really came to terms with the London stage, distrusting its artifice and opposed to the fashion for elaborate staging. When it came to adaptations of his own plays Hardy preferred amateur productions, especially out-of-London productions. His favourite company was the group called the Hardy Players, drawn from the members of the Dorchester Debating and Dramatic Society. Dorchester early became enthusiastic for staging Hardy; in 1907 a Dorchester journalist named Harry Pouncy staged episodes from *Far From the Madding Crowd* and the following year a scene from *The Trumpet Major* was presented in Dorchester Town Hall as an illustrative sequence during a lecture on "Napoleon and the Invasion of England". One thing led to another; as part of the town's "Maie Fayre" festivities three Wessex scenes from *The Dynasts* were played and the following November *The Trumpet Major* was dramatized by a Dorchester chemist, A.H. Evans, father of the future Shakespearean actor, Maurice Evans. Thus was born the first of the "Hardy Plays", performed by the "Hardy Players". Critics came from London to see the play, including Harold Child of *The Times*.

A "Hardy Play" became an annual event for Dorchester during those years prior to 1914. In 1920 the revived Hardy Players restored this tradition with *The Return of the Native*, and at Christmas they put on the mummers' play, "Saint George" for Hardy in the drawing-room at Max Gate. One of the company was the beautiful Gertrude Bugler, who had played Eustacia Vye, and to her Hardy quite lost his heart, arousing a most unreasonable jealousy in Florence Hardy. The following spring Miss Bugler added Bathsheba to her repertoire of Hardy heroines.

In 1923 Macmillan published *The Famous Tragedy of the Queen of Cornwall*, a poetic drama by Hardy. He had written it with Miss Bugler in mind as Iseult but she was unable to take the role as she was pregnant. Despite this disappointment Hardy took an active part in the production of the drama, presented at Dorchester Corn Exchange on the 28th of November. Again the London critics were present and gave the play generous reviews.

The following November saw the performance, by the Hardy Players, of Hardy's 1890s dramatization of *Tess of the D'Urbervilles*, with Gertrude Bugler as Tess. She made a deep impression in the part, even upon the West End critics. There was a possibility of a London production with Sybil Thorndike as Tess – a part coveted by every actress: who could resist that final scene with Tess stretched on the sacrificial altar of Stonehenge tranquilly awaiting arrest for murder? But Sybil Thorndike and her husband, Lewis Casson, wanted changes made to the play which Hardy would not permit. Meantime, thanks to some intervention by Florence Hardy, plans for Gertrude Bugler to play the role in London also fell through. The choice finally fell upon Gwen Ffrangcon-Davies and the play had a successful run at Barnes Theatre, before transferring to the Garrick. The whole cast came to Dorchester and put on a performance in the Max Gate drawing-room on December 6, 1925. One of the cast later wrote an account of the evening; it all went amazingly well and Gwen Ffrangcon-Davies's playing of the Stonehenge scene in the shadows thrown by the firelight was a thing never to be forgotten.

GERTRUDE BUGLER AS TESS, HARDY WAS QUITE TAKEN WITH THE ACTRESS.

Screen Adaptations

ONE OF THE major innovations of Hardy's age was the birth of the cinema. Popular almost from the day they were invented, moving pictures captured the imagination of the masses in a way that no other artistic medium had ever done before. Hardy's novels, with their dramatic scope and evocation of rural scenery, seem tailor-made for the screen, whether large or small.

The first of Hardy's novels to be adapted for the cinema, in 1924, was a silent version of *Tess of the D'Urbervilles*. The MGM movie starred Blanche Sweet as the eponymous heroine, looking much like a flapper of her day, while Alec was played by Conrad Nagel in suitably villainous mode. The film is very much a period piece, the characters more stereotypes of the silent film era than Hardy-esque characters. The next of Hardy's novels to translate to the cinema was his most lighthearted work *Under the Greenwood Tree* in 1928. It seems a fitting tribute to Hardy's reputation in his day that this was just the second "talking picture" made in the country of his birth. Made by British International Pictures, the film, like so many of its era, is rarely seen today.

Modern Interpretations

With their high production values and big budgets, adaptations of the recent years have been more successful. The 1967 film version of *Far From the Madding Crowd* was popular with audiences worldwide. The film, ably directed by John Schlesinger, had an all star cast. Julie Christie was the flighty Bathsheba, while her suitors, Troy, Boldwood and Gabriel were played by Terence Stamp, Peter Finch and Alan Bates (of whom more later). The dramatic, chilling loss of Gabriel's flock, and Gabriel and Bathsheba's desperate attempts to save the farm during a dreadful storm are scenes that stick in the memory. Although not the perfect adaptation, it is nevertheless enjoyable and obviously a product of its time, the garish technicolour and heavy make up of the leading lady placing it slap bang in the swinging sixties.

As always with classic novels, the BBC has contributed its own screen versions of Hardy's novels, with memorable adaptations of *Jude the Obscure* in 1971 starring a bearded Robert Powell, and *The Mayor of Casterbridge* in 1978, a commemoration of 50 years since

Hardy's death. Alan Bates, who had been Gabriel Oak in the 1968 *Far From the Madding Crowd*, made a convincing Henchard in this excellent version of the novel, scripted by Dennis Potter.

In 1981 came *Tess*, a paean to Polanski's dead wife, the actress Sharon Tate, who in 1969 was murdered while eight months pregnant by the notorious Manson gang. The film is dedicated to the late actress, and one cannot help but think that Polanski is drawing some parallel to his beautiful wife, struck down while so young and with so much to live for and the tragic heroine of Hardy's novel. The film stars Nastassia Kinski as Tess, who despite her German origins manages to convince as the lovely Dorset dairymaid. Peter Firth brings vitality to the part of Angel Clare; indeed the Clare in this screen adaptation is, overall, more convincing than the ambivalent character we meet in the novel itself; the drama of the final scenes owes much to his interpretation of the role. It has to be said that this is one of the most successful of the screen adaptations, it is moving and beautifully filmed, and what it may lack in tension it makes up for in aesthetic appeal. It deservedly won Academy Awards for its Costumes and Art Direction and was nominated for the Best Picture award.

The 1990s appears to be bringing about a renaissance for screen adaptations of Hardy's work. A film of *The Return of the Native* in 1994 drew a large television audience and starred an enchanting Catherine Zeta Jones alongside Clive Owen. But it has been a screen version of *Jude* (1996) that has drawn the most attention. With two of the brightest actors of the day in the roles of Jude and Sue (Christopher Eccleston and Kate Winslet) this is a film that is truly outstanding in the power of its images and stark handling of some of Hardy's most searing dramatic sequences. The partnership of Jude and Sue is presented with moving sympathy; their story unwinds implacably to its spine-chilling climax. The oddly stilted dialogue Hardy used in the novel has been wisely discarded in favour of speech better suited for our day and age. Sue comes across as a completely convincing modern girl. Jude's frustrated yearnings for Oxford and further education is brilliantly

suggested by the use of subtle visual inner-dialogue. It is hard to imagine any actor better suited to this role than Eccleston. The only criticism of the film may be that giving it heightened meaning for today's audiences has necessitated sacrificing the novel's haunting mood, encapsulating the despair and dark pessimism engulfing the pre-war generation (in this case World War One), which though not consciously aware of its imminent destruction was subconsciously experiencing (to quote the novel), "The beginning of the coming universal wish not to live." Inevitably the doom-laden essence of this most cathartic of all Hardy's books has been diverted in the, otherwise highly successful, attempt to transpose *Jude* from the last years of the nineteenth century to the closing era of the twentieth. That said it is a wholly worthy adaptation of the novel.

The 1997 Channel 4/River films production of *The Woodlanders* brings a further Hardy novel to the screen, starring Rufus Sewell (Giles Winterbourne) and Emily Woolf (Grace Melbury) and we can surely anticipate further films and television series as his novels are so wonderfully visual and so potent in their drama. It is a testament to Hardy's enduring reputation that these films continue to be made and we should be grateful that over a century after these novels were written, they still are seen as relevant to our times and our media.

NASTASSIA KINSKI AS TESS IN POLANSKI'S VERSION OF THE NOVEL

SCREEN ADAPTATIONS

Hardy's Funerals

HOMAS HARDY DIED shortly after nine o'clock in the evening of January 11 1928, His final illness was of brief duration and at first did not appear serious. He became unwell on December 11 and from then on became progressively weaker, but on the day before his death he rallied and on the morning of January 11 gave promise of recovery. In the evening he had a sharp heart attack and soon afterward died.

In the interests of his immortality the nation wished him to buried in Westminster Abbey, but Hardy himself had left instructions that he should be buried in Stinsford churchyard with Emma. After discussion a British com-

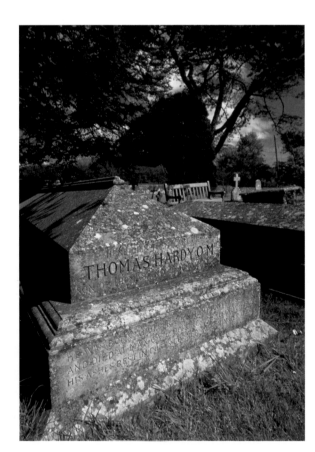

promise was reached: Hardy's heart should be buried at Stinsford, and the rest of him in the Abbey. Florence didn't like this; but she was overridden. A surgeon arrived to remove Hardy's heart; it was placed in a biscuit tin for safe keeping. The tale persists that a cat got at the tin and ate the heart. Indeed a Satire of Circumstance! Whether true or not, who can say? Had he been able, Hardy would certainly have written a poem about it.

Westminster Abbey

The ceremony which took place in Westminster Abbey at two o'clock in the afternoon of January 16, 1928, was never forgotten by those who were present. It was a curious occasion. Florence Hardy, and Hardy's surviving sister, Kate, were the chief mourners. The great throng of people present included representatives of the King and other members of the Royal Family, and many learned and other societies. The pall-bearers were the Prime Minister, Stanley Baldwin, and Ramsay MacDonald, Leader of the Opposition, representing the Government and Parliament; Sir James Barrie, John Galsworthy, Sir Edmund Gosse, Professor A.E. Housman, Rudyard Kipling, and Bernard Shaw, representing literature;and the Master of Magdalene College, Cambridge (A.S. Ramsay) and the Pro-Provost of Queen's College, Oxford (Dr E.M. Walker), representing the Colleges of which Hardy was an honorary Fellow.

They made an ungainly procession as they moved slowly up the aisle towards Poets' Corner: Galsworthy and Shaw both imposing six-footers; Barrie, an unusually small man, realizing (to quote Shaw) that he could not compete with them, "made his effect by miraculously managing to look exactly three inches high." As they all

marched, pretending to carry the ashes of whatever part of Hardy was buried in the Abbey, Kipling, immediately in front of Shaw and very nervous, kept changing his step; with the result that Shaw was in constant danger of tripping over him. A spadeful of Dorset earth, sent by a Dorset farm labourer, was sprinkled on the casket.

Stinsford

At the same hour that this ceremony was taking place in the Abbey, at Stinsford church where Hardy had been baptized and where, down the years, he had often attended services, his brother Henry Hardy was chief mourner; surrounded by Stinsford people who watched sadly while another casket, presumed to hold the poet's heart, was buried in the grave with Emma; the woman he had come "to love so passionately since he had lost her", as he had once remarked. Hardy's parents lay close by, under the ancient yew in the corner of the churchyard. In St Peter's church, Dorchester, again at the same hour, a memorial service was held, attended by the Mayor and Corporation and all the many other dignitaries who attend on such an occasion. All the shops and businesses in Dorchester were closed for an hour; the blinds were drawn; the streets were deserted, except for the crowds of people who, unable to squeeze into the church, stood in the churchyard and on the pavements outside. In this way Thomas Hardy, an exceptional man to the very end, had three funerals.

HARDY LEAVES
MAX GATE FOR
THE LAST TIME.

THE
Life

*T*he Life of Thomas Hardy 1840–1928 nominally written by Florence Hardy, has, since 1940, been recognized as having been basically the work of Hardy himself. It was originally published in two volumes, *The Early Life of Thomas Hardy, 1840–1891* and *The Later Years of Thomas Hardy, 1892–1928*: appearing respectively in 1928 and 1930.

For many years Hardy's feeling had been that he did not wish to have his "Life" written at all, but over the course of time he became aware that others, whom he perceived quite unqualified for the task, would take it upon themselves to write a biography of him, whether he wished it or not; in which case he had better set about the thing himself. The biography was to be compiled from "contemporary notes, letters, diaries, and biographical memoranda, and what the author [officially Florence] had learned in conversation with him".

Hardy seems first of all, in about 1917, to have produced an account of his childhood years and youth. He then went through all his notebooks and selected items for the composite narrative he proposed building up. He also read through, and largely destroyed, a mass of correspondence received by him over the years.

HARDY AS AN INFANT WITH HIS MOTHER.

MEMORIAL AT HARDY'S BOCKHAMPTON BIRTHPLACE.

"Materials"

The existence of the "Life", always referred to by himself and Florence as "materials", was kept a closely guarded secret. Hardy concealed the written manuscript; which was typed by Florence, also in great secrecy. There were three copies; the top copy, and two carbons. Hardy corrected and revised the third copy; Florence then inserted his changes into copy two, and finally into the top copy, which then went to the printer. In this way there was no trace of Hardy's participation in the work. By 1919 the narrative material was complete, up to 1918; thereafter Hardy continued building up the material and notes, which Florence might draw upon when writing the final chapters after his death. Hardy gave her permission to edit, augment, or delete wherever she thought it was necessary.

This, essentially, is what happened. Following Hardy's death in 1928, Florence made a number of deletions in the assembled material. Some were her own, including many of Hardy's entries about Emma, which Florence removed, motivated by jealousy. This censorship would greatly have distressed Hardy, for it contributed largely to posterity's distorted view of the first Mrs Hardy. Some of the changes to the manuscript were at the instigation of

Barrie; these included considerations of propriety, and attacks on critics. Florence inserted, again at Barrie's suggestion, early letters from Hardy to his sister Mary, and a number of anecdotes concerning his childhood and youth.

The reason why Hardy and Florence practised the deception of claiming that the "Life" was solely the work of Florence was that, by putting her in the role of authorized biographer with exceptional access to, and intimate knowledge of, the subject, there could be no dispute about authenticity, and no risk of anything being included in the text which he did not wish to be there – Hardy did not foresee Florence's expurgation of material favourable to her "rival", Emma. Concealed behind the fiction that his widow had written his life with his full knowledge and approval and with materials put at her disposal by himself, Hardy felt secure from further prying interference. This "Life" should put paid to any further ideas of a biography from the pen of some troublesome outsider! It is unfortunate that the "Life" constitutes some kind of confidence trick played on a gullible and trusting public: he and Florence were perfectly entitled to do what they did, but one can't help feeling that it was unworthy of them; especially as they were bound to be found out in the end. The earlier parts of the "Life" read best, being mainly narrative in form and furthermore containing some of Emma's own early recollections; not discovered by Hardy until after her death. Beyond Part III of the book, "Illness, Novels, and Italy" it all becomes increasingly jotty and bitty, completely in the "writer's notebook" style – except, of course, it has all been transposed into the third person.

The Last Scene

The final chapter, "The Last Scene", describing Hardy's latest days and his death, and written by Florence in a vein closer to the earlier narrative form, is extremely moving. Indeed it suggests that perhaps Florence, like his first wife, was a better writer than Hardy wished to think. The

account of his delighted reception of a huge bunch of grapes on the final morning of his life, when he unexpectedly rallied, is touching. Having sampled the grapes, and having insisted upon them being held up for everyone, from the servants to the doctor, to admire, he exclaimed gaily, "I'm going on with these!" He died some ten hours later, murmuring brokenly, "Em! Em!" Florence, an hour after his death, returned to his room to look on him alone. He wore on his face, she wrote, "A look of radiant triumph."

HARDY WITH FLORENCE AND THE INFAMOUS DOG WESSEX.

THE LIFE

Hardy's PLACE IN THE Literary Canon

WHAT EXACTLY, AS A START, is the definition of "the literary canon"? Learned men and women tell you firmly that the literary canon is what is taught in English Lit: you do" *these* authors, but *those* are no longer "done". Former great names on the literary scene have dropped into a vast black hole – and you are given to understand that it is most unlikely they will ever rise again. Occasionally a desperate bubble or two

THE IMMORTAL THOMAS HARDY

THE EVER-HAUNTING "JUDE THE OBSCURE": HARDY'S FAME ENDURES, ASSISTED BY SCREEN ADAPTATIONS.

appears on the surface – it is poor George Meredith, or maybe Edward Atherstone (*Who's he?*), and they never expected to find themselves bogged down there, in the slough of oblivion. "Do you mean to say *I* am not being taught? Yet there is that wretched woman …What's her name … Mrs Gaskell … Never met her."

But writers write to be read, rather than taught – though financially it is rewarding to be taught; even if it does mean that you run a tidy risk of being forgotten. Literature pertains to the realm of letters, says the Oxford Dictionary, it is also "printed matter". Writing, which is not always considered to be synonymous with literature, is written to be read, and enjoyed; or to weep over (but that is a form of enjoyment) or gnash your teeth over, but that, too, is a kind of enjoying yourself. Or even, something to make you yell, and hurl the book across the room, and then pick up and with a final snort drop it in the dust-bin (that is intense gratification and in a way adds up to a plus mark for the author so treated).

How long do you have to be dead, to be immortal? Thucydides, born in 455 B.C. author of *The History of the Peloponnesian War*, lived through, and fought in, that war and was sent into exile for failing to prevent the Athenian colony of Amphipolis from falling into the hands of the Spartans. In exile he wrote his history of the war, saying that he hoped it would be judged "useful by those who want to understand clearly the events which happened in the past and which (human nature being what it is) will, at some time or another, and in much the same ways, be repeated in the future." How true those words have proved! People interested in politics, and war, and peace, are still avidly and regularly reading Thucydides to discover what should be done, and what is likely to happen next. That is immortality.

But surely you don't have to live as long as that to be immortal? No. You might be Shakespeare, or Cervantes, or, coming to later in the day, Daniel Defoe, or possibly Sterne. There is no betting on anything. Nor is there any justice. Looking into the English Literature section of the *Encyclopaedia Britannica* at a pageful of portraits, *British Men of Letters: 14th-18th centuries* – among whom one female face looks out, Jane Austen – you see all Robert Southey's close friends and one good enemy. Wordsworth, Scott, Coleridge, Lamb, Byron (no friend he, but a thorn in the Southey flesh) and Shelley – a replica of the young Southey, said Southey – privately thinking that Shelley should be so lucky. But where, among these British Men of Letters, is Robert Southey? Poet Laureate, author of books, one of them at least, his life of Nelson, outstanding writer of reams upon reams of narrative verse ("Just rise half an hour earlier in the morning and you can compose half a canto with ease before taking the dog for a walk" was Southey's advice) and of course the best and most reliable reviewer of his day – and a very nice man into the bargain. "Of all the Lake Poets," observed Eliza Lynn Linton, who had known them all pretty well, "Mr Southey was the only gentleman". Where *is* Robert Southey? Sunk without trace. Not even one solitary bubble. Nobody would ever have believed it. He was *the* literary man of his day. And meantime that ridiculous old man with a glistening eye and an albatross round his neck is still stopping one of three coming out of Safeways and riveting them with his, "There was a ship …" It is all so horribly unfair.

The portrait gallery of *British Authors, 18th–19th Centuries*, includes three women, Charlotte Brontë, George Eliot and Virginia Woolf, and to our relief Thomas Hardy is there, between Matthew Arnold and Gerard Manley Hopkins – this is the 1961 edition of the encyclopaedia, so perhaps … But should he have been removed as no longer of sufficient significance, even in a little town like Keswick – where this is being written – you can go into any bookshop and find Thomas Hardy, in excellent paperback editions, with scholarly introductions and good notes and beautifully inviting covers. He is in

the public library. In fact, far from being in danger of joining Robert Southey, old Thomas Hardy is growing more and more lively with every year that passes. And it is not only his novels that you will find wherever you look; his collected poetry is there too.

So, for a while longer at least, his place in literature seems assured. It is a good sign that people not only read his books, but will argue about their respective merits pretty fiercely, too. "*The Return of the Native*! Oh no! My favourite is *The Woodlanders*!" Followed by some personal remarks that shall not be repeated here. This is what having a place in the literary canon *really* means.

AUGUSTUS JOHN PORTRAIT OF HARDY, 1923.

Index

All numbers in *italics* refer to illustrations.

A

Addclyffe, Miss 47
afternoon tea 72–3
agriculture 36–7
Albert, Prince 6, *64*, 64–5
Alhambra Chorus Line *102*
Ali-Baba and the Forty Thieves (à Beckett) 82
All the Year Round 49
Allen, Marguerite *51*
animals 100–1
Apple Pickers (Pissarro) 77
apprenticeship 21–2, 25
architecture 22–3
art galleries 80–1
Atlantic Monthly 66
Athenaeum, The 47
Avebury 33
Aveling, Edward 61

B

Barker, Granville 113
Barrie, James 63
Bates, Alan 52, 75, 134
Batten, John *51*
Becker, Lydia 96–7
à Beckett, Gilbert 82
Beechwood, The (Turner) 76
Beerbohm, Max 109
Bell, Andrew 20
Bernhardt, Sarah 83
Besant, Walter 62
Best Times (Hardy) *125*
Black and White 117
Black Beauty (Sewell) 101
Blackwood's Edinburgh Magazine 48–9
Blighters (Sassoon) 122
Blomfield, Arthur 21, 23, 24, 25, 70, 71, 82
Bloomsbury 126, 127
Bockhampton *13*, 14, *16*, 20–1, *138*
Boer War 105
Boldwood, William 53
Boucher, Léon 79
Breuil, Abbé 32
Bridehead, Susanna 92–3
Bridges, Robert 113
British Museum Reading Room 60–1, *61*
Brougham, Henry 48
Brown, Capability 70
Brown, John 65
Burges, William 23, 24
Burne–Jones, Edward 23

C

Cakes and Ale (Maugham) 54
Cardiff Castle 23
Carlyle, Thomas 23, 48, 49, 62
Caro, Avice 15
cars 128
Castell Coch 23
Cavell, Edith 121
Chamber's Journal 49
Chapman, Frederick 62
Charmond, Felice 77
Chase, The (Scott) 49
Christie, Julie 52, *134*, 134
Clare, Angel 91
Clark, Mark 20
Coast Near Folkestone (Turner) 81
Coggan, Jan 20
Coleridge, Samuel Taylor 49
Collins, Wilkie 47
Colour Schemes for the Flower Garden (Jekyll) 71
Confessions of an English Opium-Eater (De Quincey) 48–9
contraception 98–9
Contrasts: a Parallel Between the Architecture of the 15th and 19th Centuries (Pugin) 22
Convergence of the Twain (Hardy) 115
Cornhill Magazine 47, 48, 49
Cornwall 26, 31
Counterattack (Sassoon) 123
country towns 40–1
Crickmay, G.R. 25, 47
Crippen, Hawley (Dr) 110–11, *111*
crossing sweepers 41
Cunard, Nancy 126
Cytherea 47

D

Daniel Deronda (Eliot) 63
Davenant, Sir William 82
Davies, Emily 59, 96
Day, Fancy 50, 51
Day, Geoffrey 50
Desperate Remedies (Hardy) 47, 62
Dewy, Dick 13, 50, 51
Diaghilev, Serge 126
Dickens, Charles 6, 49, 63
dinners 73
Doll's House, The (Ibsen) 83
Dorchester *40*, 40, 66–7, 112
Dorset County Chronicle 66
Dream or No, A (Hardy) 27

D (cont.)

Drew, Fancy 13
Driffield, Edward 54–5
d'Urberville, Alec 90–1, 98
Durbyfield, Tess 35, 90–1, 98
Dynasts, The (Hardy) 108–9, 121, 124

E

early writing 47
Eccleston, Christopher 92, *134*, 135
Ecstasies:Deciphering the Witches Sabbath (Ginzburg) 34
Edinburgh Review 48
education 20–1
Edward VII 102, 105, 106–7
Eliot, George 48, 49, 63
Ellenore (Taylor) 49
Ellis, Havelock 76
Elmy, Elizabeth 96
"Emma Poems" 27
English Illustrated Magazine 49
entertaining 72–3
Evelyn, John 60
Everdene, Bathseba 15, 52, 53
Examiner 79

F

Facade (Sitwell & Walton) 127
fairs 42–3
fame 79
Famous Tragedy of the Queen of Cornwall , The (Hardy) 113
Far From The Madding Crowd (Hardy) 15, 17, 20, 43, 47, 50, 52–3, 67, 76, 79, 134
Far Phantasies (Hardy) 113
Farfrae, Donald 74–5
Father and Son (Gosse) 63
Fawcett, Henry 97
Fawley, Jude 74, 92–3
film adaptations 6,37 ,*51*, 52, 90, 92, 134–5
Finch, Peter 134
First World War 120–1
Fitzpiers, Eldred 76–7
Formal Garden in England, The (Blomfield) 70
Fox-Strangways, Charles Redlynch 12
Fraser's Magazine 49
Frazer, James 43
Fry, Roger 126
funerals 136–7

G

gardens 70–1
Garrett, Elizabeth 59
Gentleman's Magazine 49
George V 105
Germany 105
Gifford, Edwin 37
Gifford, Gordon 66
Gifford, Helen 26
Gifford, Lilian 119
Gilbert the Red 23
Ginzburg, Carlo 34
Godwin, William 49, 59
Golden Bough, The (Frazer) 43
Gosse, Edmund 63, 95
Grahame, Elspeth 117
Graphic 95
Greek drama 29
Grey, Sir Edward 97
Group of Noble Dames, A (Hardy) 79, 95
Guardian, The 95

H

Halliday, Andrew 82
Hand, Elizabeth (grandmother) 12, 16–17
Hand, George (grandfather) 12
Hardy, Emma (née Gifford) (wife) 11, 25, 26–7, 35, 37, 47, 52, 54–5, 60, 66, 77, 96, 97, 101, 110, 112, *116*, 116–17, *117*, 119
Hardy, Florence (née Dugdale) (wife) 34, 57, 67, 99, 101, 112, *116*, 116, 117, *118*, 118–19, *119*, 121, 129, 134, 138–9, *139*
Hardy, Henry (brother) 16, 66
Hardy, James (uncle) 12
Hardy, Jemima (mother) 12, 12, 13, 14, 16, 17, 20
Hardy, Katherine (sister) 16, 134
Hardy, Mary (grandmother) 13
Hardy, Mary (sister) 15, 16, 35
Hardy, Thomas: *141*; and agriculture 36–7; and animals 101; apprenticeship 21–2, 25; architecture 23; and art galleries 80–1; and Arthur Blomfield 21, 23, 24, 25; birth 6, 12, *13*; and Bockhampton 13, 14,16, 20–1; and the British Museum 60; and cars 128; and country towns 40–1; death 134; and Dr Crippen 110; early childhood 16–17,
138; early writing 47; education 20–1; and Elizabeth Hand 16–17; and Emma Hardy 11, 25, 26–7, 35, 37, 47, 52, 54–5, 60, 66, 77, 96, 97, 101, 110, 112, 116–17; and fairies 34; and fairs 42–3; fame 79; and First World War 120–1; and Florence Hardy 34, 57, 67, 99, 101, 112, 117, 118–19; and Frederick Chapman 62; and Frederick Treves 89; funerals 136–7; and George Eliot 63; and George Meredith 62; and Greek drama 29; and honours 112–13, *113*; influences 15, 16–17, 23, 50; and J. M. W. Turner 81; and John Hicks 21, 25; and London 21–2, 25, 55, 86; and markets 42–3; and Mary Hardy 16; and Max Gate 66–7; and monthly magazines 48; and music 84; and oral tradition 14–15; and Order of Merit 112; place in English literature 6, 62, 79, 140–1; poetry 24, 27, 47, 79, 113, 124–5, 131; and prehistoric Wessex 32, 33, 66–7; relationships 25; and religion 25; and the Royal Society of Literature 112–13; and rural customs 44; and rural poverty 18–19; and rural society 36–7; and the Savile Club 63; and Siegfried Sassoon 123; and the Society of Authors 62; and Sturminster Newton 54–5; and the suffragettes 96, 97; and superstition 34–5, 57; and T. E. Lawrence 129; and the theatre 82; and the Titanic 114–15; and village life 38–9; and Wessex 29–33; and William Tinsley 47; and witchcraft 34–5; and women 11, 52–3, 91
Hardy, Thomas (father) *12*, 12, 13, 16, 17
Hardy, Thomas (grandfather) 12, 13
Harper's Weekly 95
Hazlitt, William 48, 49
He Resolves to Say No More (Hardy) 131
Heaton, Clement 23
Heiress and Architect (Hardy) 24
Henchard, Elizabeth–Jane 75

Credits

The Publisher would like to thank the following sources for their kind permission to reproduce the photographs in this book:

AKG London 81;
Copyright © BBC 75;
The Bridgeman Art Library, London/British Library, London 97, / Christie's Images 53, 73, 122/Cider House Galleries, Ltd., Bletchingley, Surrey 41, / City Museum and Art Gallery, Plymouth 106, / Dallas Museum of Fine Art, Texas 77, / John Davies Fine Paintings, Stow-on-the Wold, Glos. By kind permission of Miss Barbara Hall 39, / The Fine Art Society 19, 126, / Fine Lines (Fine Art), Warwickshire 4, / Fitzwilliam Museum, University of Cambridge 76, 141 / Gavin Graham Gallery, London 74 centre, / Cecil Higgins Art Gallery, Bedford 17, / Imperial War Museum, London. By kind permission of the Paul Nash Trust 121, / Mallett Gallery, London 71, / Philip Mould, Historical Portraits Ltd, London 62, / Musée du Petit Palais, Paris/Giraudon 83, / Private Collection 72, 101, / Royal Holloway and Bedford New College, Surrey 88, / Schloss Charlottenburg, Berlin 109, / Christopher Wood Gallery 14, / The Victoria and Albert Museum, London 64;
Cadw: Welsh Historic Monuments. Crown Copyright 22;
Channel Four Films and Pathé Productions Limited present a River Films Production: The Woodlanders/Liam Daniel 46 (Emily Woof as Grace Melbury, Rufus Sewell as Giles Winterbourne), 76;

Corbis 24, 60, 61 centre, 70, 110 centre, / Bettmann 49, 69 right of centre, 85, 129 bottom, / Hulton Getty 70, 111, / Macduff 136 / Patrick Ward 61 main;
Dorset County Museum, Dorchester 3, 12 top left and left of centre, 23, 25, 26, 40, 50 top right, 54, 66, 69 top left, 79 (Hardy's study at Max Gate), 98, 100 below centre, 105 (Hardy and King Edward VII), 108, 113, 116, 117, 118, 119, 125, 128, 131, 132, 133, 135, 138 centre, 139;
Mary Evans Picture Library 1, 2, 5, 15, 18 top left and centre, 20, 21, 32, 34, 35, 38 top left and centre, 43, 44, 45, 47, 48, 51 right of centre, 55, 58, 63, 65 68, 80, 82, 84, 86, 95, 96, 102, 103, 104;
Hulton Getty Picture Collection 107, 110 left, 123, 127;137;
Image Select 87, 114, 115, 120;
Images Colour Library 27, 28, 90;
The Kobal Collection 99, 134 bottom/ Columbia, 129 top, / MGM 90 top left, / Paramount 89, / Renn Productions/Burrill Productions/SFP 37, 91, 94, 137/Vic Films/Appia Films 52 top left and bottom right. 135 top left.
Sarah Larter 29 (River Frome at Bockhampton) 67 right of centre, 74 top left, 112, 124, 138 bottom left;
Zoë Maggs 100 top left;
By Courtesy of the National Portrait Gallery, London 7, 59;
National Trust Photographic Library 36, 67 top, / Eric Crichton 16, / Roy Fox 42, / Fay Godwin 10 (Hardy's Cottage), / Alan North 13, / David Noton 33;
Polygram Filmed Entertainment/ Joss Barratt 78, 92, 93 top, 134 top, 136 bottom, 140 / Pictorial Press 130;
Rex Features 56, 57;
Tony Stone Images /Chris Honeywell 93 centre right

BIBLIOGRAPHY

Bennet, Daphne, *Emily Davies and the Liberation of Women, 1830–1921*, (Deutsch, London, 1990)

Hardy, Florence Emily, *The Life of Thomas Hardy 1840–1928*, (Macmillan, London, 1972)

Holmes Richard (Librarian, Windsor Castle 1870–1900), *Edward VII: His Life and Times*, (Amalgamated Press, London, 1910)

Lehman, J,. *A Nest of Tigers: Edith, Osbert and Sacheverell Sitwell in their Times*, (Macmillan, London, 1968)

Mayhew, Henry, *Mayhew's London Labour and the London Poor*, 1851 (two volumes)

Millgate, Michael, *Thomas Hardy: A Biography*, (Oxford, 1982)

Mrs Beeton's Family Cookery (Ward, Lock & Co., London 1981)

Morduant Crook, J., *William Burges and the High Victorian Dream* (John Murray, London, 1981)

Murray, Margaret A., *The Witch Cult in Western Europe*, Clarendon Press, Oxford, 1921)

Owen, Wilfred, *The Poems of Wilfred Owen*, ed.Edmund Blunden, (Chatto and Windus, London, 1931)

Purdy, R.L. and Millgate, M., (eds), *The Collected Letters of Thomas Hardy*, (Oxford, 1978–1989)

Rose, June, *Marie Stopes and the Sexual Revolution*, (Faber and Faber, London, 1992)

Sassoon, Siegfried, *Memoirs of an Infantry Officer*, (Faber and Faber, London 1931)

Seymour-Smith, M., *Hardy* (Bloomsbury, 1994)

Trevelyan, G.M., *English Social History* (Longman, Green, London, 1942)

Wood, Henry, *My Life in Music* (Gollancz, London, 1938)

Carlton Books and Molly Lefebure would like to thank the following for their help with this project:

Richard de Pyer and Mary Bennett at the Dorset County Museum.
Stephen Hebron.
The staff of the Keswick branch of the Cumbria County Library
Shelia Watson and Tahnee Wade at Watson Little.
Sandy Holton at Channel 4.
Colin Hynson for the Index.

DORSET COUNTY MUSEUM
High West Street
Dorchester
Dorset
United Kingdom
Tel: 01305 262 735

THE THOMAS HARDY SOCIETY
PO Box 1438
Dorchester
Dorset
DT11 1YH
United Kingdom